EDUCREATION

Dedicated to the British Architectural Student Association (BASA) 1960–5, which has been an inspiration to me and which saw fit to adopt Educreation as its policy.

EDUCREATION

EDUCATION FOR CREATION, GROWTH AND CHANGE

the concept
general implications and
specific applications to schools of ARCHITECTURE,
ENVIRONMENTAL DESIGN or EKISTICS

BY

PAUL RITTER, M.C.D., B.Arch., F.R.I.B.A., M.T.P.I., A.R.A.I.A., A.A.T.P I.
City Planner and Architect of Perth W.A.

PERGAMON PRESS

OXFORD · LONDON · EDINBURGH · NEW YORK
TORONTO · PARIS · BRAUNSCHWEIG

Pergamon Press Ltd., Headington Hill Hall, Oxford
4 & 5 Fitzroy Square, London W.1

Pergamon Press (Scotland) Ltd., 2 & 3 Teviot Place, Edinburgh 1

Pergamon Press Inc., 44-01 21st Street, Long Island City, New York 11101

Pergamon of Canada, Ltd., 6 Adelaide Street East, Toronto, Ontario

Pergamon Press S.A.R.L., 24 rue des Ecoles, Paris 5e

Friedr. Vieweg & Sohn Verlag, Postfach 185,
33 Braunschweig, West Germany

Printed in Great Britain by Dawson & Goodall Ltd., Bath

Contents

Acknowledgements

THE sources of help for this book have been too numerous to list. To mention some is not to belittle others.

I thank twelve years of guinea-pig students; I am also grateful for the experiences afforded me in many schools of architecture in many countries and for the eye-opening periods of sitting on the Board of Architectural Education.

Specifically I want to thank Dr. Moshe Caspi for invaluable aid, Tony Moss for patient and intelligent typing, and my family for tolerating the anti-social behaviour that goes with concentration, such as getting up at 5 a.m. for months on end.

I am grateful to the many publishers and authors who have graciously given me permission to quote.

Finally, it should be stated that the cost of the full-time research for one year leading to this book was not supported by any foundation or professional body.

Introduction

THE four sections of this book have four aims:

1. To show that a new concept of education is required and what kind we need.
2. To demonstrate the fresh pattern in the context of educational theories.
3. To indicate the general implications for education of the new concept.
4. To exemplify implementation and to show what ideas emerge from the new pattern of thinking for architectural education.

In my visits to some sixty schools of architecture and planning the world over, I have come across ideas and enthusiasm. What is lacking is an orientation. This, I hope, is now given by the criteria of educreation.

I have formulated in depth so that those who feel the necessity for radical change can see the roots of my policy and strategy. I have tried to substantiate every one of my points and I would expect to find equally careful substantiation for departure or disagreement.

Mere modification of old concepts has proved inadequate. What is sound in the old can find its way spontaneously into the new. It has become clear that the creative element, in all its aspects, is the central issue of the new concept, as memory and set skills were of the old. "Education for Creation" as a title for the book and, worse, as a phrase repeated in the book, seemed clumsy. That is how the word EDUCREATION was born: to fill a need. The need for one word to signify a new growth-orientated concept of education. The word has proved useful already in many lectures in various countries. It establishes at the outset that there is a fresh pattern of thought and action. Rather than educating for a "station in life", we educreate for life itself, the express train that runs through that old station.

A study of the many schools of architectural education and psychology has made me aware that a move towards integration is timely. At the moment, of many approaches, with some penetrating and effective, but specific, techniques, each claims that it has general validity exclusive of the others, with similar attitudes. That it is inclusive is an advantage of my concept. It integrates old and new findings and provides criteria to judge their proper and relevant application.

It is the task of many over the years to evolve the myriad of individual techniques, methods and stimulants that arise out of educreation. It is a concept of growth, and the specific techniques must change, as the substance of society will alter. Seats of learning will slide with the times. Indeed, this is its strength that it will continually throw up a wealth of new techniques and combine the power of several growing points.

I make no apology for quoting a great deal in this book. Beyond drawing attention to the need to read the works quoted it is a major part of my thesis that educreation does embrace much of progressive work and research. What better way of showing this?

Further, I feel that where my views coincide with those of another, it is only fair to give priority to the previous expression of the idea. The book, with its considerable bibliography, can be regarded as a source book for architectural education in many fields, and as a pointer to further study on many aspects of EDUCREATION. Another good reason for quotations is to counteract the mistrust of architects for anyone who has shared their training (even if he has done much else). They will take the evidence better from the work of another.

If I detail what my own school of architecture or environment might be like, in the descriptions of the third section of the book, this must not be taken out of its context. This is only one man's interpretation and the fruits of his experience. Nor is it a matter of everything or nothing. My experiments vindicate the hypothesis that educreation can be introduced from the tiniest dose (sometimes with remarkable effects) to varying amounts. This is central to the book. Opportunism—using all one's might and materials according to the educreational criteria, wherever, whenever and with whomsoever it promises to be most effective—is a basic rule.

Implementation is an essential, separate consideration. History is strewn with concepts as good as new, useful concepts, carefully explained, never applied. If you have not been turned into a cynic by this hard truth, you will appreciate the careful consideration of this aspect in educreative thought—in this book and beyond.

Context and Orientation

1.1. QUANTITATIVE ASPECT OF THE PROBLEMS OF EDUCATION

I.1.1. The Triple Explosion

(a) The population of the earth grows at an unprecedented speed.

(b) Ever greater proportions of this population gain the privilege to be educated.

(c) The body of knowledge grows fatter and fatter.

This triple explosion imposes a rate of change which distinguishes the twentieth century from all others.

In underdeveloped countries the number of people to be educated grows dramatically in all age-groups. In developed nations quantitative expansion is necessarily limited to higher education.

The Robbins Report, after analysis of the last ten years, comes to the conclusion that: " . . . university expansion has not even quite kept pace with the increase in the age group let alone the increase in the number of those with the minimum qualifications for entrance . . . "[i]

Examples of the magnitude of the problem: the French official policy is to increase the university population from 200,000 in 1960 to 500,000 in 1970. In Britain, the Robbins Report, which was accepted in principle by the Government, recommended an increase from 216,000 students in 1962 to 560,000 in 1980.

[i] ROBBINS, *Higher Education Report*, H.M.S.O., London 1963, p. 12.

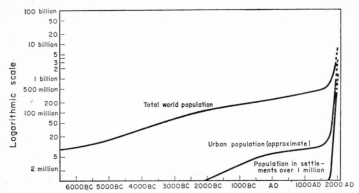

FIG. 1. Growth of world population, 6000 B.C. to A.D. 2000.
Sources: Population Reference Bureau; Kingsley Davis, Homer
Hoyt and Regional Plan Association, New York.

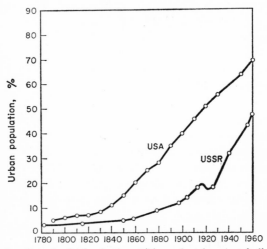

FIG. 2. Growth of urbanization. This can be taken as an indication
of the distribution of privilege. In the last decades it has certainly
been regarded as desirable to be able to move into cities. *Sources:*
U.S. Census; Lyashchenko, *Statisticheskii Ezhegodnik* (1905),
Narodnoe khoziaistvo S.S.S.R. (1959); Regional Plan Association,
New York. *Note:* Both definitions exclude rural non-farm population, but include incorporated places of 2000 or 2500 and over, and
certain other territory.

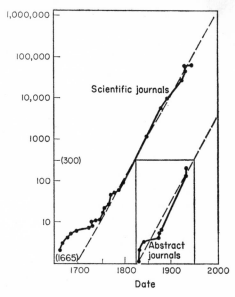

FIG. 3.   Growth of the body of knowledge. Indicated by the growth
of numbers of scientific journals and the number of journals dealing
purely with abstracts.   (Courtesy Yale University and Professor R.
Coates.)

Even these figures in no way satisfy the demand of the applications of students, but are some sort of compromise between
demand and postulated possible resources.

Taking the average from the percentages of each of the seven
most developed countries in the world, less than 8% of the
relevant age-group qualified in any higher degree.[i]

The avalanche of knowledge has been described by Bernal:

"The basic sources of information are in scientific papers and,
since the output of papers doubles approximately every ten years,
they mostly cannot be read at all.   Much of the fruits of research,
both in pure and applied science, are lost—though they are often
'discovered' again much later.

(i) Robbins Report, p. 42.

". . . Its ['information explosion'] growth is even more violent than that of the population explosion, for population only doubles every forty years. Most scientific funds are spent on research, and very little on recording and preserving the results. It is high time that all the new methods of exchanging, storing and retrieving information were available to science, otherwise the billions of dollars spent on research will be largely wasted."[i]

Innovations like teaching machines, television programmes, universities of the air, and others are taken into consideration, but it is significant that no radical departure from the organization, quality or content of education is anywhere contemplated. Yet the size of the problem is such that only a different approach to education can possibly meet the demand.

I.1.2. Selection—Hidden and Deliberate

If higher education for only some is allowed, how we determine whom to admit, in a democratically intentioned country, is relevant.

Selection is the process whereby the "chosen few"[ii] are segregated from the rest. This chapter describes the questionable nature of this very deep-rooted and multiple process as it applies in Britain. I have little doubt, however, that the study of culture patterns of other countries would show their own selection processes to be deeply rooted in prejudice also, and capable of improvement.

To understand the factors involved leads us directly to appreciate the sources for the increasing numbers who are likely to demand higher education. There are two aspects to selection for further education: there is the deliberate elimination of children by examinations and obvious choosing of candidates from applicants at the time of entry on the one hand, and the hidden selection processes on the other.

(i) BERNAL J. D., Towards a Science of Science, *Science Journal*, London, March 1965.
(ii) FURNEAUX W. D., *The Chosen Few*, Oxford 1961.

The hidden processes decide who shall submit to conscious and deliberate examination and dissemination. During recent years, a number of pieces of research have made up a jigsaw with a frightening meaning: we are very far from democracy in education. Both the deliberate and the hidden processes are dealt with in some detail as they affect materially the quantitative and the qualitative aspects of education.

I.1.2.1. HIDDEN SELECTION

Seven separate processes have been isolated, observed, measured, assessed and recorded:
  (a) The position of the child in the family.
  (b) The size of the family.
  (c) Date of birth.
  (d) Social class.
  (e) Sex.
  (f) Geographical position.
  (g) The cumulative effect of streaming.
  (h) Character structure, personality type.

Let us examine the factors in some detail.

(a) *The position of the child in the family*

A survey of 7000 children at Ilford[i] shows that the eldest child in a family is likely to be academically more successful and stay longer at school. "Educationally speaking, it seems to be a great misfortune to be a younger girl." Not only do last-born children have less access to education after fifteen, but girls significantly less than boys. Eldest children take part in leisure activities demanding skill and independence more than the youngest. "Love comics" are read far more by those who are the youngest of three or more, than by any other group, reflecting a dearth of direct love.

(i) W.E.A. (STEWART M.), *The Success of the First Born Child*, London 1963.

(b) The size of the family

"The larger the family—whatever its social standing—the less likely are the children to successfully pass the selection sieves."[i]

The significant main point that arises is that the family system, and the way it is housed, although taken for granted as the only one and the right one in every way by our society, has some evil effects. This suggests that, with modifications, a richer social pattern outside the family might be of value.

If, let us say, there is not ever a youngest daughter of a large family in a school of architecture, this is influenced strongly by the cultural selection system described above.

(c) Date of birth

" 'D' streams had twice as many summer-born as winter-born children."[ii] With neatness of administration, we punish winter-born children, particularly if they are also born of manual workers.

(d) Social class of the family

"Of manual workers' sons reaching eleven between 1931-40, only 1·7% reached university (for white-collar workers it was 8·5%). Of manual workers' sons reaching eleven between 1946-51, only 1·6% reached university (for white-collar workers it was 19·2%)."[iii]

One hundred children subdivided as they progress through school.[iv]

(i) JACKSON B., *Streaming, an Education System in Miniature, London*, 1964, p. 139. Also LYNN R., *Environmental Conditions Affecting Intelligence in Educational Research*, Vol. 1, No. 3, June 1959.
(ii) JACKSON B., *Streaming, an Education System in Miniature*, p. 29.
(iii) FLOUD J., *Social Class Factors in Educational Achievement*. HALSEY, FLOUD J., ANDERSON, *Education, Economy and Society*.
(iv) JACKSON B., *Streaming, an Education System in Miniature*, p. 137, table 39.

	At birth	In 'A' stream at 7	Pass 11	Educated at 18
Middle class	25	15	12	7
Working class (non-manual workers)	75	24	12	3

"Children coming from working-class homes still fail to realize the expectations raised by their score at eleven-plus." Children do not, even roughly, have equal chances.[i]

Research shows that the lack of success of children of manual workers is due to their leaving education earlier. Those who continue to A-levels show that they are as successful as other social groups.[ii]

Children of educated parents tend to have more education than those of parents with less education.[iii]

But streaming engrains the social differences disastrously: ". . . streaming worked as a major form of social as well as academic selection. There were only five chances in a hundred of a professional's or manager's child going into a 'D' class." This remained true in all kinds of streaming, Jackson found.[iv]

(e) Sex

The Robbins Report shows that education-wise this is still a man's world: 85% of boys of non-manual fathers born in Great Britain in 1940-1 had no degree educations, but neither did 97% of manual workers' sons. For girls, the percentages are 91% and 99% respectively. The totals for enjoyment of degree

(i) KELSALL R. K., Getting on at the Grammar, *Times Ed. Supp.*, March 15, 1963.
(ii) Robbins Report, p. 52, *Statistics of Education* 1961, H.M.S.O.
(iii) Robbins Report, p. 51.
(iv) JACKSON B., *Streaming, an Education System in Miniature*, p. 29.

education of those born in that year are: non-manual 12%, manual 2%.[i]

(*f*) *Geographical position*

The Robbins Report records that the difference between the percentages of children who are absorbed into grammar schools varies from 12% in the well-provided area down to 7%. What is more, the table given suggests that the "social class" of the area influences the figures, to the advantage of the higher class. Again, the social factor counts.[ii]

(*g*) *Streaming*[iii]

Streaming is dividing a group of pupils too large for one class, the criterion for division supposedly their academic capacities. It is a far more widespread and powerful factor in education than even very experienced teachers think: Thirty-eight teachers attending a course on the subject, particularly interested in the field, radically underestimated it. It is little known that even at the age of five 5% of a sample of 134 schools show streaming. At the age of six, 25%—a quarter of the child population—are virtually segregated into sheep and goats for good. At seven, nearly three-quarters, and ten, 95%.

The moving from stream to stream hardly ever occurs, although the possibility is used to defend streaming again and again. Research has shown why it does not occur. Good streams improve pupils, but bad streams make them worse. The system works to make it easy for the selector to demonstrate he was right.

"Streaming emerged as a technique to reduce the special problems facing state education in the 1920s and '30s . . . it

(i) Robbins Report, p. 50 (Reverse % for effect).
(ii) Robbins Report, p. 54.
(iii) Data from Jackson B., except where stated.

developed from temporary strategy into one of the settled institutions of our educational system."

No country outside the United Kingdom "streamed" children in a study of twelve countries carried out by Unesco. And no country showed as great a variation of academic results. The highest and lowest standards were twice as far apart as in some other countries.[i]

How is streaming determined? Jackson culled from nearly 600 schools:

	%
Class teacher recommendation	79
Infant school report	67
School arithmetic test	57
School English test	56
An experienced judgment by head and staff	55
External reading test	54
External intelligence test	43
School reading test	42
External arithmetic test	28
External spelling test	21

Jackson adds: "A large number of schools preferred to group children as 'A', 'B' or 'C' without much use of objective tests; 37% used none at all. The most popular methods were all 'internal,' private to the school concerned. Less than half the schools employed any intelligence test."

It is impossible to have any confidence in this sort of selection, even within its framework of reference, even if one believes in streaming.

What is particularly nightmarish is the cumulative effect of streaming:

" . . . streaming by ability reinforces the process of social selection observed. . . . Children who come from well-kept homes and who are themselves clean, well clothed and shod, stand a

(i) *Streaming, an Education System in Miniature*, p. 122.

greater chance of being put in the upper streams than their measured ability would seem to justify. Once there they are likely to stay and to improve in performance in succeeding years. This is in striking contrast to the deterioration noticed in those children of similar, initial measured ability who were placed in the lower streams. In this way the validity of the initial selection appears to be confirmed by the subsequent performance of the children, and an element of rigidity is introduced early into the primary school system."(i)

Jackson concludes: ". . . streaming reflects social background, privilege, accident and handicap." Just those who might need special help face more handicap.

Criticizing the streaming system, Jackson says: "Our society is one of opportunity and possible plenty. We reduce its potentialities by an educational sieve designed for a society of scarcity. In the past this sieve served well enough. It could be argued that when society's resources were more limited it was sensible to pioneer the way forward by concentrating on the education of a small band of pupils. Streaming is a means to this end."(ii)

Specifically, we can fault the way streams are selected: ". . . . if, instead of assessing children on tests examining the speed and accuracy of their logical faculties [verbal selection tests are tests of urban (not rural) vocabulary] . . . we divided children according to their scores on a 'creative' intelligence test, where what counted was enterprising, divergent thought . . . gold and iron would be more confused . . . And if we . . . defined human excellence in items of imagination, sympathy, tenacity, courage, as well as rational speed, then the present structure looks . . . limiting . . .".(iii)

We must agree that "streaming has serious, far reaching social implications. It reflects and continues culture patterns . . ." and "I think there are enough patches of evidence to suggest that

(i)   *Streaming, an Education System in Miniature*, p. 19.
(ii)   DOUGLAS J. W. B., *The Home and the School*, London 1964.
(iii) *Streaming, an Education System in Miniature*, p. 38.

streaming may have some small connection with fostering future delinquency".[i]

". . . the huge selection machine that we have built . . . has its own law. Two code words summarize it: if a child has 'SUPREMO' he is likely to be gold. If he is found to be 'WORSWUN' the system gives him little chance":[ii]

"Strong	*W*eaker build
*U*rban	*O*ther children in family
*P*arents educated	*R*ural
*R*ight birthday	*S*ummer-born
*E*motionally stable	*W*orking class
*M*iddle class	*U*nstable home
*O*nly child	*N*ervous."[iii]

(*h*) *Character structure, personality type*

Extroversion is already a handicap at school. The work of R. Lynn[iv] shows this. A more clear-cut test of the relative excellence of ability of children and their school records, intelligence tests and creative ability was carried out by Getzels and Jackson.[v] This shows that though they do as well in classwork, extrovert, creative children are less popular with their teachers, and their values do not coincide with those of parents or teachers, unlike the introvert, high I.Q. children.

Conclusions

It is sobering to read that "very few of the teachers had much knowledge about teaching methods, school organization, or the

---

(i) *Streaming, an Education System in Miniature*, p. 126.
(ii) To this, according to Musgrove, we can add "introvert" and "extrovert". The words then become "supremio" and "worsewun".
(iii) MUSGROVE F., *Youth and Social Order*, London 1964.
(iv) LYNN R., Two Personality Characteristics related to Academic Achievement, *British Journal of Ed. Psych.*, 1959.
(v) GETZELS and JACKSON, *Creativity and Intelligence*, New York 1962.

possibilities of education outside the system which prevailed in their present school or the school they attended in childhood. Most seemed to think that some method of early selection was universal—an original fact of life, rather than an artefact of British life."[i]

"Teachers' attitudes are slower to change [than formal proposals], and so long as they believe and think about types of children there will be types of children. Streaming goes deep and in some form it is likely to be our concern for many years to come."[ii]

If, in describing the selection, I suggest that girls of poor and large families should have a better chance in our society, I do not want to suggest that more of the inferior type of education now available is necessarily a good thing. Far from it. More can be gained by radically improving what we have. If we do not rethink and reform, it may be better not to extend the school-leaving age, or the number of places at universities for that matter.

I.1.2.2. DELIBERATE SELECTION

(a) *Eleven-plus examination*

The eleven-plus examination formally endorses the injustice of streaming. On top of this it is itself very unreliable and more and more authorities are replacing it by a later, more liberal, selection based on choice.

The National Foundation for Educational Research reports that under the best eleven-plus selection techniques we know, there is still an "irreducible error" of 10%. About 70,000 children are likely to arrive at the wrong school (according to this eleven-plus criterion) each year.

"The evidence set out in this book gives strong reasons for believing that much potential ability is wasted during the primary

(i) JACKSON B., *Streaming, an Education System in Miniature.*
(ii) Ibid., p. 142.

school years and misdirected at the point of secondary selection."[i] The scale of the total waste and misdirection is terrible.

It is obvious that the distateful state of affairs laid bare and here summarized should be changed—to this the ideas of this book are highly relevant. Administratively: "Our next step is to end all early selection. If there is no division of roads at eleven-plus, twelve-plus or thirteen-plus, then selection at seven may also disappear."[ii]

(b) *Selection for university entry*

O-level and A-level exams are as notoriously unreliable as those set as eleven-plus, but no figures have been compiled and no comprehensive research made. However, a grammar school headmaster entered twenty-eight pupils for an English language examination under two separate boards. The results were ludicrous: one board gave twenty-seven passes and one failure; the other gave twenty-five failures and three passes. The boy who came top in the one examination came bottom in the other.[iii]

And Hart and Rhodes report in their book *An Examination of Examinations* that in an essay type paper, the same candidate will get widely different marks from different examiners, and different marks from the same examiner marking the same paper on different days.

While hoping for the varying numbers of A-levels required by the various schools, students make several applications. This has demonstrated that there is little agreement on the part of selectors. Happily several interviews make acceptance more likely.

"If the performance of candidates who have been accepted by a particular university in a particular year is compared with the performance of other candidates who were rejected by that

(i) Douglas J. W. B., *The Home and School*, London 1964, p. 119.
(ii) Jackson B., *Streaming, an Education System in Miniature*, p. 142.
(iii) Davy J., *The Observer*, February 14, 1965.

university but nevertheless managed to gain admission elsewhere during the same year, then there seems to be no clear evidence that there is any difference at all between the standards achieved by the two groups. There is a significant difference between those who are accepted the first time and the second time of trying. The selection at universities is done with a mixture of "empiricism, tradition and personal experience which cannot always be expected to produce the most valid results."[i]

But this is not the chief point I want to make at this juncture. What I primarily want to pin down is the incredibly fine and unfair thinning out and grading that precedes selection at university entrance level. And still: "The problem of selection is mainly that of picking out those people who have not the capacity for gaining a university qualification and ensuring that they do not gain admission."[ii]

Yet only 4% of the 1962 age-group (of whom 7% had entrance qualifications) obtained entry to universities in Britain. Of those who qualified for entry about 15% less entered universities in 1962 than in 1954! Selection is not improving, but it becomes less relevant year by year.

Further at this point, it is a sobering and sad reflection that of this highly refined *élite* the current approaches to education manage to eliminate up to 36% of students from one faculty in one university down to 3%, but never lower (of e.g. 1957 entered graduates). The average over all students entered that year is 14%.[iii] Furneaux reports a 15-20% failure rate for universities generally and 5% for highly choosy and pampered Oxford.[iv]

The Robbins Report lays most of the blame at the "customary rates of failure at institutions", not in any way at entrance selection. It is shown that standards are revised to keep to a "customary" number of fails each year. A scandalous state of affairs.

(i) Furneaux W. D., *The Chosen Few*.
(ii) Ibid.
(iii) Robbins Report, pp. 190–1.
(iv) Furneaux W. D., *The Chosen Few*.

Beyond the shortage of places, and while there is little doubt that university education must grow immensely, the educational boards of the professions sit behind locked doors and indicate how many newcomers should be allowed so that their position as professionals does not become intractable.[i] This is a false approach in our age:

"The suggestion that the possibly limited number of professional scientific positions might mean that we are 'over-producing' scientists strikes me as comparable with the notion of taking the best available estimate of the number of clerks required in fifteen years' time and restricting accordingly the number of people to whom reading and writing should be taught."[ii]

Professor Bondi's comments are valid for all the professions. A narrow, narcissistic or national image of any group, profession or otherwise is no fit gauge for the numbers required in the twentieth century. It obscures the real issues of education and is blind to world needs.

We can conclude that the deliberate selection is inefficient, but that its irrelevance is even worthier of note: it takes our attention off the real issues, the right of a young person to study if he wants to and is qualified.

I.2. QUALITATIVE ASPECT OF THE PROBLEMS OF EDUCATION

I.2.1. The Critical Situation

The desperate position in education in general, the urgent need for a specific and practicable set of directions, was expressed by Peter Cowan's comment on Lord Llewelyn-Davies's oration to the Society of Industrial Artists and Designers.[iii] "He left us

(i) The Willink for reduction of entry to the medical profession (1957) is now reaping its terrible effect. It helps doctors with current pay claims!
(ii) BONDI Prof. HERMANN, Turning a Training into an Education, the *Observer*, January 7, 1962.
(iii) December 2, 1964. Reported in *A.J.*, December 23, 1964.

feeling that unless something is done rather quickly we shall continue to stagger from crises to crises . . ."

This is no empty threat. At the risk of making the reader grow pale, I quote Alfred North Whitehead's ghastly correct prophecy of his address to the Mathematical Association of Great Britain in 1917:[i]

"If, in the troubled times which may be before us, you wish appreciably to increase the chance of some savage upheaval, introduce widespread technical education and ignore the Benedictine Idea. Society will then get what it deserves." And technical education was brought in, particularly in Germany, with greatly admired efficiency, and the "savage upheaval" was without precedence.

We are warned again in the sixties: "The challenge to education today is to question its assumptions, to sort out essentials from inessentials, to review its structure, in the perspective of a fast moving world . . . if at this critical juncture education fails to fire the imagination of the coming generation—if, above all else, it fails to provide a meaningful picture of the living universe —the vast, exciting potentialities opening out before us can crumble into dust and the way will be open for a phase of sophisticated technically efficient mechanized barbarism . . ."[ii] And in our radioactive age, "crumbling into dust" is putting it mildly!

"Our national education is based on an uncritical belief that the existing curriculum is good and the pupils must adapt themselves to it. . . . Instead of trying to adapt the children to fit the curriculum, we have to adapt the curriculum to the children . . . and the results are satisfactory."[iii]

Huxley explains why the race must take a hold of itself. "In earlier times, when the rate of technological and demographic change was slow, societies could afford the luxury of their

(i) WHITEHEAD A. N., *The Aims of Education*, New York 1949.
(ii) BARRACLOUGH Prof. G., *Times Ed. Supp.*, Jubilee Number, December 2, 1960, p. 80.
(iii) LYWARD G. A., *Respite from Pressure*, p. 119.

collective neuroses. Today political behaviour dictated by obsessive memories of the past (in other words by venerable traditions that have lost their point, and by old, silly or actually diabolic notions raised to the level of first principles and canonised as dogmas) is apt to be fatally inappropriate."[i] And this also applies to education.

The work of Reich,[ii] from the twenties onwards showed with a unique crystal clarity why society suffered from inertia and why it may be increasingly ready for a radical departure in education, and also how this process should be orientated. We are losing enough of our fear of freedom to look and act differently. There is more life and urgent, pressing need.

Change in the quantities to be educated in developed countries depends solely on the proportions winning through to higher education. But the quality of education is about to undergo a radical development at all levels.

For fifty years or so the ideas of A. S. Neill,[iii] Bertrand Russell,[iv] Whitehead,[v] Herbert Read[vi] and others, and indeed their experiments, have been regarded as ideals or oddities with little relevance. But now, with a growing momentum, the influence of this pioneering is felt in every conceivable aspect of education. The capacity for life of the pioneers is becoming an increasingly common commodity. The process is supported by affluence, and its by-products, in the century of the common man.

I.2.2. Bias Against Creation

The most significant aspect and evidence for this view lies in the growing number of research projects and books which, in the

(i) HUXLEY ALDOUS, the *Observer*, October 22, 1961.
(ii) REICH W., *Character Analysis*, London 1958. Also *Ether, God and Devil* and other books.
(iii) NEILL A. S., *Summerhill*, London 1964, and many other books.
(iv) RUSSELL BERTRAND (his early book on his and Dova Russel's School).
(v) WHITEHEAD A. N., *Aims of Education*, New York 1949.
(vi) READ H., *Education Through Art*.

B

academic fields of sociology and education, produce the statistical and objective evidence of the ineffectiveness of our education and deliberately point to the attitudes hitherto regarded as ideal, impracticable and odd. Ironically, an age, which relies less on insight than any previous era, is persuaded to put its faith in the spontaneous and the creative by evidence obtained with statistical tools; blunt, currently fashionable, regarded as the only really respectable scientific communication:

The unification of science and art; the integration of the multitude of specialized subjects is under way. Just how popular and general such concepts have become is exemplified by Koestler's vast collection of evidence and the original thought in his book *The Act of Creation*. He recognizes the part played by education but does not deal with it.[i] But it arises more clearly out of Koestler's book than before that it is not a matter of having education, based on either science or art (the false discussion alive in architecture today), but to educate in that which is common to both. The rest looks after itself.

We can extract far more from the human organisms: bodies, human minds, human beings and groups. We would not tolerate a machine running as inefficiently knowing, as we do, just how superb the "design" is and how well it might run. The Behaviourists here show, even if on a shallow level, just how surprisingly much animals can learn. But the rapid development in aids confuses the issue. Though computers, for example, are undoubtedly useful, we cannot gauge their relevance or use them properly until we have developed the natural brain and other organic powers to something like their capacity. And that is a great deal.

The bias of our culture pattern to use only one aspect of human ability has been examined in some detail.

Evidence still being assembled already shows clearly that our education favours, arbitrarily as far as the needs of the country are concerned, a certain kind of person.

(i) KOESTLER A., *The Act of Creation*, London 1964.

Musgrove writes: "We have fashioned institutions of higher education which can achieve their ends most easily with a certain personality type: which can relatively easily be made to feel guilt and self-reproach and to drive itself without much steering . . . he is rewarded for, and confirmed in, these particular dimensions. Individuals who are stable and extrovert seem to do less well in the activities which are valued by grammar school and universities, even though they are of similar intelligence."[i]

Broadbent reports an experiment which shows that with such work "the more extrovert the greater the deterioration with prolonged work".[ii] And, particularly at the borderline of university admission, extroverts probably tend more often than introverts to be denied a place.

Furneaux shows that in an engineering department of borderline applicants $25\cdot7\%$ were neurotic extrovert and $21\cdot4\%$ neurotic introvert. Yet admissions from this borderline group were only $6\cdot2\%$ extrovert and $37\cdot5\%$ introvert, suggesting a powerful bias.[iii]

All this suggests that initiative and creativity, at a premium in growing numbers of creative design professions, are not adequately fostered nor diagnosed at times of assessment, and that they are unpopular virtues in institutions of learning.

We produce insecure children who compulsively find answers. We structure our education so that reward is for those who give "THE" answers, can remember facts, and can keep quiet in class. Initiative, rebellion, high spirits, artistic exuberance, opportunist quick thinking, a sense of responsibility, capacity to give love, sensitivity, insight and the desire to see beyond and below pat answers, the eagerness to learn unusual subjects, are not valued.

To correct this situation we must make a deliberate attempt to select, bearing in mind that the child most likely to succeed in

(i) MUSGROVE F., *Youth and Social Order*, London 1964, p. 4.
(ii) BROADBENT D. E., *Perception and Communication*, London 1958, p. 148.
(iii) FURNEAUX W. D., The Psychologist and the University, *University Quarterly*, 1962, p. 17.

creativity and adaptability has been at a disadvantage with the usual educational arrangement all his school life.

The reliability of the school-leaving examination results—as a tool to assess the success of students at universities—is largely an indication that memory examinations continue to be the chief criterion.

Thus it well may be true—and indeed obviously is—that good examination passers stay good examination passers, by and large. But if other aspects, creative and initiative for example, become recognized and utilized at all levels of education, then the examination results as such, in which Furneaux and others place trust, become less important. The danger lies in accepting recommendations for selection procedure without bearing in mind the need for change as the tasks at schools begin to vary from those expected at universities, and as educational goals change at least in emphasis.

I.2.3. Broadening of Horizons

We must deliberately broaden our horizons to extend over an era unlike that which nurtured us and which dominates our imaginations. There is the traditional idea of training someone for a "station in life" as if it was the only one. We ignore the other possibility that a man may have many stations in life; that, like the small exception at the moment, careers and occupations could be far more varied than they are today.

It is generally conceded that:
1. Originality thrives from a variety of application.
2. Once one enjoys one's "work", and has as much time for "hobbies", the dividing line between them is fragile.
3. Talents which are manifold are exploited only in specific directions through our specialized education which takes for granted that a normal man can qualify or train or be interested only in one field.

Given these three points it is reasonable to assume that talents might be developed severally and more widely, that occupations, hobbies or work will satisfy a greater range of outlets and that associations—functional associations with other human beings—will range across a more numerous set of groups.

We must stretch our fields of vision beyond the narrow concept of "swotting" for exams, "hating" to work for a living, "dreading" retirement, "escaping" for holidays, "rat-racing" for positions in hierarchies, "keeping up" with the Joneses, "fearing" restrictive trade union practices and automation, "time being money", and living "by the clock". It is time to recognize that an educational system might encourage development towards these beckoning freedoms. Stipulating such future possibilities is not to be confused with suggestions leading to revolutions. My concern is to note that we will have them (all being well!), and that a decisive measure to have them sooner rather than later is to have an appropriately changed and changing and deliberately orientated education.

This suggests a fundamental departure from present concepts—from the "venerable traditions that have lost their point—old, silly or actually diabolic notions raised to first principles and canonised as dogmas"—and implies this at all levels of education.[i]

It is my belief that a sweeping simplification of the learning process will come about and that far vaster areas of knowledge will be accessible to each man through a unitary approach applicable with salutary effect to all sciences, as well as sundry other fields. The indications can be found in many directions, the crying need is obvious, the advantages that would accrue incredibly great, far-reaching and significant. The search for means of making the exploding volumes of information in the world meaningful and available is highly relevant here.

"There is no field of study which is likely to last the student more than a small fraction of his life . . . I see education as an

(i) It is not an affront to the underdeveloped countries to stress quality in educational advance. It is the responsibility of those who have plenty to look ahead and stress the ultimate need for quality—and, as I demonstrate, often the qualitative criterion leads to quantitive improvement also.

integral part of life at all stages. Many advances, many old techniques and many whole sciences will become obsolete and new ones will gradually take their place."[i]

I.3. THE PLIGHT OF PROFESSIONAL EDUCATION

If the strong accusations drawn from Huxley, Whitehead and others, and endorsed by the research quoted, have relevance to professional education, grave dissatisfactions should be observable. Indeed it is, in medicine, architecture, civil engineering, law and science (not to speak of teacher-training colleges).

I.3.1. Medicine

Professional education as we know it today, and indeed the general attitude to education as held by our society, is dominated by the Victorian examination-bound thinking from which it emerged. A typical example of the formalizing of courses for the professions is described by the secretary of the Association for the Study of Medical Education: "In 1858, the training which had evolved for this new kind of general practitioner became required by law and was controlled by the General Medical Council, which set out a minimum course of studies, relating both to knowledge and to practical training, which all must complete before graduation.

"The aim of these studies was to train the student in everything which he would need to do as a G.P. by the time he took his finals. Gradually in Britain, the studies became divided into two parts—one concerned with basic medical science and the other concerned with a more apprentice type clinical training. This system worked admirably in this country for about one hundred years."

And thence the dilemma:

"We have thus kept in existence the structure of a family doctor system, although it is true to say that most of our general

(i) BERNAL J. D., *Science Journal*, March 1965,

practitioners were trained to do a job that can no longer be done and are as yet uncertain as to what new job is required of them. Meanwhile, the inevitable disruption of medical education has been made worse, more in some schools than in others, by the continued attempt to train G.P.s for a job which no longer exists by a form of apprenticeship to specialists which cannot be successful anyway."[i]

Trends in medicine are remarkably close to those in architecture. At the World Health Organization conference of the European region, Dr. John R. Ellis said: "Medical education has been weakened by attempts at comprehensive coverage. Undergraduate students have become progressively less able to think for themselves and at the same time efforts to teach them everything have been redoubled in the conviction that safety lay in this direction. Thus a vicious circle has been established. This could now be broken only by the deliberate acceptance of new education objectives."[ii]

At the same conference, Jonathan Fearnley said: "A radical revision of our whole concept of the scope and purpose of medical education is becoming a matter of urgency." Mr. Fearnley criticizes the *status quo*: "For the first two years they will laboriously dissect the whole body, learning anatomy in the same relentless detail. They will follow the same biochemical 'experiments' to the same foregone conclusions. The emphasis throughout is on facts and a good memory rather than ideas and a creative mind."

". . . the whole question of the relation of medicine to the social problems of today is badly neglected . . . there is an unavoidable tendency for the student to see medicine as a series of unrelated parts rather than an integrated whole".[iii]

Further evidence comes from Sir George Pickering, Regius

(i) Letter from Hon. Sec., Association for the Study of Medical Education, to W. Allen, taken from *The Practical Training of Architects*, R.I.B.A., London 1962.

(ii) Repeated in *The Times*, September 25, 1961.

(iii) RITTER PAUL, Medical Education Criticized, *A.J.*, November 22, 1961.

Professor of Medicine at Oxford University, who said: "Today a medical student is avidly lectured at and ruthlessly examined in a large number of basic sciences, and one of the greatest problems is to preserve the infantile characteristics of curiosity and capacity to learn."

Finally, back to the secretary of the Association for the Study of Medical Education, describing the aim in remarkably educreational terms: ". . . the content of knowledge and experience of undergraduate years must be selected for its relevance to the processes of learning and not to its relevance to future practice. When we have done this, then obviously we will allow for great individual variation amongst our students, realizing that if we have achieved the importance of undergraduate education, then any gaps in knowledge and experience which an individual has, can be made good in the post-graduate period. Conversely, any gaps which may exist, and there are sure to be some, will never be made good unless the objectives of undergraduate preparation have been achieved."[i]

I.3.2. Science

In education for science we meet once again a similar diagnosis of the new needs, and the false current directions:

"There has been a constant pressure to make the training of science students more vocational, more a training in skills and less an education.

"This seems to me short-sighted and fallacious, even from the narrow points of view of those wishing to increase immediately the supply of skilled graduate scientists. For science is, above all, a subject full of change. New concepts, new theories, new experimental equipment supplied by an ever-expanding technology, these are the very nature of the subject. Thus a student trained in a narrow discipline, trained to be proficient in certain skills, will find, before long, that these skills are out of date, that his is a back number, who has acquired at the university nothing

(i) Quoted in *The Practical Training of Architects*, R.I.B.A., London 1962.

but a knowledge of that, after a few years, ceases to be of much use.

"What is required of a scientist is that he should have a flexible mind, that he should be able to absorb and acquire and, if possible, produce new ideas. Training him for this cannot be merely a training in particular skills or an imparting of special knowledge."[i]

I.3.3. Structural Engineering

Structural engineering in many ways seems to be getting the worst of both worlds, to quote Frank Newby, a quite exceptional engineer, educated in the manner peculiar to Cambridge and Oxford: "An engineer is a checker for society—checking that a building is structurally stable. The engineering student is in fact given little encouragement or time to carry out creative design, or, in other words, to create the problem to be solved."

"Structural models are very seldom made or tested,[ii] and he gets no feel for structural materials or for the deformation of structures; neither is he given any indication of the function of structure in a building. Theory is in fact divorced from practice. He is trained to be a two-dimensional stress man or a confirmation man with no creative ability. How can he then come to be a full member of a design team?"[iii]

Dr. Christopherson sketches an answer—in line with educreational possibilities: ". . . what has to be done is to make the subject of design as presented to the undergraduate so fascinating that anyone who has talent in that direction will leave with a very strong bias towards design, and will thereafter do the kind of job which will ensure that he never regrets his decision.

(i) BONDI Prof. HERMANN, Turning a Training into an Education, the *Observer*, January 7, 1962.
(ii) Under Prof. Coates my structural awareness studies for the first year of the School of Architecture were accepted as a joint architect–engineer first-year exercise in 1962. This includes making and testing models. See Section III.
(iii) NEWBY F., Lecture on architectural education at Queen's University, Belfast, 1963,

"But I suspect that in most universities we are a long way from doing anything of the kind. Very often what is done is first to teach the student to draw, after a fashion, and then in most cases to give him some design work to do, which may err either on the side of being too much a matter of routine, of producing minor modifications of a standard article, or of being too ambitious— the kind of project on which a team of draughtsmen would in practice have to work for a year—so that the student cannot attempt much more than an outline, and an outline which often enough will not face him with the kind of practical problems which are at once the bane and the delight of the designer's life . . ."[i]

I.3.4. Architecture

In architecture the traditional has been fully exposed.

"Our present pattern of architectural education derives from a time when the division between art and science was widest. Although this division has been challenged in recent times, particularly by Walter Gropius, and is now rarely defended, the form and content of our education has so far undergone little change."[ii]

"It is sad to reflect that students have so often been trained for the kind of work that was current when their teachers were going into practice—in other words by teaching with an eye to the past, which is quite right, but also without an eye to the future, which is quite wrong."[iii]

"The young graduate architects we meet in our offices today have been through a programme spread over five years of unrelated, unrealistic design programmes, on the one hand, and a hotch-potch of formal lectures in building technology on the

(i) CHRISTOPHERSON Dr. D. G., Vice-Chancellor, Durham University, at conference on design methods. *Collected Papers*, Pergamon Press 1963, edited by Jones and Thornley.

(ii) DAVIES RICHARD LLEWELLYN, The Education of an Architect, *A.J.*, November 17, 1960.

(iii) HOLFORD Prof. Sir WILLIAM, *Architectural Education.*

other. The idea that a student arrives from his university and after one or two years is stamped as a qualified architect is a confidence trick played on both the young student and society."[i]

The architectural profession has been the most vocal about the inadequacies of its education. This does not mean, as some modest architects believe, that it is the worst. On the contrary, it shows an earlier and better awareness of the plight which affects the others equally. But due to this same modesty, perhaps, or other factors, innovators and critics have again and again pointed to the medical and engineering traditions (Professor Llewellyn Davies, Professor Page, Mrs. Layton, Professor Ling, etc.) as models to be copied. The criticisms quoted from within those professions make it so very clear how mistaken this view is.

The basic reforms really required will apply universally to all kinds of education. However, if there is a technique that has a future it is the studio attitude, the project attitude, of the architect. It gives time to think with others, but even this, as we will see, needs complete transformation.

I.3.5. False Starts to Reform

The danger inherent in reforms on invalid principles, or in improvized improvements, cannot be overstressed. Such things give false confidence, take our attention right off the central task of working up a series of new basic principles, a pattern fit to develop into the future.

i. A mistake of many innovators is their preoccupation with organization, course structures, subjects, and syllabus as if these are basic, as numerous articles show.[ii]

In fact course structures, the whole question of first degrees and second degrees, faculty allegiance and the rest, matter only in terms of administrative convenience. I do not deny that a

(i) SUGDEN D., The Office Man's View of the New Graduate Architect, *A.J.*, August 5, 1964.
(ii) e.g. HARPER D., A New Educational Framework, *R.I.B.A. Journal*, June 1960. KRETCHMER and THOMAS, Joint Education, evidence submitted to the Robbins Committee, *A.J.*, December 12, 1961, etc,

professor may, for example, get vastly more funds by being in a science faculty or with technology. This may be worth while, but should not be confused with the educational process which really matters and which stands in urgent need of new thought.

ii. Another characteristic of amelioration is solving yesterday's problems not tomorrow's. The "innovator" has a vivid memory of his own shortcomings and interprets the solutions of his son's problems in an idiom suitable and perhaps enlightened for his days of education.

This tendency should be recognized by each of us and consciously counteracted. It was recognition of it in myself that led to the fresh notion of educreation.

It is not necessarily always a matter of changing more than is being changed now. It is a matter of changing according to criteria that really lead us towards growth and renewal. The innovations must lead to the future pattern not fit the pattern of the past. I will give examples of innovations which suffer from the above weaknesses.

i. Joint training ideas, originating from the diagnosis that professions do not understand each other, have been studied for three years, and the first agreement is a statement bound by syllabus and examination-centred, truly the lowest common denominator of the professions involved.

Worst of all, in an age of rapid transition, of need for mobility, growth is precluded. A permanent advisory body is recommended. "One of its tasks should be to ensure that syllabuses do not in future diverge unless it is shown necessary that they should."[i]
Truly the opposite to educreation, particularly when one reads the stale tale "called a common syllabus" under its many heavy headings. This is worse than nothing. This is far too great a price for "joint training". There is no virtue in all learning together if it is outdated, useless gibberish.

ii. At a different level, and for some years, Professor Lord Llewellyn Davies has lead an attack on traditional architectural

(i) The Hall Report, Joint Committee on Training in the Building Industry, November 1964.

education. Faulting its weaknesses and recognizing its strength, he made the recommendation that didactic teaching of many fundamental subjects should precede design. He suggested that the rationality of his suggestion was borne out by engineering and medical education. He claimed that it was logical to go on teaching in the didactic way in the early years of a course as this lead straight on from school, where pupils were used to being taught in this manner.

Logical as the diagnosis and cure may sound, the disastrous error lies in the false premise: it is assumed that didactic teaching in schools is right and will remain. It is assumed that teaching didactic first and design afterwards is the way human beings learn to design best. It is assumed that the engineers and the doctors are satisfied with their education and, perhaps more important, the public with their performance, when neither is the case.

The forbidding permanence of present university legislation makes the introduction and permanent paving of such educational blind alleys frightening.

Ironically, research into architectural education at the Bartlett School, where Lord Llewellyn Davies's didactic-teaching-first approach prevails, is lead by Dr. Abercrombie, who argues in her book[i] on her research on medical education against didactic lessons and for free group-discussion teaching.

iii. Professor Page's recommendation brings up, once again, the invalid parallel of medical education: "The scientists have a large responsibility for the first academic stage, the practitioners for the second practical stage. I think architecture should be similarly handled . . ." (The medicals, as quoted, are trying hard to get out of it!) Having prescribed ineffective medicine for architects, in an aggressive manner, he confesses a few lines later: "Unfortunately nobody really knows of what the discipline of architecture consists at the moment. . . ."[ii]

(i) ABERCROMBIE Dr. J., *The Anatomy of Judgement*, London 1960.
(ii) *A.J.*, January 20, 1965. New Year number on research.

It seems remarkable that a professor admonishing architects vigorously for their unscientific attitude should lay down the law on a matter on which he admits ignorance, in fact "nobody really knows". He is recommending the experiment prior to hypothesis!

iv. The editors of the *Architects' Journal* see the improvement of architectural education as the process of shifting from an art school training to a science-based training—the prime example of advice to leap from the frying pan into the fire.

Scientists, as has been shown, have an enormous house to put in order and as has been suggested by Whitehead, Koestler, Bondi and others, the solutions to their problems will be those that apply to the arts also.

v. The report on diversification says: "The course of studies undertaken during the first three years should provide the student with a foundation of knowledge of the whole field of building . . . until the student has a sound knowledge of basic principles it is not appropriate to consider specialization in his studies", forgetting, of course, that what it requires "foundation of knowledge of the *whole* field of building" has long been shown as impossible due to the vast and ever expanding field.[i]

"Not appropriate" applies to what is now normal and what the writers have experienced. It is quite appropriate and practical and in fact inevitable (if we judge what actually happens and not phoney syllabuses) that students specialize *before* they have knowledge of the whole field of building, and often do so effectively.

The whole idea of diversification demonstrates the bankruptcy of thought on education: students are diverse. The rigid standard syllabus forces them all into similar, familiar packages. Then we come along and prescribe diversification! We even tell the

(i) The responsible senior students of a well-known school of architecture compared the syllabus and the actual teaching average in building construction over five years. The result bears out what any teacher knows but most hide, with a splendidly loyal hypocrisy—saving the face of the institution—the syllabuses are not covered by far.

students what they might be interested in with lists! (See quotation from Sec. of Association for Study of Med. Educ.)

We have forgotten already, for example, that many students were vitally interested in industrial building in my day (1946-51). They were beaten back. "That's not architecture", was the verdict of the schools and of the externals.[i] So what happens? In 1964 there was a big conference on how to bring industrialized building into education! I suggest that we should learn from experience. Instead of prescribing titles for diversification accept that live students' interests will lead them diversely, way beyond the guesses of some committee as to what is fitting for them.

To summarize, it is clear that the dilemmas of the professions are similar. Architectural education has gone further in taking measures to stem the tide of criticism. But here, more clearly than elsewhere, the outdated basis for reform and the pathetic filling of gaps of knowledge leave us feeling "that unless something is done rather quickly we shall stagger from crises to crises . . .".

Two years on the Board of Architectural Education have confirmed me in the belief that without a new pattern, without new criteria, we do stagger, and I resigned.

Given a pattern like educreation we can find our feet; we do not have to pretend we know before we start looking.

I.3.6. B.A.S.A.

In the reform of architectural education the British Architectural Students' Association (B.A.S.A.), has played an outstanding part particularly between 1960 to 1965 (the present day).

(i) The most remarkable example I know happened as recently as 1962 when the staff of our school had agreed a man should have a distinction and the well-known "progressive" external examiners wanted to fail him. After a battle lasting until 7.30 p.m. a pass mark was presented. The man went to Illinois and a year later Buckminster Fuller wrote of him, "He is an inspiration to his teachers". He had always been that to me and, more important, to his fellow students.

A succession of highly capable and responsible presidents, such as Jeremy McKay-Lewis and Hilary Chambers, and their executive committees, have arranged conferences and publications which have had remarkable and complementary qualities. On the one hand, they were the height of respectability and mature in their conception. On the other, the speakers brought together were, almost every one, in the forefront of their subjects, many highly original. The inspired selection of lecturers and discussion group leaders realized what had been largely pious hopes in the professional circles: the widening of the architectural horizon and the horizons of architectural education, opening up the doors to what was there, fertile or barren, in sociology, the psychology of perception, teaching machines, economics, environmental studies, design methods, computer aids, etc., etc. In many cases the R.I.B.A. took the cue and some similar lecture was held at R.I.B.A. a year or so afterwards. (Contrary to B.A.S.A., selection of R.I.B.A. lectures has seemed somewhat barren.) B.A.S.A. conferences, with their very concentrated working sessions have become so well known that awake heads of schools, teachers, architects and others have often attended them and come away astonished at what they have learned; out of the mouths of babes and sucklings . . ..

Significantly, for example, it was at the York B.A.S.A. conference that the very important, long awaited statement about the new course at the Bartlett School was given jointly by Professor Llewellyn-Davies and John Weeks.

The reports published and resolutions passed by B.A.S.A. have had influence far beyond the normal students' literature. Deservedly, of course. Not only have the speakers had authoritative voices, but the quality of the resolutions have been remarkably forward-looking, practicable and well put. Those passed on teaching techniques in Oxford 1960, were passed to all heads of schools and still offer a very worthwhile goal for most departments, though in small part they have now been accepted in many places already.

A list of some of the speakers makes interesting reading:

Dr. M. L. J. Abercrombie, perception.

Dr. Dennis Chapman, sociology.

Prof. Boris Ford, education.

Ian Michaels, education.

Prof. R. Coates, engineering.

Prof. H. Kay, teaching machines.

John Smith, background to education.

Prof. Page and Alexander Hardy, environmental factors.

Paul Ritter, educreation.

Prof. Llewellyn-Davies, John Weeks, The Bartlett's New Course.

Henry Swain, user requirements.

Prof. Sir Leslie Martin, education.

James Gowan, architectural design.

D. G. Thornley, J. C. Jones, G. Pask, design methods.

I.4. EDUCREATION—EDUCATION WITH BIAS TOWARDS CREATION

Coining the word "educreation" makes vivid that I am describing a kind of education, opposite in many ways to present practice; one that is biased towards creation and growth, flexibility, adaptation, development. It is not "narrowly" objective, it is not afraid of emotion or feeling: educreation has a profound bias.

What distinguishes educreation from traditional education? Three primary factors will release enormous potential in our young *without* a corresponding increase in the number of teachers.

I.4.1. Self-regulation to Replace Compulsion

The tendency to learn and create is innate. Individual and group hunger for skills, appetite for experience and curiosity lead to programmes of work which take the place of the enforced traditional syllabus, its set courses, lessons and the authoritarian educational attitudes and systems that go with it.

To incorporate this fact into a workable system is long overdue.

Whitehead wrote in 1923: "If you have much to do with the young as they emerge from school and from the university, you soon note the dulled minds of those whose education has consisted in the acquirement of inert knowledge. . . . The craving for expansion, for activity, inherent in youth is disgusted by dry imposition of disciplined knowledge. Discipline . . . should satisfy a natural craving for the wisdom which adds value to bare experience."[i]

A. S. Neill's pupils who decide one fine day that they must have O- or A-levels and go at it like mad without coercion from outside are an example. So is their success.[ii]

Whitehead goes on: ". . . the principle of progress is from within: the discovery is made by ourselves, the discipline is self-discipline . . . The teacher has a double function. It is for him to elicit the enthusiasm by resonance from his own personality, and to create the environment of a larger knowledge and a firmer purpose. He is there to avoid the waste . . .. "[iii]

The quotations are as apt but more embarrassing for us forty-two years later.

I.4.2. Co-operation to Replace Competition

Co-operation, as the very context of education, replaces competition which is usually regarded as the sole means of spurring on effort. Its techniques are carefully taught. The help each teacher or student can give to each other teacher and student are maximized. Here lies the way to make democracy a more efficient way of organizing society's efforts. Competition continues, of course, as a game, subservient to co-operation.

Co-operation has proved itself at all levels. The qualified professional says: "To collaborate with other designers while

(i) WHITEHEAD A. N., *Aims of Education* (New York 1949). The Rhythmic Claims of Freedom and Discipline, originally published in the *Hibbert Journal*, July 1923.
(ii) NEILL A. S., *Summerhill*, London 1964.
(iii) As note (i).

developing individually is undoubtedly possible, since the great potential of the group situation is that the individual within the group can flourish to a greater extent than when working on his own."[i]

And at primary school, where streaming is the ultimate in refined use of competition, ". . . in most of the streamed schools it was an offence for one child to turn to another for aid with an arithmetical problem. This was 'copying' and to be punished. Yet in most of the unstreamed schools this turning of one child to another was constantly encouraged by the teachers and rewarded with small words of praise." All children improved somewhat in the unstreamed schools, compared with the streamed, and the weakest children gained most.[ii]

I.4.3. A Therapeutic Attitude to Replace Moralist Judgements

If the urge to learn and create is impaired, which is a very likely situation in a society severally and obviously diagnosed as sick and deficient, then a therapeutic attitude (i.e. what impairs the urge and how can we help?) takes the place of the traditional coercion, moral denouncements of "lazy" and the social pressure to keep up a good name or be sentenced to a bad reputation.

The therapeutic approach has also proved its worth. Paul Goodman,[iii] a pioneer in the use of therapy in higher education reports that Professor U. E. Whiteis tested whether the increasing failure of learning and the high rate of drop-out are due to "lack of disciplined intelligence" or the interference of "emotional maladjustments" of the students.

Professor Whiteis employed a kind of Rogerian and Sullivanian psychotherapy in one class but not in an equivalent class. The results were fairly spectacular. The therapeutic class had almost no absences, scored progressively better in academic tests and only two of its members were dropped by the college as

(i) R.I.B.A., *Guide to Group Practice and Consortia*, London 1965.
(ii) JACKSON B., *Streaming, an Education System in Miniature.*
(iii) GOODMAN P., *Community of Scholars*, p. 120.

against nine. Goodman mentions other experiments at St. Louis and New York with similar results. He concludes: "My guess is that the success of all such programs comes from taking the students seriously as human beings, with sentiments and purposes that make up a whole existence."

Goodman brings the sinister "therapy" sound down to earth: "What was the 'therapy' employed by Professor Whiteis? It was non-directive interpersonal contact. In his words, he gave 'acceptance and understanding' rather than 'cajoling, coercing, ordering, forbidding, threatening, advising, etc.'. He allowed students to express their hostility, guilt, secret wishes. In this atmosphere, it seems, it was possible for the students to feel again the spontaneous interest that any young person might take . . .."

"It does not matter if this is called 'therapy' or not; I would prefer a use of language that would call it precisely the normal state of things: the lively response of normal students to a teacher who knows something and pays attention to them as human beings."[i]

The less sophisticated voice of the battling school-teacher is in accord: "Many years ago Freud, Adler and Jung made important discoveries about the hidden springs of conduct, but so far as we (teachers) are concerned they might never have lived."[ii]

I.4.4. The Powerful New Pattern

It may be said that though the ideas of self-regulation, co-operation and therapy (love in education) are each relatively old, the lack of their success to date lies in their weakness in isolation.

Educreation combines these three powerful factors. They reinforce each other mutually. The combination gives each one more force, more points of application and greater range of effectiveness. The new pattern is germinal to whole new ranges of more effective teaching and learning techniques.

(i) GOODMAN P., *The Community of Scholars*, p. 120.
(ii) MACKENZIE R. F., *A Question of Living*, London 1963.

After a considered and scientific study of higher education Marris thinks it feasible to propose the "spontaneous university": ". . . imagine a university which is entirely spontaneous. Each student is assigned a tutor, who first draws out of his pupil the range of his interests, and then suggests a scheme of study which seems mutually attractive. The student then sets out to explore it, crossing the conventional boundaries of academic disciplines wherever his interest leads him, and initiating his own research as original questions arise.

"The programme would differ from a graduate school in the diffusion of intellectual context. The research project is the starting point from which to discover a widening range of related problems, rather than a concentration of previous knowledge on a specific problem. At the completion of his studies, the student takes no examination: he consigns his findings, for what they may be worth, to the university store, and relies on the personal recommendation of his tutor in getting a job. The spontaneous university assumes that there is nothing specific a student must know, irrespective of his particular interests. And it can only teach those who find intellectual inquiry intrinsically meaningful. . . . As the wealth of knowledge grows beyond the grasp of any introductory synthesis, the limitations of the spontaneous university may begin to tell less against it."[i]

Here we have a self-regulatory picture. Most attractive to freedom-loving people who have that degree of health and strength to realize how they could enjoy and benefit from a period like that. It becomes practicable if we also recognize the therapeutic needs of a large majority and the possibilities for better use of the limited number of teachers through co-operation. It can be conceived as a concept allowing change in a time of transition. All three criteria of education are essential for effective implementation; at least they must be borne in mind if not applied.

(i) MARRIS P., *The Experience of Higher Education*, London 1964, pp. 70 and 71.

To try to use any one of the above in isolation has broken the hearts of many teachers (D. H. Lawrence for one).[i]   To realize the new pattern of educreation and develop accordingly, making use of all three approaches with a team of techniques, is infinitely more effective. Discipline–syllabus–moralized competition forms a workable and meaningful pattern for an authoritarian society. The constellation of self-regulation–co-operation–therapy is equally full of meat and meaning for the century of the common man.

The educational pattern is today failing and breaking down because the wild new waves of life emerging like the brooms of the sorcerer's apprentice become increasingly difficult to harness—because the set syllabus is an ever more ridiculous phenomenon obviously out of date; because imposed moral standards and competition appear clearly as arbitrary and unhealthy.

Over the past fifty years environment has been recognized as a decisive factor, at the expense of previous neat, hereditary preconceptions. This is one of the outstanding changes in man's attitude to himself. Education in its widest sense is almost synonymous with environment. The changes imminent in education mirror the decisive findings in the art and science of discovery.

On the one hand, often intellectually, we have got to know nature well enough that we are not afraid any longer, that we can work with her in us instead of against "dark forces" we do not comprehend. But on the other, in our flesh, muscle, imagination and emotions there are blocks against acting as we might. More life than we have been reared to tolerate rouses anxiety. And this brings with it the myriad rationalizations, "folly", withdrawal through fear, whether discretion is or is not the better part of valour, and downright opposition from obstructionist to ferocious.

It is crucial that educreation allows for opportune implementation, that it is economically viable (more education per pound

(i) MOORE H. T., *The Intelligent Heart*, 1950.

sterling!)[i] and practical, in that it uses the outstanding, odd, exceptional talents and enthusiasms hitherto specifically discouraged.

The creative bias, the essence of educreation as a diametric departure from education, is indigenous in the combination of the three tenets—self regulation, co-operation, therapy. It will emerge from any system, based on this attitude. What is more, the system itself will have the capacity and tendency to grow with the times, to act as a catalyst to the advances of society so that the young ask questions and are not afraid to act according to the answers they discover.

(i) Lord Bowden in a speech on education in 1964.

CHAPTER II

The Basis of Educreation

II.1. THEORIES OF LEARNING

Those not widely read in education or the psychology of learning may assume that, as in physics or biology, we have an organized body of facts and a theory which represents a sound and generally agreed base. But it is not so. Fragmentary theories and bits of knowledge float about, manned only by their creators, often oblivious of anything beyond their own little limited world.[i]

Summing up the situation[ii] an academic observer says:

"Theorists now differ not so much in their biases about the nature of learning as in the areas they prefer to study and the methods they prefer to use . . . [there is] an increasing recognition of the boundary conditions of theories and an increasing respect for specialization."

Yet this seems to be going in the wrong direction, for according to the same man:

"Most psychological interpreters of learning would probably recognize as ultimately desirable a broad, formal theory from which a wide range of learning laws could be predicted with a high degree of precision. There is, however, much scepticism about the practicability of such a system in the near future."

No wonder. The book which ends with that sentence begins

(i) An examination of the bibliographies of books on theories of learning makes this obvious.

(ii) HILL W., *Learning: a Survey of Psychological Interpretations*, San Francisco 1963.

with ". . . it is almost impossible to give an exact definition of learning that will be generally acceptable to psychologists . . ."[i]

J. A. Deutsch, at the beginning of his attempt to "explain some of the experimental evidence amassed by psychologists," has an even stronger view of the situation:

"Remarkable techniques have been developed for the purpose of collecting data about the behaviour of animal organisms under rigorously controlled conditions and for assessing these by elaborate statistical procedure. In this way a large mass of scientifically impeccable evidence has been built up and the pile is daily augmented. We cannot call it an edifice, for in spite of the general agreement about the method of making the bricks, there is no accepted way of putting them together. There is no concord among psychologists about what the facts they have accumulated are evidence for. This does not mean that they are merely in disagreement about the edifice they wish to erect; they have not decided even what constitutes a building. That is, not only do they disagree about the explanation of their findings, but they are not clear about what it would be to explain them. As a result it is not sufficient only to put forward a theory to explain the facts; it is also necessary to put forward a theory to justify the type of theory put forward. This is the reason for beginning with a discussion on explanation. There is little agreement on this topic and no general consensus of opinion on the various issues involved, which is not very surprising, as no one has been clear about what the issues are."

At the end of his book he claims no more than to have given "a coherent explanation of some phenomena".[ii]

Just as the present chaotic state of sociology can best be understood if its origins are traced, so with the psychology of learning. As sociology, in its quest for scientific objectivity and respectability has been divorced from applied social sciences, so the theory of learning has been detached from educational

(i) As Hill does not give a definition it is impossible for him, not just "almost".

(ii) Deutsch J. A., *The Structural Basis of Behaviour*, Cambridge 1960.

endeavour, or connected only to a narrow stretch of the whole waveband. (Both sociology and psychology can be seen to be so extreme as a reaction to the anti-scientific, moralistic and metaphysical attitudes dominant in the nineteenth century in those fields.)

The early psychological laboratory work originated in Germany[i] and dealt with the analysis and study of the components of conscious awareness only. There was a twofold development from this. On the one hand the Behaviourists from Watson[ii] through Pavlov[iii] in the U.S.S.R. onward (the Connectionists' theories), limited by their severe definition of what "behaviour" meant, studied an artificially isolated bit of life, largely rats in mazes. They were keen to see what happened not just what was felt and thought. On the other hand, the Gestalt School (cognitive theories), beginning with Wertheimer,[iv] noted some specific characteristics of man's and ape's perceptive and cognitive patterns and, over the years, through Wolfgang Köhler[v] and Kurt Koffka[vi] and others, a whole network of experiment and related theory grew out of this in Germany. The work moved largely to the U.S.A. in later years.

As might be guessed, there were attempts to combine these two approaches. However, this proved in vain for the approach and experiments of the Gestaltists, which was, according to Russell,[vii] typically German, were so different and the results quite unrelated to the American rats, which "rush about frantically, with an incredible display of rustle and pep, and at last achieve the desired result by chance". No new concept proved sufficiently broad to integrate both approaches on a higher level.

(i) WUNDT W., founder of the first psychological laboratory in an institution of learning in 1879.
(ii) WATSON J. B., Psychology as the Behaviourist Views it, *Psychol. Rev.*, U.S.A. 1913, Vol. 20, pp. 158–77. Also *Behaviourism*, Chicago 1930.
(iii) PAVLOV J. P., *Conditioned Reflexes*, Oxford 1927.
(iv) WERTHEIMER M., *Productive Thinking*, New York 1945. (Wertheimer's first paper was published in 1912, a year before Watson's.)
(v) KÖHLER W., *Gestalt Psychology*, London 1930.
(vi) KOFFKA K., *Principle of Gestalt Psychology*, New York 1935.
(vii) RUSSELL B., *An Outline of Philosophy*, London 1927.

The Behaviourist movement has gathered vast momentum in the U.S.A., and its mechanistic concept with its narrow rationalism, measurable cause and effect, stimulus and response (S.R.), has suited the current mental climate of much of science; and its cynicism about man, and his creative capacity born of ignorance and inability to understand himself.

Just this partial picture of the mechanistic approach was useful to men afraid to look at themselves, surrounded by emerging fascist tendencies, the epitome of conditioning[i] (of course, one can condition for democracy also, as Skinner insists). But a careful reading of Skinner's voluminous work—he is the most influential Behaviourist today—led me to pin-point one line that seems to me the key[ii] to his approach, and of the remarkable, self-imposed limitation of Behaviourism. What is more, it shows how oblivious and proud they are of the very limiting factor, purely and simply because it leads to some measurement, the sacred cow of materialists.

"I had the clue from Pavlov," writes Skinner.[iii] "Control your conditions and you will see order." To me this means roughly that if you cannot understand the subtleties of life, hold it, hit it, measure the loudness of the screams and you will have something concrete, even a general law about reaction to hitting perhaps, but not much of the subtlety of life.

Skinner's work has found incredible reservoirs of learning ability in a variety of animals. He has refined the techniques to teach them. No wonder he is itching to get his hands on to children. But happily, there are even better ways to tap the undoubted human reservoir. Skinner bases his moral right to condition people on the fact that it is happening anyway through advertising, propaganda, drugs, etc.,[iv] and that conditioning

(i) REICH W., *Mass Psychology of Fascism*, New York 1946.
(ii) SKINNER B. F., *The Behaviour of Organisms*, New York 1938, and *The Science of Human Behaviour*, New York 1953.
(iii) *Cumulative Record*, London 1961, p. 80.
(iv) SKINNER B. F., *The Behaviour of Organisms* and *The Science of Human Behaviour*.

can be benign and civilizing. (But two blacks don't make a white.)[i] His persuasive powers are considerable.[ii] (They need to be. The world remembers Aldous Huxley's Brave New World, Orwell's 1984, science fiction, etc.) He just leaves out of account the possibility that we have other educational methods which might raise the standards of life in a more efficient and reliable way than conditioning.

Russell's contention that animals did in their experiments what the experimenters wished them to—an incredible statement for the mechanistic, rigidly objective, psychologist–behaviourist— was more than a joke. This was borne out by an experiment on the experimenters;[iii] sure enough, two random samples of rats behaved as "genius" and "stupid" according to the "objective test" after two sets of experimenters had been given the same kind of rat but with two kinds of labels! Devastatingly, the result fitted the false labels not the objective facts! The incredible narrowness of Behaviourism is in remarkable contrast to, yet perhaps the explanation of, its prolific growth.

". . . once we have arranged the particular type of consequence called a reinforcement, our techniques permit us to shape the behavior of an organism almost at will. It has become a routine exercise to demonstrate this in classes in elementary psychology by conditioning such an organism as a pigeon. Simply by presenting food to a hungry pigeon at the right time, it is possible to shape up three or four well defined responses in a single demonstration period—such responses as turning around, pacing the floor in the pattern of a figure-8, standing still in a corner of the demonstration apparatus, stretching the neck, or stamping the foot. Extremely complex performances may be reached through successive stages in the shaping process, the contingencies of reinforcement being changed progressively in the right direction of the required behavior. The results are often quite dramatic.

(i) See his *Walden Two*, New York 1948, a conditioned yet humane democratic Utopia.
(ii) As note (i).
(iii) PETERMAN P., *Gestalt Theory*, London 1932.

In such a demonstration one can see learning taking place. A significant change in behavior is often obvious as the result of a single reinforcement."[i]

". . . In a more academic environment they have been used for demonstration purposes which extend far beyond an interest in learning as such. For example, it is not too difficult to arrange the complex contingencies which produce many types of social behavior. Competition is exemplified by two pigeons playing a modified game of ping-pong. The pigeons drive the ball back and forth across a small table by pecking at it. When the ball gets by one pigeon the other is reinforced. The task of constructing such a "social relation" is probably completely out of reach of the traditional animal trainer. It requires a carefully designed program of gradually changing contingencies and the skillful use of schedules to maintain the behavior in strength. Each pigeon is separately prepared for its part in the total performance, and the 'social relation' is then arbitrarily constructed. The sequence of events leading up to this stable state are excellent material for the study of the factors important in non-synthetic social behavior. It is instructive to consider how a similar series of contingencies could arise in the case of the human organism through the evolution of cultural patterns.

"Co-operation can also be set up, perhaps more easily than competition. We have trained two pigeons to co-ordinate their behavior in a co-operative endeavor with a precision which equals that of the most skillful human dancers."[ii]

". . . rarely in the history of science has a more ambitious theory been built on shakier foundation." And with this comment of Koestler's I refer the reader to the full and brilliant

(i) SKINNER B. F., *The Science of Learning and the Art of Teaching*, p. 100.
(ii) "The reactions of Dr. Skinner himself, as a pigeon conditioned by our society, are well exemplified by the following: 'Since it is difficult to write teaching machine programs, bad programs undoubtedly will be written and marketed but if the market place has its usual effect, we can look forward to the emergence of highly efficient programs in the not too distant future.' "—(GOODMAN P., *The Community of Scholars*, p. 9.)

criticism of past learning theories in his book.[i] We must know our enemies and the results of the theories of Behaviourism do threaten us currently in the indiscriminate acceptance of teaching machines.[ii]

As one might expect, the Gestalt theorist appealed to the artistically orientated and was developed in their work.[iii] But direct observation of animals continues—with some fascinating results. The work by such men as Bernhard Rensch[iv] at Munster and others regularly reported (with English summaries) in the fascinating (but inordinately expensive!) *Zeitschrift* für *Tier-psychologie*[v] gives information on the attitudes and characteristics of the animal as whole, or in response to alternate choice situations, within relatively free conditions. Control is minimized whereas, as we have seen with Skinner, to Behaviourists it is the crucial factor.

Sudden recognition of solutions to whole problems through "insight", activities for their own sake; reward actually disturbing activity (what a contradiction and change from "stimulus response" rigidity!);[vi] preference of the new over the old, i.e. innate curiosity; preference for regular patterns. These kind of fascinating discoveries have been made through the Gestalt approach. As control is less, the influence of the research worker on the experiment is not likely to be so decisive either.

Whereas Behaviourism is exclusive, Gestaltism, by its very nature, is inclusive, organic and a far more open approach. Any integration of the many facts so far found in psychology of learning will have to be organic because we are organisms;

(i) KOESTLER A., *The Act of Creation.*
(ii) See Section III.1 for a fuller discussion.
(iii) ARNHEIM R., *Art and Visual Perception*, London 1956; GAMBRICH E. H., *Art and Illusion*, London 1960; ELLIS W. D., *A Source Book of Gestalt Psychology*, London 1938; NORBORG-SCHULZ C., *Intentions in Architecture*, London 1963.
(iv) RENSCH B., Wirksamkeitasthetischer Faktorer bei Wirbeltieren, *Zeitschrift fur Tierpsychology*, Band 15, Heft 1958.
(v) Publisher, Paul Parey, Berlin.
(vi) MARRIS P., *The Biology of Art*, London 1962.

C

inclusive because it involves the whole of the organism; and open to allow for development. The worth of Gestalt work is likely to be greater than that of the Behaviourists.

In a small book such as this it would be out of place to discuss at greater length the battles, trials and tribulations of the short history of learning theory. But in giving a representative bibliography, further study of any topic which seems relevant to the individual reader is easily available. Koestler's *The Act of Creation* (760 pages) represents a splendid source book and a theoretical framework highly stimulating and in line with my own approach in many fundamental principles. It lacks a therapeutic approach, however, and ignores the work of Reich, which restricts its usefulness decisively, limiting the application of his learning theory.

II.2. Philosophies of Education

Beyond the psychologies of learning there are the views of education which emerge from a sociological or cultural or philosophical viewpoint. Here we can also broadly divide the theories into two: on the one hand those who see education as the socializing process, meaning that this is the manner in which the child learns to fit into the existing society; basically a static process. On the other hand there are those who declare that education is the means for fulfilling life, and this means changing society; basically a dynamic concept.

The intricacies of discussion on this issue can be boring. Thelan[i] has shown that the way these views are expressed indicates differences that make debate usually meaningless. A similarity to the gulf between Behaviourists and Gestaltists.

Progressive writing can be very woolly, lending itself to countless interpretations. On the other hand, doctrinaire Behaviourism may sound very liberal. An example of each is given below. First, John Dewey,[ii] perhaps the most famous of the

(i) THELAN A. H., *Dynamics of Groups at Work*, Chicago 1954.
(ii) DEWEY JOHN, *The School and Society*, Chicago 1949.

liberal philosophers of education. Given the advancing society of our time, he declared we must "make each one of our schools an embryonic community life, active with types of occupations that reflect the life of the larger society and permeated with the spirit of art, history and science". *For a fascist* this might even describe fascism!

And now Skinner, whose Harvard following is well nigh fanatical:

"In the light of our present knowledge a school system must be called a failure if it cannot induce students to learn except by threatening them for not learning. That this has always been the standard pattern simply emphasizes the importance of modern techniques. John Dewey was speaking for his culture and his time when he attacked aversive education practices and appealed to teachers to turn to positive and humane methods. What he threw out should have been thrown out. Unfortunately, he had too little to put in its place. Progressive education has been a temporizing measure which can now be effectively supplemented. Aversive practices can not only be replaced, they can be replaced with far more powerful techniques. The possibilities should be thoroughly explored if we are to build an educational system which will meet the present demand without sacrificing democratic principles."[i]

While Skinner is right that Dewey did not give us a working pattern to replace the old, one would not guess from the style of Skinner that he wishes to construct a system of conditioning,[ii] of stimulus and response machinery and programmes which, albeit orientated to democracy and humane social behaviour, have absolutely no place for spontaneity and creativity, insight, or pleasure in learning, as such.

[i] Skinner B. F., *Cumulative Record*, p. 177.
[ii] 300 years earlier the idea was already about:
"Many children imputing the pain they endured at school to their books they were corrected for, so join these ideas together, that a book becomes their aversion. . . ."—(Locke John, *Essay Concerning Human Understanding*, Book 2, Ch. 33.)

It is fascinating that, within the framework of each psycho-analysis, or Behaviourism or Gestaltism, both philosophies static or dynamic can be found. It is the educreational approach which integrates the two concepts on a more generalized plane of diagnosis and remedy. Constraint to a static world practice has been so much easier to imagine and enact. It is rooted in our culture and has a long tradition. But momentum has been gathering for change, not surprisingly. However, the view taken by A. N. Whitehead in 1916[i] and repeated by many since, has at long last, with the practical therapeutic approach, gained the methods necessary to turn "wants" into obtainable "facts", ideals into policies.

The limitations of existing theories and the need for a comprehensive working hypothesis is emphasized by each new discovery relevant to learning, perception, thought, memory, etc. In recent years there have been experiments going beyond the limiting aspects of the two main schools and much of this, as well as material from neglected workers in biology and sociology, has been integrated by Koestler.[ii] Today, the relevant facts have to be painstakingly collected from scores of specialist journals in dozens of artificially separated fields.

The last five lines of Koestler's text read:

"The ominous trend towards over-specialization, its dangers to the creative mind, and the educational and administrative reforms needed to remedy it, are outside the scope of this book."

They are the *raison d'être* of this one.

Research and thought on this subject have led to a wider theory than Koestler's, and to a demand that goes beyond a "broad formal theory from which a wide range of learning laws could be predicted". But it need not "fulfil the high degree of precision" as Hill[iii] goes on to say. As the charm and virtue of hand craftsmanship is its lack of "dead accuracy", so, similarly, in theory of education; having arrived at a high degree of preci-

(i) WHITEHEAD A. N., *Aims of Education*.
(ii) KOESTLER A., *The Act of Creation*.
(iii) HILL F. W., *Learning*.

sion would be a sign of loss of very desirable qualities (as in Behaviourism). What is more, there is no virtue, no value, beyond a neurotic craving of our time, for objectivity, numbers, precision in the central issues of such things as learning or eating or loving.

I see the demand for a theory which is so broad that it does not fit education exclusively but allows us to see the learning process as indigenous to the life process itself. (A natural development from Reich, and Koestler's aim also.) Furthermore, the theory must be capable of comprehending existing systems and diagnose their lacks. (Reich's work here is crucial.) Finally, it should lend itself to predict reliably aims and values, for the future, and point to the techniques and policies for implementation; a theory which applies to individual and group alike; which does not leave one with the cause–effect dilemma of whether the individual changes society or the society changes the individual; which throws up teaching techniques for the skills and disciplines demonstrated as common to science and art, artistic creation and scientific discovery.

And so the principles of the chapter are regarded as common to all life, many of them common to all phenomena in the universe as we know it. They represent the outline of a philosophy built up from observation, from hypothesis and experiment, and from constrained practical use. To state them is to try to show the common nature of life process and educational process. As we develop educational ideas, so we could develop ideas on all other aspects from these root postulates. They combine much that has been written in the last twenty years and I feel indebted particularly to the works of Wilhelm Reich, Bronislaw Malinowski, L. L. Whyte, Arther Koestler, J. Bell Pettigrew, A. N. Whitehead and H. W. Heason.

Together the principles represent not so much descriptions of events, of entities, but indicate the meaningful questions we can ask about relationships. It is a checklist for a dynamic understanding of reality always taking into account what is decisive: the point of view, i.e. the relationship to a relationship.

II.3. OUTLINE FOR AN INTEGRATED PATTERN APPROACH AND CONCEPT

II.3.1. Basic Concept—The Fundamental Factor

We take "Relationship" as the definition of existence. So any form of existence is a relationship. The nature of existence is determined by the relationships of or in relationship. This it seems to me, is the ultimate in "reality-thinking".[i]

Our philosophical and scientific traditions have concentrated on "entities" rather than relationship. Even when relationships are considered, entities are seen "in relation" rather than the relationship, which is far more. "Man" seen as a relationship of relationships makes very good sense. Even the Christian—that voluntary custodian of the idea of "individual"—must admit relationship to be basic: to God, to fellow men, to temptation leading to heaven or hell, depending on the relationships of a lifetime. Entity we can define as a complex of relationships the form of which has definition, impact or meaning in its relationships, according to criteria to be established.

If relationship is the common denominator, its nature must have reality. It is this which allows us to conceive the world as one (e.g. it's all made of atoms), to connect and relate by original thought and action. But atoms are themselves relationships which become increasingly plainer. A structural "entity" approach is proving futile for definitions. Reich's theory of primordial energy,[ii] a basic energy (he called it orgone) is the best working hypothesis for the relationship approach I have met to date.

One of Buckminster Fuller's axioms is "Unity is a complex, volumetric plurality at minimum two".[iii]

(i) "The word 'between' describes the spatial relation of three objects—one is between two others; and so on . . . one can abstract the word 'betweenness'. As it happens, it expresses an idea we seldom wish to talk about." I wonder why?—(CRAWSHAY-WILLIAMS R., *The Comforts of Unreason*, London 1949, p. 63.)

(ii) REICH W., *Cosmic Superimposition*, Rangeley, U.S.A. 1951.

(iii) McHALE J., *Buckminster Fuller*, New York 1962, p. 113.

Fuller's work represents a remarkable parallel from a structural "synergetic" point of view. Relationship (as "synergy" implies) is his starting point. The basic elements, two "open" triangles forming the basic tetrahedron.[i]

Whether you say with Descartes, "I think, therefore I am", or, as Reich might say, "I feel, therefore I am", or, "We are, therefore I am", or, "I am as I think I feel", as one might formulate it, we cannot get away from the two-or-moreness, that all experience is relationship.

It is easy to try out and test the postulate that relationship, pattern, two-or-moreness is basic to existence. As soon as you imagine, or look, or feel, the pattern is there. There is the imaginer, and the imagined, the onlooker and the seen, the feeler and the felt. And it is likely that study of the pattern, the relationship is more fertile than that of merely the entities as "relating". We have a hard task to overcome the habits of thought, the language, logic and symbolism borne of our tradition which has been to think in entities.

To summarize: I recommend a change from thinking in terms of "entities in relation" to the relation of entities (themselves relationships). A profound difference.

The relevance of this basic tenet to learning is very obvious. The patterns of child–society, child–teacher, child–child, child–teaching aid, the learner and the learnt, the associations of ideas, the attraction of knowledge, memory, etc., gain from a relationship approach. The illuminating quality clarifies and penetrates where confusion and incomprehensibility reign. It has helped me to sort out, again and again, the mountains of dissimilar and conflicting writings on various subjects collecting on my desks. It leads to a sense of direction and effective action.[ii]

I think that the reason that Behaviourism, in spite of its severe

(i) BUCKMINSTER FULLER, World Design Science Decade, 1965–75, Phase I (1964), Document 2, *The Design Initiative*, Illinois 1964, pp. 23, 25, 31.
(ii) I needed a working concept—that's how it came into existence. I found it useful; it evolved through its use. Because it is useful I like it. And its evaluation will continue—"there's modesty in my megalomania".

theoretical and practical limitations, has got so far so rapidly, is its basis on relationship, albeit in a very little isolated bit of learning. The Stimulus-response (SR) concept, though born of causal and mechanistic thought, has become so intimately related that it really is applied as a concept of relationship not as the cause and effect of the two entities.

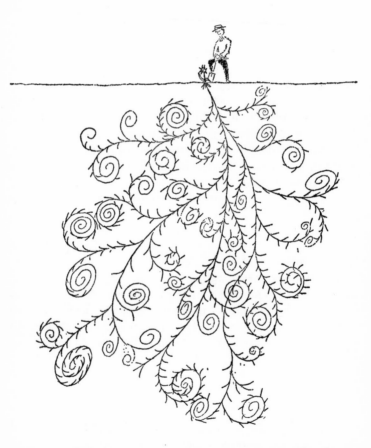

FIG. 4.   Discovery! a cartoon with factual "roots" and profoundest implications.—(By T. Bestwick after Karel Čapek.)

The relativity theory and many other developments in this century, use more and more "relationship thinking" in the extension of our understanding of the cosmos. Gravity and much else will yield to comprehension, I think, with this approach and its working methods.

II.3.2. Basic Tentative Tenets

The basic tentative tenets of an integrated pattern approach or concept are summarized below.

Any kind of event or existence is a relationship of relationships, perhaps to infinity.

All specific relationships can be seen, found meaningful and identified and qualified by defining their behaviour as seen in terms of the following common qualities of all relationship:

(A) It is dynamic; movement is ubiquitous and always obeys the three-beat cyclical formula pattern:

1. Attraction $\rightarrow$ (fusion–liberation),
2. Fusion $\rightarrow$ (liberation–attraction),
3. Liberation $\rightarrow$ (attraction–fusion).

The Temporal priority of beat is irrelevant to origin.

(B) It has form; the form of movement and structure (frozen movement) is the resultant and combination of three tendencies:

1. To spiral (in the widest sense).
2. To branch (in the widest sense).
3. To balance (symmetry, etc., in the widest sense).

(C) It has organization along the following principles:

1. *Self-regulation*—inherent tendency to control the functions and growth of an entity on predetermined lines, in its freedom of interaction with the environment more or less constrained.

(a)

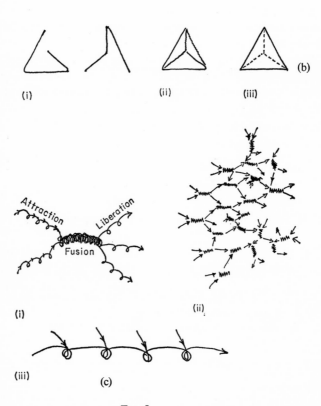

FIG. 5.

2. *Co-operation*—the tendency to behave as a meaningful part of a whole, a concrete or abstract pattern, an organ, an organism or a group.

3. *Creative bias*—the total of possible relationships within any environment is an indeterminate number of combinations. From this number the creative bias tends towards:

(i) growth;

(ii) structuralization;

(iii) transformation—any relationship stretched beyond the integrative strength of its attraction–fusion–liberation pattern by an attraction from outside the self-regulative, co-operative organization (or entity) will tend to disorganize (in organizing elsewhere or otherwise).

Each of the above qualities, A, B, and C, includes all the others. The understanding of phenomena follows the line of investigation along the framework given. I do not claim it's the only frame-

---

FIG. 5 *opposite.* (a) Wilhelm Reich's diagram of the creation of particles and life. Spiral energy waves "superimpose" and creation takes place.

(b) Buckminster Fuller's diagram of the creation of the tetrahedron —the minimum structural system, basic to all others in the universe. Fuller says that "two flat spirals" (triangles) combine to form the tetrahedron. (i) The two "flat" spirals. (ii) They fuse into a tetrahedron. (iii) The basic structural form.

(c) Developed attraction–fusion–liberation diagram. This is a dynamic generalization of events in the universe. It forms a common denominator for physical and non-physical—animate and inanimate phenomena, in terms of a "basic energy" concept. The learning process, design process, research process, etc., are decisively clarified by the application of this concept (model, formula, diagram). But a two-dimensional diagram of a complex relationship, that we can really only comprehend in terms of space and time, is bound to be weak. It does, however, give an indication of the attraction–fusion–liberation pattern of cycles, and cycles within cycles. It indicates the concept of movement in terms of spirality, branching and balance (direction). (i) Basic diagram. (ii) Growth and pattern development diagram built up of basic patterns. (iii) Each diagram loop, in any phase, can be regarded as minor fusion showing that the 3 beat applies at all levels of hierarchy.

work, but it is the one that seems to make most sense to date and answers, otherwise highly elusive, meaningful and urgent questions.

We have a remarkable confirmation from Buckminster Fuller's structural approach; which has been used in microbiological formulations as well as in enormous man-made structures. ". . . we do not have any such thing as a closed triangle in a plane; all triangles are merely spirals, very flat spirals . . ."

And what is even more remarkable in its parallel evidence: when Fuller's two spirals fuse they create the basis of all structure . . . a tetrahedron! Reich's fusing orgone spirals create matter and energy.[i] Fuller works with structure and so begins with triangles. Reich starts with function and arrives at spirals through study of energy movement.

The concept of attraction of the two " open " triangles, their fusion in structure and their liberation as capable of behaving as a structure conform neatly to the three-beat formula. It is a moving discovery to note such diverse approaches arrive at such related conclusions. This encourages the belief that the validity of the general concepts are indeed general. Maybe their useful application in this book will encourage the development of this unpopular unifying kind of science which takes little note of the academic pigeon holes, and therefore finds slow acceptance, little co-operation from research funds and no relevance to any of the narrow syllabus-bound "educational" courses. (Except as side-shows occasionally!)

The above common qualities of relationship A, B, C, occur within the constraint of rhythm, ubiquitously and simultaneously. Their meaning and relevance to learning can now become more specific. We will describe the three common qualities with their three sub-sections more fully in the context of their relevance to education and educreation.

(i) REICH W., *Cosmic Superimposition*, Maine, U.S.A. 1951. Also BUCK-MINSTER FULLER, World Design Science Decade, 1965–75, Phase I (1964), Document 2, *The Design Initiative*, Illinois 1964, pp. 23 and 25.

II.4. INTEGRATED PATTERN APPROACH TO EDUCREATION

II.4.1 Definitions

To distinguish, say, the taking of nutriment when eating an apple pie, from learning (i.e. what is an apple pie?), we can define the field of learning as that aspect of any relationships of which are born, or through which are developed:

(a) Capacities for communication (expression and absorption);
(b) Knowledge and memory (structuralized and stored information and acquisition of skills);
(c) association and bi-sociation (deduction, design, judgement, creation).

Learning need not be through education, which is a deliberate process. It covers relationships, with inanimate objects: a door teaches you not to bump into it. It also covers a number of processes which involve innate, permanently absorbed or structuralized skills. From the cell which has "learnt" how to grow, to the young gosling who by "imprinting", attaches himself permanently and irrevocably to whatever is more like mother goose when he is a certain number of minutes old (albeit tin can or human being), to the birds who know how to whistle without ever meeting other birds.

It is obvious that whatever is involved cannot be imagined merely in terms of brain paths, nerve cells, etc. The structuralization of knowledge might be in terms of energy patterns which are evoked, created, in the growth of relationships.

The code, the phenomenon of storing growth pattern, is one of the fundamentals we have to postulate. We can call it "miraculous" or just "an unknown", as with all fundamentals. We shall find out much more about its characteristics in the course of discovery. For the moment it's important to remember that it cannot be comprehended in terms of existing frameworks of knowledge and is therefore a challenge and an arrow to further research. To be able to disturb or influence the process tells us only a little about it (note behaviourists).

To accept it as an important principle is not precluded: we observe lawful, inborn behaviour, the concept means something that is useful.

Bearing all this in mind educreation is the deliberate encouragement of learning. Although the deliberate effort to teach, by one organism to another (usually the mother) is found in many species, the conscious effort to give opportunity to learn in abstracted forms and for specific goals is limited to man and marks his educational efforts of the past.

The consciously designed effort to gain not a static goal or known aim but an increasing capacity to develop, create so as to be able to design and plan to change efficiently and influence the collective growth process positively, that is the next stage: educreation.

"The controls of a skilled activity generally function below the level of consciousness."[i]

II.4.2. The Dynamic Quality of all Relationships

The nature of relationship-dynamic is rhythmic movement. The three-beat formula attraction–fusion–liberation and again attraction–fusion–liberation is the common functioning principle of all such rhythm. It can be felt and is applied intellectually to comprehend the patterns of behaviour.

The three words in the formula seem the best general terms to cover an infinite number of variations within the three-beat rhythm pattern:

> Attraction covers phenomena that have been called: association, compulsion, excitement, drive, urge, instinct, tension-charge, crises, etc., etc.
>
> Fusion covers amalgamation, crystallization, integration, combination, bi-sociation, super-imposition, fulfilment, climax, convulsion, orgasm, creation, mating, etc.

(i) KOESTLER A., *The Act of Creation*, p. 42.

Liberation: repulsion, dissociation, division, satisfaction, discharge-relaxation, liberation from and liberation for, to be freed from urge or compulsion, disintegration, etc.

Our cause and effect tradition will make us start with "attraction" as the first beat. But that is the only reason. As relationship is basic to the rhythm the whole pattern exists all the time. The temporal sequence is only useful to isolate phenomena for understanding them. It does not indicate a temporal origin. It is not a matter of cause and effect. The "fusion" beat is the creative aspect and from this arises capacity for new patterns.

Thus, it might have meaning to have the formula written fusion–liberation–attraction, fusion–, etc. But the very difficult thing for us is to appreciate is that the temporal priority is irrelevant.

Each beat, as we are dealing with a "common functioning principle"[(i)], can itself be seen as a three-beat pattern. Take a very obvious relationship between boy and girl. They walk hand in hand. A feeling of love (attraction) leads to the squeezing of hands (fusion), a letting go and a feeling of happiness (liberation). Yet the entire walk, to the place where they will cuddle, can be taken as attraction, the cuddle as fusion and the liberation the pleasant feeling afterwards, and so on.

Let us now examine the three-beat rhythm in learning relationships. One would expect (in a sick society such as ours will be demonstrated to be in the next chapter) that it is as important to comprehend the three-beat pattern in disorganization and transformation as in organization.

Most schools of educational psychology have had to assume "motives", "instincts", "urges" or "drives". The important thing is to realize that in learning we deal with a spontaneous phenomenon:

" . . . we eat because we like a good dinner: we subdue the

(i) A common functioning principle, a phrase coined by Reich, indicates the notion that a common rhythm of behaviour runs through microcosm and macrocosm.—(REICH W., *Cosmic Superimposition*, Maine, U.S.A. 1951.)

forces of nature because we have been lured to discovery by an insatiable curiosity . . ."

"It must never be forgotten that education is not a process of packing articles in a trunk . . . its nearest analogue is the assimilation of food by a living organism."[i]

We doubt insight so we must set up experiments to see everything in laboratory conditions before we believe it. So at McGill University they paid students well to be comfortable physically but inactive with all their senses. After some hours, discomfort proved too much; they wanted to be let out in spite of the good pay. They also deteriorated at problem solving. So the laboratory showed what common sense has long known. Mental and perceptive activity and learning are not something that have to be forced on man; on the contrary, he needs it—he needs to interact with the outside world in that way just as he does when he eats, is social, or breathes. And self-regulation in all these things is part of the organic make-up.

But even though you may call it by any other name the fact that a child wants to learn and work and play and co-operate as eat and breathe deeply, are signs of health.

In sick societies the "attraction" (relationship) of learning is disorganized by cultural phenomena, taboos, repressions, traditions. In our society, for example, the baby learns to associate venture with smacked hands, curiosity with being naughty; later, naïvety with derision, initiative with frustration, being interested with being sissy. We destroy the spontaneous pattern and try to make up for it by a culturally enforced one of compulsion–competition (aggression)—moralistic—judgement. This weakens the learning process decisively into "education".

That is why "The main educational tasks in many of these schools must be therapeutic".[ii]

(i) WHITEHEAD A. N., *The Aims of Education*, p. 44.
(ii) PINION F. B., *Educational Values in an Age of Technology*, Oxford 1964, p. 56.

Why " . . . the academic problem at present is to unblock the intellect in the young, to prove that it is possible for persons to display intellectual virtues without embarrassment or punishment and to use them in the community and the world without futility".[i]

And that, "The premature amassing of knowledge diminishes enlightenment and the exercise of intelligence".[ii]

It is interesting that Lord Llewellyn-Davies's educational changes emanating from the Bartlett School of Architecture are in danger of making just this mistake.[iii]

As certain species have only just held their own against the attack of certain diseases to which they were particularly prone, so man has suffered from "armouring" and the emotional plague. While this vital theme will be discussed more fully in the next chapter, it is interesting to note the effect of this illness on the learning process.

(a) *Attraction*—instead of allowing self-regulation and the skill hunger, curiosity, appetite for the new, to be the leading principles, we coerce into arbitrary, limited channels the unwilling, resentful child, who becomes frightened of life or being attracted to the new. He may be attracted to learning by an ulterior motive—the love of a person.

(b) *Fusion*—is abortive. Instead of pleasurable learning, good in quality and extensive in quantity, absorbed and integrated efficiently, we get parrot answers, no relation between question and relevance. And where fusion takes place it might be with emotional aspects and needs in relation to the teacher or parents' approval. This results in inferior kinds of learning.

(c) *Liberation*—hatred for subjects, learning in general, inability to use acquired knowledge in creative, original ways, liberation for limited coerced attraction only, due to the above. Permanently contracted learning life—instead of life-long learning

(i) LLEWELYN-DAVIES, Deeper Knowledge—Better Design, *A.J.*, May 23, 1957.

(ii) WHITEHEAD A. N., *Aims of Education*.

(iii) LLEWELYN-DAVIES, Education of an Architect, *A.J.*, December 17, 1960.

development. (Verdi's operas; Strauss's Oboe Concerto; work of Goethe.)

All this is reflected also in the ascendancy of administration, the topsy-turvy concepts and undue snob respect for research, the fact that school and learning was, and largely still remains, a dirty word, not only for children—it sticks for life.

Shakespeare's description is the epitomy of the armoured character in the rigid society:

> "Then the whining school-boy, with his satchel
> And shining morning face, creeping like snail
> Unwillingly to school."
>
> (Shakespeare, *As You Like It*, *c*. A.D. 1600.)

What volume of centuries of man-made cruelty is summed up in these words? At the above date this view of education must have been well established. Three-hundred-and-sixty-five years later our system is still based on the notions that it cannot be left to children whether to go to school or not.

But it is generally valid that ". . . inventive genius requires pleasurable mental activity as a condition for its vigorous exercise . . . science is almost wholly the outgrowth of pleasurable intellectual curiosity."[i]

Whitehead also developed a three-beat theory for learning. He calls his three beats romance–precision–generalization and couples this concept with his view of the discipline as arising spontaneously:

To the child it seems "he has been given free access to the glory of the heavens". The teacher has sent it to look through the telescope.[ii]

". . . when this stage of romance has been properly guided another craving grows. . . . Now is the time for pushing on for knowing the subject exactly, and for retaining in the memory its salient features. This is the stage of precision."[iii]

(i) WHITEHEAD A. N., *The Aims of Education*, p. 54.
(ii) Ibid., p. 44.
(iii) Ibid., p. 45.

Imposition is diagnosed as disorganization of the learning process:

". . . a block in the assimilation of ideas inevitably arises when a discipline of precision is imposed before a stage of romance has run its course in the growing mind . . ."[i]

I even found that Whitehead saw his rhythm also as a common functioning principle.

". . . there is not one unique threefold cycle of freedom, discipline, and freedom; but that all mental development is composed of such cycles, and of cycles of such cycles . . . I call the first period of freedom the 'stage of romance', the intermediate period of discipline I call the 'stage of Precision', and the final period of freedom is the 'stage of Generalization'."[ii]

"In no part of education can you do without discipline or can you do without freedom; but in the stage of romance the emphasis must always be on freedom, to allow the child to see for itself and to act for itself."[iii]

". . . the discipline should be the voluntary issue of free choice, and that the freedom should gain an enrichment of possibility as the issue of discipline."[iv]

The discipline that Whitehead speaks of is the wrapt intent, complete absorption in play, in work, in love, in giving birth.

"First-hand knowledge is the ultimate basis of intellectual life."[v]

Learning crystallizes in fusion. The fusion with actual experience is a much more powerful all-inclusive experience than the intellectual one. Within all the kinds of work the spontaneous interest, the spontaneous learning process, is so much more effective than the instilled or compelled one. We need merely to think of the different qualities involved in memory (examination swotting, a sort of special skill like balancing a tightrope; it is memory of the shortest duration). To generalize: anything—if remembered in an interesting context—comes back easily. If it

(i) WHITEHEAD A. N., *The Aims of Education*, p. 44.
(ii) Ibid., p. 42.   (iii) Ibid., p. 44.   (iv) Ibid., p. 40.   (v) Ibid., p. 61.

was compulsively learned it is either compulsively remembered (to the exclusion of other creative activity on the theme) or compulsively forgotten. The emotional content of learning (i.e. it is a process which always involves the whole of the organism) comes out most clearly in the elated *eureka* feeling when one has understood something, whether really original or only new to the learner.

When the deprived rat associates an action with getting food it learns a habit. The Behaviourist's skill is to get results by placing a passenger on the attraction–fusion–liberation vehicle of hunger; with the hunger satisfaction fusion the habit is created. It goes to the depth of the rat's being. All manner of mutilation still leave it trying by any means to perform the usual ingrained habit.[i]

The child who eats compulsively because eating has been identified with love in his personality, has used the love fusion to carry the eating compulsion.

Such techniques are dangerous because they are anti-creative, anti-critical just because they are efficient.

The teaching machine seduces the pupil by offering regular little fusions (he gets the right answer) because the questions are so simple. This, too, may well engrain such small-step learning to the detriment of other kinds of much postponed reward activities like research . . . like thinking of questions . . . like seeing the difficulties instead of the step to the next small reward.

The encouragement and techniques of Synectics[ii] towards the creative association (bi-sociation) of previously unrelated matrices according to Koestler, is an educreative way of aiding the three-beat rhythm in problem solving. The attraction, the fusion and the liberation stages are understood and helped in their spontaneous functions. Good teaching of many kinds does the same thing.

(i) KOESTLER A., *The Act of Creation*, London 1964, p. 458.
(ii) GORDON W. J. J., *Synectics*, New York 1960.

II.4.3. Form

Spiralling, branching and balancing (symmetry) are the tendencies of all movement. A study of form, the relationships of the forms of movement to the forms of structure, has in recent years produced some books. Dramatic illustrations have been possible through modern techniques. But nothing has matched the immense, largely original study of Pettigrew[i] on this subject. This, together with the theory of Reich, made me set out on further investigation on the subject, and brought me face to face with a number of highly detailed, life-long studies on movement (i.e. of the blood or of the amoeba). Each ended in the conclusion (among others) that spiral movement was "innate" and not explicable in known terms. For ten years I have now observed, read and found this phenomenon recurring. From DNA and the movement of atomic particles to nebulae. I have not concentrated on branching or balance to the same extent. They are equally self-evident. If expanation is beyond us, maybe impossible, then rather than hide our ignorance let's make it obvious. The three qualities of movement become part of our hypothesis; we do not explain them but use them to explain. It is useful to find a concept to form which applies to relationships of the abstract as well as the concrete and, indeed, the relationships between abstract and concrete.[ii]

(i) PETTIGREW J. B., *Design in Nature*, London 1908. The sub-title of the book is: "Illustrated by Spiral and other Arrangements in the Inorganic and Organic Kingdoms as exemplified in Matter, Force, Life, Growth, Rhythms &c., especially in crystals, plants and animals. With examples selected from the Reproductive, Alimentary, Respiratory, Circulatory, Nervous Muscular, Asseous, Locomotory, and other Systems of animals. Three vols., 1,400 pages, 2,000 figures". A source book indeed.
See also BURTON W. K., Theory of Crystal Growth, *Science News*, 21, Penguin, August 1951. COOK T. A. (a) *The Curves of Life, being an Account of Spiral Formations, their application to growth in Nature, to Science and to Art*, London 1914; (b) *Spirals in Nature and Art*, London 1903.

(ii) The sick society has been diagnosed as using this tendency in a compulsive way by CRASHAY-WILLIAMS R., *The Comforts of Unreason* (a "must" for every student). See also FREUD S., *A Philosophy of Life, New Introductory Lectures on Psycho-analysis*.

The relevance to learning is vital. It explains what we can observe and conceive as part of self-regulation; the spiralling movement is the rhythmic nature of problem–hunch–solution (attraction–fusion–liberation) which, or the promise of which, accompanies the repeated application of energy. It ensures that we tend to return again and again to spiral deeper and deeper into the detail of a field or soar, similarly, towards more and more general formulations. It is this which ensures that a student is attracted to that which is relevant for the future—often even before his teachers get around to it.

The worry of so many people that a child, left to study what it wants to, will become very one-sided and not a "balanced personality" in its education, is shown unwarranted by the very basic tendency to balance and symmetry. The child will tend from "art" to "science" even if it is in the service of a very specific thing like music, if he is the exceptional little Mozart. Normally, it will be far more general and result in a more even coverage of useful and relevant phenomena than our syllabuses.

The tendency to branch ensures "diversification". It is the branching, born of interest, which leads into other fields. Branching can be seen downwards, as in analysis, which leads to specific fields, and upwards into specific interpretation. It is the emergence of the specialist, the development of the exceptional in each person.

To summarize: the observation of healthy learning justifies the hypothesis that through the three-beat rhythm and the three basic tendencies in form, to spiralling, branching, balancing we can identify and describe behaviour.

II.4.4. Organization

(a) Within organic and inorganic patterns there are relationships of hierarchies where the lower sub-whole is always subservient to the higher sub-whole—or organ or organism; the lower can only fully be understood as part of the higher. This principle applies as far as we can divine.(i)

(b) Each relationship contains the self-regulating principle of its members and the creative principle of freedom of choice and spontaneity in interaction with its environment. This is why all beeches are similar on the one hand, and all and every one different on the other. This is the meaning of common and individual aspect in every species.(ii)

The above principle is applicable to the hierarchies within the learning process itself, i.e. once a skill is learnt and becomes ingrained, embodied, fused with the person, like typing, it is very difficult to alter the technique without deliberate strong attraction–fusion–liberation through another learning process, brought about by some good strong reason whereby the whole person (self-regulating organism), say moving to a foreign country, must get used to a different kind of letter position. And the old still remains in the background.

We have much to discover about learning in such a way that makes development easier, makes the new attractive and not

----

(i) Koestler describes his hierarchical concept thus: ". . . it means a special type of organization (such as a military hierarchy) in which the overall control is centralized at the apex . . . with branches downward. At the first branching out . . . say, digestive, respiratory, and reproductive organ-systems; each of these is sub-divided into units organs on lower levels of the hierarchy with their own co-ordinating centres . . . the organs in turn are sub-divided into organ-parts; and so the branching process goes on down to the cellular level and beyond . . . each sub-organization retains a certain amount of autonomy . . . a living organism or social body is not an aggregation of elementary parts or elementary processes; it is an integrated hierarchy of semi-autonomous wholes consisting of sub-wholes, and so on. Thus the functional units on every level of the hierarchy . . . act as wholes facing downwards, as parts when facing upwards".

(ii) In Koestler's terminology the code of each sub-whole acts within a matrix of choices, freedom—and the strategy is the actual choice made due to the relationship with the environment. The code of the sub-whole is often rigid as part of the whole: the salamander's legs, cut off and grafted on in reverse, will continue to walk backwards while the salamander moves forward with its other legs. Considerable documentation will be found in Koestler's *The Act of Creation*.

frightening. "Relaxed learning", as contrasted to compulsive or compelled learning, gives the learner far more ability to face the new. Educreation fosters this and so the techniques that go with it. At the moment, and for a long time, we have been altogether like the typist, trained to think in a certain limited way and resisting change. If pattern thought should replace cause and effect thinking there has to be a strong desire (attraction) to learn to do so—no easy matter.

Perhaps the most relevant aspect of the hierarchical is found in the self-regulation principle as the social organization of education. From this arises the basic nature and the present need to learn co-operation. We are inevitably associated as individuals, to groups, and form sub-wholes with them, governed also by principles of self-regulation. Once we recognize this consciously it is clear that co-operation between people is a multiple skill and, as the learning of other skills, should be an important indigenous part of education. The behaviourist Skinner, in his *Walden II*,[i] fills the need by conditioning. One has sympathy with his desire and with the simplicity of his idea; but there are far better and fuller ways of learning to live and work together. (Of course, a public school education of the famous English brand is as much conditioning as Skinner recommends, and less efficient; but they start comparatively late in life. Jesuits are supposed to excel in this.)

The real shortcoming of all these types of learning is that they do not allow for flexibility, a therapeutic approach, growth and change. And just that is vital in our age and with our immense issue of new problems. We know enough to know that we don't know what many of them will be and how the solutions will look; that is why we must imbue the young with maximum capacity for development, teach the advantage of having eyes and ears wide open without conditioning—so that shutting them at times does not go against the grain either.

The concepts of relationships and their dynamic form and

(i) Skinner B. F., *Walden II*, New York 1948.

organization, help towards a fuller comprehension of observable phenomena.

(a) *Self-regulation*

Self-regulation in bringing up our six children has been a "creative experiment" for us.[i] We learned, against all the black prophesies, in spite of the adverse environment at school and the world at large (but with the aid of many life-positive people and friends) that the children have the capacity to let their organisms regulate themselves within the hierarchical contraint of their relationships within the family, the schools, and so on. These are not absolute, of course; the self-regulated child takes an active part in changing the group to which he belongs. In birth, sleeping, breast-feeding, eating, drinking, play, work, learning and social skills the children have powers that are wasted in traditional upbringing and education. The waste becomes extreme when routines, created in the image of machines, are forced on the children.

The particular success in the social field is perhaps the least expected. Most people, even those who agreed with our ideas, but found them impractical ideals, thought the children would find school and co-operation particularly difficult. Instead, the one adjective that is common to practically all the school reports from various schools and many teachers is "co-operative". It seems that, paradoxical for an authoritarian society but obvious for an educreational one, self-regulation is a sound base for healthy co-operation.

That self-regulation, taken as a child having his own way all the time leads to the "spoilt child", the unhappy person, has also been observed. This, too, makes very good sense within the theory. It is a theory of relationships, and to reduce the right and the privileges of all those associated with the child is an artificial state, a symptom of sickness of the group, insecurity on

(i) RITTER P. and J., *The Free Family, A Creative Experiment in Self-regulation for Children*, London 1959.

the part of the parent. This means that the self-regulatory tendencies have too little interaction (attraction–fusion–liberation), too few problems, too little to do to keep the organism energetically toned. For as with muscles so with the organism as a whole. There is an optimum of tasks and problems and application that give health. And just as repression will harm permanently as grossly overworking muscles will also result in permanent disability, so the flabbiness of muscles persuaded and influenced into constant sedentary activity (or inactivity)! are paralleled by the child's whole organism when not allowed to face problems, not allowed to apply itself within the self-regulatory drive, within the framework of his relationships, to the social and physical environment.

This concept is useful to counter the arguments of those who either think a child must have all his own way (impossible anyway —there is no such thing), or that a child can't be allowed all his own way so that he must deliberately be drilled to learn Latin or to do without. Society bullies children in eating, in defecation and urinating, in their sex-play, when to sleep, what to play with, and restricting movements most cruelly. A child's life holds more than enough problems in ninety-nine cases out of a hundred. (See again *Walden II*, Skinner's Utopia.) Educreation orientates the whole process in a direction applicable and useful for our and the foreseeable times.

(b) Co-operation

We have already taken self-regulation as a starting point to the observation of what is a healthy learning rhythm. In terms of educational organization we see that it does away with the need for authority. Children will and do go to school voluntarily if, literally, it serves their interest. But once there, the interaction with teachers, "consultants", fellow children and equipment provides the relationships of learning with the richness and the relevance the young demand and do not get at the moment.

This brings us to the second principle, of co-operation.

Co-operation is the means whereby an organism associates with and relates to groups. As such it is a skill basic to man's needs which is learnt quickly and easily—by the self-regulated child. The sick society with the aggression-competition background makes it difficult; or to many it becomes so ideal a notion that they regard it impossible.

The relationship between competition and co-operation puzzles many people. Competition is subservient to co-operation. It is a playful organizing or aggressive disorganizing phenomenon, depending on the context, i.e. whether it acts within relationship or against it.

Like a team of athletes in training for relay events, the human race needs to get ready for a more than usually important match! Co-operation becomes essential, as to the athletes. Each man may still run his one hundred metres hoping his time is fastest, but what matters most is the total time and ability at the take-over, co-operation. No man could run the four hundred yards quicker by himself, if the take-over is learnt—but if not—if batons are dropped each time—then one man might be better.

This example illustrates not only the necessity of co-operation and its basic advantages. It also shows that co-operation has to be learnt. Finally, it makes clear that to compare crudely the futile attempts at co-operation of people untrained in a task with one highly trained person—whatever the outcome—shows only one thing: co-operation is still to be learnt.

(c) Creative bias

The creative potential explains why a child will build, make and learn rather than behave destructively. We must not confuse the expression of the need for physical prowess in throwing, pushing, hitting and smashing with innate destructive tendencies. The difference can be determined easily: the healthy child will have the outlets for the physical prowess. This means that if he hits or pushes it will not be where it is, obviously or explained as, anti-social. He will have the self-control and desire not to harm and damage his group membership by his aggression. (This is the opinion based on observation, hypothesis and experimental results.)

II.4.5. Disorganization

Strained beyond certain levels of tolerance a relationship becomes acutely or chronically impaired. If acutely, it will pass through crises of energy release in the tendency to become whole or healthy again.

If chronic, the energy channels are altered, structurally blocked or totally transformed.

The basic rhythm (attraction–fusion–liberation) does describe unhealthy activity as well as healthy. And the division into distinctive phases allows the diagnosis of where the blockages occur, and where remedial application is likely to be effective.

Disorganization we have already found an influence on all the other concepts because we live in a sick society. Once we understand the tendencies towards disorganization we are in a strong position to develop positively; the creative bias is always there, and man can learn to use it increasingly. Dying, letting oneself flow towards love or music—every attraction is the disorganization of a previous relationship macroscopically in space or time or microscopically.

In learning, disorganization is obvious in the children who dislike it because of mistreatment. Attraction to doing what you are forbidden, to holidays rather than school, to favourite mistress rather than subject, to examination results rather than interest, to satisfying parents' pride rather than curiosity, to compete rather than co-operate—all these and many more are signs of disorganization; the relationship of learning of child and environment, has been stretched beyond endurance, beyond its elasticity through the repressions and the armouring which emerge in a sick society. And this is why the tenet of disorganization, which has general natural relevance also, is spectacularly relevant to diseased conditions of our society.

The quality of the relationship varies, from sick to healthy. Both chronic and acute sickness affect the function of eating, loving, learning, etc., in similar ways. How the influences arise can best be examined by noting the nature of the attraction–fusion–liberation.

Take a person who feels "sick" after eating: the person may have been starving and eating too fast (overstrong attraction), or so excited—energy elsewhere tied up—that digestion (fusion) was impossible, or, having gall-stones, so sensitive to the results of digestion, bile-production, that pains set in and affected the quality of the liberation decisively. Similarly, the disturbed learning process and its relationships lend themselves to examination, useful analysis and diagnosis all the time.

It is interesting how the self-regulating and the co-operative tendencies interact in man and how awareness of the process can help: a specially succulent plum will attract you to eat one more, when otherwise you would not have done; attraction stronger than self-regulation. Conversely, one deeply in love hardly notices other girls which, the week before he "fell" (fusion) in love, would have been attractive. Self-regulation stronger than attraction. Not a "moral" self-regulation but the attraction–fusion–liberation energy economy is absorbed in the love relationship—and minor attractions are not strong enough to "disorganize".

II.5. THE THERAPEUTIC ATTITUDE TO A SICK SOCIETY

II.5.1. Multiple Diagnosis

I define as a sick society one which perpetuates with its culture pattern, an incapacity for health: the biological, psychological, sociological symptoms of this are all aspects of a disturbed basic energy economy.[i]

(i) This crucially useful concept came to me from the work and method of Wilhelm Reich. See REICH W., *Character Analysis*, London 1958, and other references in this book.

History and newspapers make the symptoms vivid. But why sickness? Why not just human nature, death instinct, original sin, or any of many other names for the phenomenon? Well, sickness infers careful diagnosis, compassion, concern and remedy—a more useful and effective pattern of events than follows from other attitudes.

This standpoint is adopted in this book because it allows the best insight into the problem of education as a whole. It obviates the laying of blame at the feet of this or that group. Regarding the whole as an ailing organism, a developing pattern,[i] I am concerned with the growth processes that will remedy, in its myriad relationships, the malady sapping society.

As Professor Allport paraphrased Kurt Lewin's[ii] standpoint: "Remedial efforts, he insisted, should be introduced into a community prepared to study the results of its own social action." This is now applicable, urgently and usefully to educational groups large and small. It emerges only from the willingness to grant the standpoint that a society may be sick. This is not a new concept.

Workers in a variety of fields have come to the conclusion that within their own disciplines can be found the criteria whereby society may be pronounced "ill", "diseased", "unhealthy", "disintegrated", "unbalanced", "anxiety-ridden", "neurotic", "emotionally plagued", or just "sick", and have explained this state variously.

Strict academic sociology cannot as yet accept the concept that "society is sick". Concentrating on obvious structure, it has formulated no fundamental laws on the functions of societies. There is no measure of health, no reliable yardstick. But many workers in the social sciences have gone beyond the limitations of the orthodox sociology and the tendency is gaining momentum.

(i) Sprott W. J. H., *Human Groups*, London 1958, uses the term "dynamic entity".
(ii) Prof. G. W. Allport's foreword to *Resolving Social Conflict*, Lewin W., New York 1948.

Burgess[i] sees society as responsible for not "providing adequately for the social roles essential for the mental health of its members". Halliday[ii] diagnoses the "weakening of the psychological bonds of members of groups within society", and the production of "social evils" instead of "social goods". The emotional disintegration and psychological unhealth of the members reflects, according to his analysis, the socially unhealthy or sick society.

As early as 1936, Frank[iii] saw that the "concept of a sick society in need of treatment has many advantages for diagnosis . . .", and thought that the so-called social problems are the result of "frantic efforts of individuals lacking any sure direction . . ."

Karen Horney[iv] and Erich Fromm[v] base the origin of the sick society as they see it on its cultural patterns. Kardiner[vi] finds that "the outstanding feature of the basic personality structure of Western man is its emotional insecurity and consequent anxiety".

In 1908 Freud[vii] wrote in an article in which he expressed the opinion that sexual abstinence (insisted upon, more or less, by civilized societies) created a chain of events which finally "contains all the elements needed for lifelong neurosis". In 1907 von Ehrenfels[viii] had said much the same. But even more direct is Freud's statement dating from 1930:

"There is one question which I can hardly ignore . . . would not the diagnosis be justified that many systems of civilization—or epochs of it—possibly even the whole of humanity—have

---

(i) BURGESS W., *Mental Health and Mental Disorder*, London 1956.
(ii) HALLIDAY J. L., *Psycho-social Medicine*, London 1948.
(iii) FRANK L. K., *The American Journal of Sociology*, Vol. 42, p. 335, 1936.
(iv) HORNEY K., *The Neurotic Personality of Our Time*, New York 1939.
(v) FROMM E., *Fear of Freedom*, New York 1954, and *Sane Society*, London 1956.
(vi) KARDINER A., *Psychological Frontiers of Society*, New York 1945.
(vii) FREUD S., *Civilized Sexual Morality and Modern Nervousness in Sexual Problems*, Vol. 1908.
(viii) EHRENFELS V., *Sexualethik*, Vienna 1907.

become neurotic under the pressure of civilizing trends? . . . I would not say that such an attempt to apply psycho-analysis to civilized society would be fanciful or doomed to fruitlessness.

"But it behoves us to be very careful . . . The diagnosis of collective neuroses, moreover, will be confronted by a special difficulty. In the neurosis of an individual we can use as a starting point the contrast presented to us between the patient and his environment, which we assume to be 'normal'. No such background as this would be available for any society similarly affected; it would have to be supplied in some other way. And with regard to the therapeutic application of our knowledge, what would be the use of the most acute analysis of social neuroses, since no one possesses power to compel the community to adopt the therapy. In spite of all these difficulties, we may expect that one day someone will venture upon this research into the pathology of civilized communities."[i]

It becomes obvious that some saw the origin of the diseased state in the individual and some in society. This dichotomy was recognized as artificial by a number of people. And although Frank had already, in 1936, called his approach "socio-psycho-somatic"[ii], the cross-disciplinary approach has made only slow headway. Academic and professional organization then, as now, militates against it.

Burgess[iii] in 1956 advocated a "marriage of psychiatry and sociology", and Reich[iv] (who had for some time stressed the connection between psycho-analysis and sociology) suggested in 1933 that psycho-analysis was the "father" and sociology the "mother" of his psychosomatic approach, which he later called "sex-economic".

To give credence to the approach of those few who saw a unitary basis to sickness of mind, body and social relations,

(i) FREUD S., *Civilization and its Discontents*, London 1930.
(ii) FRANK L. K., *The American Journal of Sociology*, Vol. 42.
(iii) BURGESS W., *Mental Health and Mental Disorder*.
(iv) REICH W., *Mass Psychology of Fascism* (first English language edition), New York 1945.

Pearse and Crocker[i] at the Peckham Health Centre established that, even with relatively superficial examination, over 90% of their sample of humanity had discoverable physiological disorders.

Halmos,[ii] in what he called a "bio-social" approach, related sociological symptoms of sickness of society to physiological principles.

Reich's[iii] theory of an energetic, unitary basis to the psychological, physiological and sociological ills, and indeed also to the healthy functioning in these spheres, was a milestone. "The disturbance of energy flow acts deep down at the basis of bio-social functioning and thus governs all functions of Man." It provided a clinically and experimentally tested hypothesis and was far from the often metaphysical speculations of those who went before (and have come since) and sometimes used similar words. It gave a most effective key to the puzzle of the interconnection and relatedness of what proved to be various aspects, or symptoms, or expressions of the same basic energy, obeying the same general laws and having "common functioning principles".

II.5.2. ORIGIN AND FUNDAMENTAL NATURE OF THE EMOTIONAL SICKNESS IN INDIVIDUALS AND GROUPS

Why is society sick? To understand origins and nature of a disease helps prophylactic and therapeutic endeavour. However, because of the involvement of all of us in the emotional sickness, information about this becomes, as a rule, too much to take in. Things can be so bright that instead of seeing them they blind us. Medical theory has remained detached and aloof.

My analysis shows emotional sickness as part of a general valid pattern of disease of organisms. If the rhythm of attraction–

(i) PEARSE and CROCKER, *The Peckham Experiment*, London 1943.
(ii) HALMOS P., *Solitude and Privacy*, London 1952.
(iii) REICH W., *Character Analysis*, 3rd edition, Maine, U.S.A. 1949, and London 1958. Also *Function of the Orgasm*, New York 1945.

D

fusion–liberation represents the satisfaction of essential needs, then an interruption of this rhythm, illness, is either temporary: the organism recovers totally in its ability to enjoy the rhythm. Or the disruption is too great for the organism to recover entirely: an elastic limit is broken. Part of the organism's pattern has become chronically unable to attract–fuse–liberate. This is easily understood in terms of physical injury, broken bones, etc. How does it work in emotional sickness? Here FUNCTION, not structure, is destroyed: i.e. in emotional sickness destruction of a function means the destruction of some of the capacity for

FIG. 6. The time-honoured authoritarian face of our school buildings. The image symptomatic of the deeply engrained fear and respect attitude to education. "Crawling like snail unwillingly to school": cartoon by Paul Ritter.

attraction–fusion–liberation in the emotions. How does this happen and why, is this so serious?

Assume that love or food is withheld from an individual or a group beyond the elastic limits of the organism, as described. This would then be a relationship which is "disastrously" unsatisfactory. Now relationships represent energy processes and in life energy manifests itself fundamentally and directly in the emotions. It is the *most direct* contact with the energy rhythms of attraction–fusion–liberation, and can be felt as inner streaming, warmth and coldness, etc., beyond the usually recognized emotions. Here diseased patterns can easily arise. This has been reliably, severally and clinically established.

This is why there is emotional sickness—why its symptoms manifest themselves most deeply in the emotions, and why the emotional disturbance is basic to the mental, physical or social symptoms in the affected organism or group. The traumatic event—the disaster—disrupts the energy function, as has been described. The diseased condition is kept chronic by the specific characteristics of the emotional sickness—discovered and described first by Wilhelm Reich in 1945: the energy which does not stream any more in its healthy paths is bound up and blocked in interconnected, integrated, mutually reinforcing elements of patterns of tense, immobile muscles, a condition accompanied by some tense, irrational mental attitudes and blocking of sense perceptions and tense taboos and authoritarian social relations.[i]

(i) The most decisive evidence of the energy pattern of bodily, mental and emotional defences lies in therapy. The bound-up energy in the tense muscles shows itself dramatically: if, by massage, and as an integral part of the therapy that Reich evolved, a "muscle knot" is broken, sometimes quite dramatically with the outcry of pain—not a muscular pain but the unbearable type of pain of a tense muscle trying and not being able to release itself—a vivid memory of the traumatic experience that was at the root of the chronically tensed muscles appears—out of the blue. And with this release of the bodily, muscular tension a characterological symptom, like an extreme pathological fear of wasps, can suddenly disappear. I speak from personal application of such therapy.

To experience this kind of thing repeatedly makes it so obvious that it's hard to remember that not everyone sees it like that.

We have here a pattern of defence against the reactivation of the disastrous situation, of the immobilized function. Irrational fears, anxiety, inability to think clearly, prejudice and many other familiar common "only human" traits are expressions of this. The organism has really set up a "once bitten twice shy" attitude to put it simply. Wilhelm Reich called it "character armour". And it is no exaggeration to call it "armour". It resists penetration with the strength of the desperate fear of re-experiencing and feeling an extreme pain, the original disaster.[i]

It is, of course, part of the nature of the armour that its very irrationality must remain hidden and unnoticed to the person or group involved so that it can remain effective.

With regard to the origin of the emotional sickness the point made by the above theory is this: There is no temporal, historical origin, in time, of society's sickness. Yet psycho-analysis, and the religious concept of original sin, have led virtually all past thinking onto those lines. The origin of the emotional sickness lies in the capacity of the organism, or the group, to defend itself against complete destruction, as its reaction to blood poisoning or any other disease. It can erupt at any time in any of a myriad of circumstances, and world history is good evidence of this.

Like some other diseases the emotional sickness is catching. It is passed on not only in highly organized fashion as in systems of education, but in many subtle ways through direct energetic contact. The emotional sickness like others has its quiet or virulent manifestations, and sometimes breaks out in plague proportions.[ii]

The disease is the most serious one of mankind. It alone now

(i) The suffering involved in the emotional sickness if part of the reaction-relationship, *not* the effects, pure and simple, of the original "dis-ease" or disaster. This idea may have increasing relevance and use in medicine generally.

(ii) Countless variations of the simple principles above fill the textbooks of medicine, criminology, psychiatry, history, anthropology, religion. Like a field of diseased wheat, or myxomatosis rabbits—it's difficult to find the healthy to establish the nature of disease by comparison. That's why sociologists refuse understandably to accept the theory of sick society.

threatens the destruction, self-destruction of the race. The greatest danger lies in its hidden quality.

This book would make no sense if there were not a theoretic and demonstrated therapeutic complement to the diagnosis. As with tuberculosis in certain circumstances, the cure may be something that stretches over generations it relates so closely to environment. Possibilities and hope lie in the fact that although his own disrupted functions are hidden from each individual, the functions disrupted differ: thus each has the capacity to make another aware of some disrupted functions. The lame can lead the blind, who can carry them. Individuals and groups can make each other aware.

The decisive difficulties lie first of all in the newness of the whole concept or diagnostic attitude taking the place of time-honoured moral blaming. Secondly, in the great energies involved in making another aware: for this, the first step in a deeply felt therapeutic process, tends to evoke immense hostilities —increasing with its effectiveness. These have to be dealt with positively—a complex matter. The hostility is, of course, part of the defence of the organism or group against having the original, extremely painful, terrifying, traumatic experience reactivated.

Because of man's ability to use his intellectual insight to lead him to a creative use of the emotions, i.e. his life energy, we can live in hope and work towards therapeutic endeavours, though the limitations of application are severe, to ignore them is to invite disaster, so experience shows.

We are still in a crude stage of using the awareness that results from such acts as reading this book, for example. The therapeutic attitude is as yet in its infancy and a multitude of techniques await discovery to dissolve the blockages to life in our maimed and crippled minds, bodies, emotions and culture patterns.

The educreation described in this book is born of the creative and health orientated force at the base of all life, I think. The application recommended carefully takes into account the limited capacities for new things of most of those who are involved and which are the norm together with the irrationalities and anxiety in us and about us all. This leads to the opportunism and realism which make the most of the possibilities in each situation.

Sex repression, in the final diagnosis, is the epitome of the cutting off of feeling, of life, of changing healthy attraction, fusion and liberation into more or less diseased, sadistic or masochistic variations of the function. As one might deduce, so common is the occurrence, that these have become regarded as "normal" and the words "sadism" and "masochism" are falsely reserved for only the most obvious and outrageous symptoms of the emotional sickness. The example which follows shows just how fallacious this is. It is a matter of teachers' attitudes to the attraction and love of adolescents—sexually the most alive age group.

II.5.3. Relevance of a Therapeutic Attitude to Higher Education

Let us look at a fairly vivid example of the English sick society as it manifests itself in the taboos of our schools carrying on where parental repression leaves off. A similar situation prevails abroad, and let us not think that corporal punishment is the only or the worst one. It merely makes sadism obvious. We can regard the next small section as an introduction to further education.

The difference between new students is immense. There are those, increasing in number, whose schools and sixth forms used enlightened teaching procedures. Then there are those from the large percentage of schools the methods and emotional climate of which come to notice only through children's reports or the odd newspaper report.

But to understand and remind just what goes on in that jungle in which parents put such trust—that ludicrously inefficient and cruel (both to teacher and taught) system geared to bringing the harvest of O-level and A-level fruits (dependent on three-hour examinations!) and satisfaction to countless sadistic teachers (and sadistic pupils), consciously or not.

"HEAD AND WOMAN TEACHER FINED FOR SPANKING[i]

"*Punishment Went Too Far*

"A grammar school headmaster ordered two girl pupils of seventeen and eighteen to undress partly and tuck up their knickers before spanking them on their bare buttocks with the back of a hairbrush . . .

"Mr. . . . prosecuting, said that the two girls . . . had paired up with a sixth form boy and another youth. They had been rehearsing scenes from Shakespeare in the school's Green Room when the school had finished for the day.

"They engaged in kissing and cuddling. There is no question of anything more serious.

"Both girls were subsequently called to the head's office and given the option of a spanking on the understanding that nothing more would be said about the Green Room incident.

"Describing the spanking of the younger girl, Mr. . . . said . . . told her to take off her jumper, skirt and underskirt, tuck her blouse into her knickers and tuck up her knickers so that her buttocks were exposed.

"He then told her to lean over the end of the table with her legs apart, and also to hold his hand and look at him.

"Mrs. . . . stood behind her and began hitting her on each buttock with the back of a hairbrush. When she stopped . . . made the girl stand between his knees, bending over as if to touch her toes . . ."

"He hit her with the same brush about the same number of times. When he had finished, he said: 'She does not look very sorry. Perhaps she had better have some more.'

"Both hit her again, . . . taking her over his knee and holding her hands behind her back. Later he placed his hands on both buttocks and asked if it hurt.

"A doctor examined the girl '50 or more' hours afterwards and found considerable bruising covering 72 square inches."

(i) *Daily Telegraph*, July 3, 1964, a prominent and long item.

The Chairman said the magistrates had borne in mind the "excellent character of both defendants".

Just how cowed children, or should we say women old enough to be married and mothers, must be to allow this sort of thing hardly bears contemplation. The education committee's ruling that "things had gone too far"—in other words that they did not object on principle—is typical. The denial of the right to kiss and cuddle—especially for people of the ages of seventeen and eighteen—especially after school hours, and after acting Shakespeare together! (What would Shakespeare have said?)

One also wonders what the alternative was to "hearing no more about the incident". And it is worth while contemplating what else might have happened in the many years of that school—and many, many other schools—reigned by the foibles that become supreme through our authoritarian education. (Huxley's "actually diabolic notions canonized as dogmas".)

That there was no public outcry demonstrates just how hardened the English public is, and how widespread the attitudes that condone if not support this kind of thing. It is not the physical cruelty of having a few stinging blows on the bottom that is involved, but the immense damage to the feelings and sensitivity of these young women and thousands like them who by the bullying of teachers and prefects (and parents) are reduced to fear, not respect, authority. It is such people who need to let off their hate first, possible in therapeutic approach, and then be loved back into self-respect and made to feel secure in the knowledge that others respect their persons.

Yet in November 1964 the National Union of Teachers submitted a report to the Central Advisory Council for Education which said that in the interest of the majority of children the right to decide when to use corporal punishment should remain with individual teachers, in spite of much evidence which shows punishment to be harmful.

So frightened are our children in primary schools it seems that "in most cases the knowledge of the possibility of corporal punishment was a sufficient deterrent of anti-social behaviour", and many teachers who use it not at all or rarely are therefore in favour of keeping the right to use it.

This very clearly shows the authoritarian and fearful basis of much of our primary education. In secondary education it gets worse in many instances. Directors of education are quoted as "believing in original sin".[i]

Let us raise the implications of the newspaper report to the level of scientific investigation in the most permissive of educational systems, that of the U.S.A. The original mind and the lively rebel are still penalized:

Getzel and Jackson[ii] had a hunch that the high I.Q. adolescent and the highly adjusted adolescent were revered and singled out for praise in the U.S.A. quite unjustifiably. They tested with two sets, both exceptional schoolchildren, whether the "highly creative" were not at least (statistically) equally praiseworthy.

In the elaborate investigation it was found that the "creative" did as well or better than the high I.Q. individuals in school work as a whole. These adolescents had a better sense of humour, were more lively, postponed decision for vocation, had more relaxed parents, and fewer fact-stuffed magazines in their homes. But (in spite or because of this) they were less liked by teachers and parents generally, and therefore discriminated against.

As a corollary to this we may say that in spite of being liked less by the body of teachers and parents, highly creative children have as good a scholastic record as high I.Q. ones.

Other useful pointers which apply to education in Britain in many ways, are worth noting:

The U.S.A. has a name, "overachievers", for those who seem to produce better scholastic performance than their I.Q. measurement is deemed to warrant. This is regarded as a pathological

(i) For example, Nottingham. See WILSON C., in *Task*, December 1964, p. 49, which gives a ghastly picture of the "blatant bloodsport" still allowed and enjoyed in Education, i.e. the Advisory Centre for Education at Cambridge found that one firm alone sold 3000 school-straps (for hitting children) a year. They advertise in the *Scottish Educational Journal*!

(ii) GETZEL and JACKSON, *Creativity and Intelligence*.

symptom and the child regarded as in need of therapeutic treatment (of the "adjustment" kind). Getzel's and Jackson's work suggests that the reverse may be true, that the high I.Q. group displays characteristics that give cause for concern and points to application for therapy rather than the "highly creative" low I.Q. group with its "overachieving" individuals. This is not to say that high I.Q. does not go with creativity.[i]

The qualities described for the highly creative child are those which show more life. What is more it is possible by therapy or therapeutic attitude to increase the creative aspect and reduce the compulsive I.Q. aspect. And if this is possible, then surely it must be the direction in which we wish education to go.

Getzel's and Jackson's research is one of a number which have shown that our education is anti-life and anti-change.

The work of Musgrove[ii] is similarly concerned with the favoured treatment of certain types in the world of education in accord with those described in the American work. He goes further and shows how the very institutions we have formed "can achieve their ends most easily with certain personality types".

In other words, although university education becomes more and more the prerequisite for a satisfactory occupation, the choice of entrants and nature of the education, the character of staff all tend towards one personality type and a neurotic one at that, as described by Musgrove. He is not only concerned that we keep good student material from achieving proper educational development but with the ill preparation of the wrong kind of personality for what are the present and future needs of society.

"It is perhaps of little consequence that the universities should be staffed predominantly by neurotic introverts. (But, if both staff and students score high in these dimensions of personality, the result is unlikely to be a particularly hilarious kind of

(i) It does, but, on the other hand, they report D. W. MacKinnon as saying that "among creative architects the correlation of the two variables is a value not significantly different from zero". Here is food for thought.

(ii) MUSGROVE F., *Youth and the Social Order*, p. 4.

community.[i] No doubt hilarity is an irrelevant criterion by which to judge the life of a university; but it is doubtful whether work of the highest intellectual originality will be produced where there is no dash of frivolity.)"

And Zweig's book[ii] confirms this sad picture of students at old and new universities "becoming old before their time", the students anxious, harassed, guilt-ridden, unadventurous, and the atmosphere "heavy and joyless".

Clinical investigations show that a stay at a university (in the States, and this differs not too greatly perhaps from country to country) increases the incidence of "hypochondriasis, depression, hysteria, psycopathic deviate, schizophrenia and mania".[iii] The only comparison between college and non-college people in the States shows nearly twice as many college people "seriously maladjusted".

The Kneale Committee published its findings on examinations at Oxford noted that twenty-one in 1964 and twenty-six students in 1963 took their "Final Honours Schools as in-patients of an Oxford mental hospital . . ." and this is the élite of the élite, supposedly.

The trend towards neuroticism has been accepted as part of academic education,[iv] and the "real" world after college has been regarded as a curative measure.[v]

So all is not well at our universities. Taking the colossal, fresh problems described in the first chapter, in addition to the above, indicates vividly that a more creative and extrovert education is required. We need the extrovert's skills as well as the introvert's.

"The intelligent extrovert must not be denied the qualifications necessary for entering positions of high responsibility." Beyond

---

(i) I call it little "swots" taught by big "swots".
(ii) ZWEIG F., *The Student in the Age of Anxiety*, London 1963.
(iii) Ed. SANFORD N., *The American College*, New York 1962.
(iv) WEBSTER, Some Quantitive Results, *Journal of Social Issues*, 1956.
(v) TATE and MUSICK, *Adjustment Problems of College Students*, Social Forces 1954.

"narrowly defined intellectual exercises" Musgrove[i] feels that the skills of human relationship should be assessed: ". . . quiet unruffled confidence in human crises; an outgoing and reassuring approach to colleagues, subordinates and clients; tact and capacity to tolerate uncertain and ambiguous human situations; concern without hypersensitivity; an interest in and concern for actual concrete individual instead of ideas about individual and formulae which embrace an abstracted aspect of a faceless multitude. Some of our new institutions of higher education must recast their curricula in these terms."

To summarize the chapter, we can say that we not only have multiple diagnosis of society as sick but also a theory that explains the origin of the condition. This theory is useful in that it allows us to understand the nature and roots of the sickness and gives clear indications for remedial action. Study of the educational system demonstrates that a creative and therapeutic approach in all its aspects is required to deliver us from the evil.

(i) MUSGROVE F., *Youth and Social Order.*

CHAPTER III

General Implications of Educreation

III.1. STUDENTS

III.1.1. The Crisis of Entry

Any curative process has its crises. At such times special energies are released, used for progress or frustrated. The therapeutic approach to education shows clearly that to arrive at college from home and/or school is just such a crisis. The very change is an immense stimulant, the expectations high, enthusiasm ready to be released, yet all mixed with anxiety.

From this we can deduce that particularly at the beginning of a course, using the immense energies mobilized for the challenge and opportunities imagined, there is a golden chance to raise the awareness of the individual and to give means for using, orientating and harnessing his energy into worthwhile, rewarding efforts. Today, we do the reverse with a vengeance.[i]

Of the many thousand students I have spoken to in many parts of the world, not one could say that the first year he had experienced had harnessed the enthusiasm with which he entered on his university studies. But bitter disillusion was remembered by many.

(i) "The undergraduate . . . fresh from school arrives unprepared for the impersonal, lonely place that university first appears to be. . . . He probably faces, for his first year at any rate, work that is repetitive of his sixth form studies. Already sick of text books, he embarks on a course that demands ever more of him. Lectures that don't involve his intelligence, and tutorials that are barren of encouragement just where he needs it". *Sunday Times*, October 13, 1963, Oxbridge student's report, "Youth—Humbug!"

Nowhere in the course is the aim more vague, nowhere in the course is a student more lost, than at the outset; worse, his person is degraded by the traditional rites, overt or hidden, to make sure he feels inferior to staff and senior students.

The initiation rites or rags still found in some places have a function. At least they make the student feel he is at the beginning of something considerable. However, the lack of understanding of the function and the sadism and violence and indiscrimination that characterized such rags obscure the meaning and have ill-effects. I describe a fairly vicious one below. (Initiation proposals are detailed in Section III.)

In Liverpool in 1942, freshers at the hall of residence underwent a number of ordeals one of which was to get up, having been tipped out, at 5 a.m., run round the fenced tennis courts with fire hoses playing on the naked bodies while they sang very loudly, "How green we are, how green we are."

When any individual was deemed to have gasped and sung loud and long enough, he was let out. He then ran the gauntlet of whipping seniors lining the cross-country course within the grounds. This included among other obstacles, a bucket full of urine in which his head was submerged under the pretext of getting hold of an apple with his teeth, and an enormous pit of cow dung (nearby cattle made this easy), over which the fresher was told to jump but was tripped on taking off so that he landed flat on his face.

Finally, one by one the exhausted body of men ended up in a light-well where the hoses again played on them, washing them down. Typically enough, what led to the end of this rag tradition was not its cruelty but the allusion to sex: the littering of the light-well, outside the servant accommodation, with prophylactic sheaths. These, blown up like balloons, or a sanitary towel, were the only "dress" allowed.

On top of this sort of thing the student's energies and enthusiasm are sapped by humdrum lectures and exercises. Worst of all, if he does not excel in the latter, he begins his course in many an institution with "FAIL" written on his work, perhaps repeatedly—and only because he cannot master adequately some detailed skill of marginal importance usually presented with extreme irrelevance. We segregate the new students from the old, and this ensures that they remain "green" for the maximum length of time. It all adds up to the most fearful waste of energy and gigantic, pitiful dissipation of enthusiasm.

The height of the tragedy is that the momentum lost at the beginning can never be fully regained. The opportunity to have the flying start of his enthusiasm is lost irretrievably. The world, straining for better human resources, just cannot afford this idiocy. It is a loss for each individual aiming for greater health and richness in life. We must no longer tolerate the spiteful spectacle of turning potential, purposeful zest into cynicism and nihilism or just depressed drifting, frustrating the invaluable energy released for the crises.

Those who, through insecurity or lack of purpose or perspective of the world, have a supreme sort of self-centred arrogance, will become therapeutically debunked in the awareness studies and through group work. This arrogance of haughty high-school boys is itself a disease. It was deliberately and ruthlessly crushed by the old rags and initiations. This had a thoroughly bad effect all round. It made sure that the vicious circle of arrogance breeding violence to meet arrogance was continued.

The alternative is clear: Through a sense of worth and belonging, through friendship and co-operation (instead of fear and competition) the fresher can become more secure. This allows him to become more aware—see himself as others see him, hear himself as others hear him (you know the shock of hearing a recording of your voice). And the increased awareness leads to therapeutic action which leads to better, more creative work and a fuller life.

This chronological account of the interaction is a partial picture only. It is as inadequate as an elevational view of a four-dimensional phenomenon. But it may indicate what I mean.

It is one of those common mistakes to think special attention to foreign students would be bad because we are judging with the modes of conduct of the typically British withdrawn stereotype in our minds. But as virtually all other cultures have far warmer and intense social relations there is no harm at all in making the extra effort to integrate the foreigner and bring him to a reasonable state of feeling he belongs. That one is a "bloody foreigner," whatever the polite or vivacious interest shown by the native, is a familiar impression.

I came to England at the age of fourteen, but my own experience has been underlined by the observations I have made of the older foreign students I have taught. And at a guess I would also judge that every British student enjoys immensely a warm foreign welcome from a body.

III.1.2. The Basis of Real Respect

Some good starting points are the formal introduction of teachers through personal philosophy lectures to students, the integration into the groups of students of all years into which any school can be divided, "vertically", and the machinery, detailed later, to give the student a sense of belonging quickly, at the outset, when it is crucial. He can soon see that tutors need not be feared as "sir", to be respected for their authoritarian position or age, and that their experience and humanity makes it irrelevant whether they are addressed as "sir", absent-mindedly, or "you bastard" in the heat of argument by the emotionally inflamed student. Respect for tutorial staff arises out of their wisdom, understanding and empathy.

The new student may be bewildered and amazed at the different philosophies expounded to him by the great range of teachers who introduce themselves. But whereas today we lack any sort of credo, and have as the result aimless drifting into the atomic or the population explosion, the multiplicity will have the effect of stimulating the student to develop his own beliefs and to learn the weaknesses and strength, consistency and inconsistency of the views held by others.

Whitehead knew: "It should be the chief aim of the university professor to exhibit himself in his own true character—that is, as an ignorant man thinking, actively utilizing his small share of knowledge."[(i)]

"There is one place in particular where the teacher is concerned with the individual and also with society needs. We need to give deep thought to the way in which a small group like a 'class' and the large groups like an institution work. This developing brain of psychology has very much to offer the teacher. It is related also to questions of leadership and authority which affect both teaching methods and the quality of life, more than explicit instruction, which affect a student's moral and political views. A democratic school (the term must go undefined) will teach the values of democracy by exemplifying them; if the staff in fact respect their pupils the pupils will more readily respect foreigners, blimps and the unpitiable."[(ii)]

The aimless drifting is particularly prevalent in British universities where the liberal attitude of extreme scepticism, supreme irresponsibility and good financial backing combine. While a critical attitude is healthy, scepticism too often is a defence against believing anything which might lead to action. The irresponsibility arises out of a feeling of hopelessness in the face of political parties and the massive stupidity of the world.

Without any political bias (for I believe politics demonstrate the emotional plague at its most virulent and that includes student politics), I feel it is high time youth felt involved in the miseries and problems that beset this world. Buckminster Fuller's World Design Decade Globe is a good tool. Built to a large size so one can get inside, it should have plotted on it, to be used with the help of a computer, the data that allows one to see the history of the world, its resources, conditions; the present state invites the student to do something about it, and to give predictions. Students should live around the concept that the world is one, made most vivid by Fuller's quip to those who

(i) WHITEHEAD A. N., *Aims of Education*, p. 48.
(ii) MICHAELS J., B.A.S.A. Conference Report.

wanted to know what it was like on a space-ship: "You've never been off one!"

Generations who think of the world as one, on such lines, will find it increasingly difficult to ignore the problems that are in fact ever more obviously becoming everybody's concern.

This feeling of responsibility is no longer too much: the resources, the communications and the technology of man make solutions feasible and the main difficulty is to overcome with the therapeutic attitude, in time, the emotional plague, restrain outbursts, most dangerous through power politics of the states of the world.

This is not the place to produce solutions, to show how students' contributions may be far more than a mere demonstration of good faith. What is relevant here is that the feeling of belonging to the world as a whole, responsibility for the unborn children and those growing up, and for its present-day citizens, can become the central driving force of the university community and the sub-groups within it. It can become the done thing to care! Fancy!

It seems to me that although the problem of enough food, shelter, contraception, therapeutic approach, are paramount, it is up to the universities to back quality in life not just mere quantity. Such can be the criteria for any philosophy: does it lead to quality in loving, learning, eating, breathing, feeling? In a materialistically orientated age, when the reaction of the extreme poverty of the poor and under-privileged is exploding in "everything for everybody" as long as the land, the soil, the water, the trees, the road space, the steel and the oil last, it is vital to add quality to privilege. We should counteract the mad rush for pink counterpanes—keeping up with the Joneses, may be, but perhaps rather the reaction to being under-privileged: as working class, and perhaps more basic, as children and young people.

The functional advantages of 'quality thinking' replace the waning, first imposed, now exposed Victorian (Christian!) ethics, with their commandments—and reality that belies them—which makes hypocrites of everyone and has bedevilled every thinking child and usually still does.

If the quality of life matters and a therapeutic sympathy, not blame, attaches to those who inhale bad air, eat bad food, drink bad water and resort to poor loving and sex (not morally bad, qualitatively poor), then reform is more likely. As key pleasures are forbidden to the young, the forbidden is associated with pleasure (or have you not noticed?) So to say "Thou shalt not" becomes a spicy phrase by association, and so is not a good way of achieving the desired end.

The therapeutic attitude makes sense of the teacher who smokes and yet believes smoking is bad, believes in good environment yet wears uncomfortable clothes out of sheer habit, and, to take an extreme case, who goes to prostitutes and yet realizes it is as much a sign of poverty of his life as breathing the foul air of the city he lives in. He displays, more or less, a tragic and hopeful picture, a good example of what can be achieved, and a bad example of what happens when it can't; which has a positive effect on the student. The variety of tutors will give a far from uniform picture. The more healthy persons would select themselves to an increasing extent for educreation, which is more than can be said about education.

Once talking about the "virtue" of quality (rather than quantity, normal to the materialistic age), the difficulty is that, especially separated by a "generation", as teachers are prone to be, it all sounds, at least for the moment, too much like hot gospelling and is likely to bring out the defences of the young. The key is sincerity. The students have the capacity, in a therapeutic environment, to understand and take into account, without loss of respect or the need to blame, all the weaknesses of their elders, if we are open about it.

Perhaps a good example is the approach to smoking, Circulars to teachers tell them not to smoke in front of the class so as not to be a "bad example". This ignores that teachers are very rarely regarded as examples to be copied in class—their outside privileges are envied, if any. And if they smoke in secret only, the effect is to regard it as a special privilege and aim for it. To hide is to entice in a moralistic, authoritarian climate.

My own daughter, at fourteen, smoked to join with the whole of the rest of the class puffing clandestinely. (Not particularly influenced by teacher).

"What the hell?" I asked, sniffing the smoke in the air in a house otherwise not so polluted (!).

"What can I do?" she asks. "I have to practise somewhere. They all smoke."

"I understand," says I, and leave her room pensive. Now what? Idea! I rush back: "Go in tomorrow and tell them, 'I've given it up.' That way you won't lose face, the phrase sounds big."

She saw the sense at once—and has not smoked since. There was no place for "forbidding it" in our approach, as the others who were smoking had it forbidden by their parents—and no doubt enjoyed it largely because of that.

This indicates that if one could have approached this class with sincerity, instead of moral preconceptions, most of them would have been in the position of my daughter. And smoking among many students has just such a status origin of one sort or another.

In the light of the taboo on kissing and cuddling prominent in so many schools (a visible peak of the iceberg of puritanism in spite of a relaxation on censorship), it is little wonder that the university, with its relative freedom in private affairs—away from home at last—egged on by the daring of one's comrades, leads to insensitive, qualitatively inferior, "necking", "petting" and intercourse, largely the reaction from repression and disapproval of home and school. The contact, if poor, is still sought. Human beings are social and seek the comfort and warmth of others—by healthy or sick means—when desperate, desperately.

The therapeutic attitude, beyond giving the student a sense of belonging which is good social contact, makes him aware of what is happening in him. It is not a matter for advice until he asks. Then the advice should be a matter of helping him to recognize the questions which he can only answer himself. Questions of motives, real quality, real enjoyment, guilt, etc.

III.1.3. Sexual and Social Metamorphosis

More and more freedom in sexual matters is a trend standing out a mile. No one in his senses, and alive, can but see this as qualitative potential and as one of the major hopes for mankind. More sex—less aggression—is the simple energy economy. But that this means pleasure–anxiety, temporary inability to recognize one's own interest and that of one's groups—this is a necessary by-product with which we can cope only on a therapeutic level.

Sexual behaviour is the most dramatic in its emergence from middle-class atmosphere. This is specially applicable to universities where the more down-to-earth attitude, which often prevails among the working classes, is so very poorly represented. Strongest guilt feelings, and serious possible consequences combine to make the subject a hot potato. But it is crucial and cannot be shelved.[i]

The most fruitful and constructive approach is through the recognition of the problem of transition from a moralistic to a spontaneously moral society. To see that the sickness of society is nowhere more vivid than in its sex; that here, as with work, food, air, clothes, not quantity but quality counts, and that a therapeutic attitude will improve quality and lessen insistence on quantity for ulterior and not pleasure motives.

I make this one of the central themes of my own introductory talk on my philosophy of life to first-year students. The effect is remarkable: the group's bluff is called and the result is all the more powerful. Bluff is, after all, only the defence, hiding really sterling qualities in each of the members of any group.

A good experiment is to compare the discipline (where discipline has to be kept in a class) before and after you have made clear to the children or near-adult students that you are not afraid of any aspect of the subject of sex nor any obscene interpretation of it however extreme. That you are feelingly associated

---

(i) The architectural students of Oxford having heard of a lecture I had given at Cambridge years before, invited me to lecture on "Sex". This I did. They were afraid to say so on their posters! There it was just "RITTER"—I had to point out that the two words were not synonymous!

with it and appreciate their feelings, that you know that humour is attached to the field as to any other, and that it can be funny for a variety of ways (or very, very sad). To get rid of the sniggering undercurrent that pervades most of society, in the framework I am describing, is a specifically rewarding task. This opens up the way for those in a group to help each other in the emotional difficulties that meet the fresher in immense intensity and profusion. This can bring about the security to allow awareness and therapeutic development and growth of character and personality.

The answer is not to ban mixed halls of residence but to make them universal! The therapeutic approach helps decisively in the emerging love relationships of students with their ecstasies, agonies and crises. It helps development in the hard work of getting to know each other—or hastens the realization of incompatibility.

To the sincerity and help of tutors we can add the matrix of friendship of students to each other. Yet the cultivation of trust may be slow for some: no wonder.

All his life the student has striven to outdo his competitors, to excel individually. There was always something to lose at school if his ideas got to another, who then got the better mark. All personal relations were influenced by this. Honesty was often quite impracticable both to teachers and fellows. To hide one's mistakes, pretend excellence (in a very modest English manner) where there was none, was the recognized form of behaviour, particularly for all those who could not satisfy, in the narrow waveband of present educational requirements.

With this background, a tremendous change is asked of the student if his work and thinking are to be on a genuinely co-operative basis. Beyond a whole host of new work techniques, and preliminary to these, the emotional readjustment is considerable. No more fear of failure but appreciation for helping another with his thinking; accredited for showing the ability to recognize and mark the weak spots in your own work (instead of trying to hide them); functional leadership by him who knows best; sharing of tasks; genuine appreciation of individual talent; respect for need for individual expression, privacy and interests. All this depends for its origins and effectiveness on feeling secure. The power springs from being one of a community, a group with common aims and joint ways of achieving them.

In the last analysis, if an educreative approach is adopted as policy, it is not limited to the staff–student relationship. The constructive ripples of life influence everything and anything from cleaner to director of education or vice-chancellor. And, it is taken as agreed that staff in such an environment will wish to continue to develop as the other participants.

The therapeutic attitude of educreation is not something that cures the student in his first year and then loses its importance. It is a way of life and attitude to the world. As a way of life it may be initiated in the first year of higher education, or earlier, or much earlier, but success merely means the capacity to continue to apply the idea, to continue to grow alive, develop, create, and wish to learn. Not just until the end of university life but until the final "transformation".

As an attitude to the world it can replace all those vindictive, blaming, moralistic or highly idealistic and unreal pieces of metaphysics which we have so long called our personal philosophies.[i]

III.2. HUMAN TEACHERS[ii]

III.2.1. The Confused Position

The human being is the best learning aid if it is in proper working order and efficiently installed. Empathy and all it entails cannot be taken over by machines. But the situation today is unsatisfactory on three counts:

(a) Staffing of universities is heavily weighted towards "neurotic introverts" not teachers: in plainer language, little swots who

---

(i) A concept of Primary Truth and Secondary Truth is fundamental to the effectiveness of this philosophy. It will be explained in the context of the chapter on implementation.

(ii) Everything recommended in this chapter applies to all levels of education though the comments are angled at university level.

have grown into big swots. Musgrove makes this clear.[i] And every personal experience of University education confirm it:

"An important branch of psychology is concerned particularly with the complex processes of learning, and therefore with correlative processes of teaching. The primary state of education has profited from this work of the psychologists; at the secondary stage the suggestions are heard but largely disregarded; at the stage of university and professional education barely a whisper of a suggestion has penetrated the smooth outer coverings of complacant amateurism".

Another experienced research worker who has particularly examined the training of professions finds the situation in this respect extreme: "University teachers behave as though students don't have any emotions and as though university teachers don't have any either. This is nonsense and the sooner we face the fact that teaching and learning gives us pleasure—why should we not say so?"[ii] And one might add, "Why should we not protest when it does not give pleasure?"[iii]

At the moment, "The academic hand is not aseptic enough to end the student's 'personal' development—it is left to the rugger pitch, the union, the bedsitter or the pub. This, however, is uneconomical because the training thus acquired is not necessarily and automatically transferred to work situations".[iv]

The position as described is certainly not likely to fulfil the requirements of Ian Michaels: "An educational system is one of the means by which society changes itself; one duty of the system is to produce critics and rebels".[v]

To summarize point (a): University teacher selection shows a bias towards emotional and intellectual deadness.

(i) MUSGROVE F., *Youth and the Social Order*, London 1964.
(ii) ABERCROMBIE J., comment in B.A.S.A. 3rd Report on Architectural Education, 1963, p. 60.
(iii) MICHAELS I., B.A.S.A. Conference Report. B.A.S.A. 3rd Report on Architectural Education 1963.
(iv) ABERCROMBIE M. L. J., *The Anatomy of Judgement*, p. 15.
(v) MICHAELS I., comment in B.A.S.A. 3rd Report on Architectural Education, 1963, p. 27.

III.2.2. Present Application and Duties

(b) The application of staff is chaotic. Without training in teaching, the newly appointed finds himself trying to cope with demands for enforcing discipline (often the most vehemently stressed aspect from above), giving lectures on separate courses in the main (an inferior teaching method also imposed), and usually a syllabus that is impossible to cover. He finds that, introducing his own ideas and using more dynamic methods, projects and programmes, is often strongly opposed.

He is marking work on the very narrow basis of his own experience, usually without any really valid general criteria. He is vaguely supposed to make cultural and social contact, but has no guidance and often little opportunity. The position has been well described by Marris after his research into four very different colleges and universities:

"Students are afraid of the staff, not because teachers are personally unsympathetic but because collectively the staff represents an authority they are bound to respect. It is scarcely possible to talk on equal terms with someone from whom you are used to accepting knowledge of which you are ignorant, appraisal of your performance, correction of your mistakes, and perhaps reproof for breach of regulations. The fear of exposing intellectual naïvety to a teacher whose judgement has power to wound your self-esteem is matched by fear of emotional naïvety. The staff appear as an older generation, who for better or worse have settled their personal lives. The successful seem too remote from the students' uncertainly: the unsuccessful, embarrassed and embarrassing. The attempt to foster conversation in an atmosphere of social equality becomes an uneasy pretence in which neither staff nor students can altogether believe.

"But students do want to know the staff better, and believe that they can learn from them, apart from their studies. They grow tired from time to time of undergraduate discussion, which begins to seem repetitive, unpractical and pretentious, and would like to talk to someone older. The younger students are often passing through a period of estrangement from their parents, and it would be easier for them if they could occasionally treat a member of the staff as a source of parental reassurance. They also feel a general hostility towards established authority, which finds a rational outlet in challenging ideas and attitudes. Some of these will become the orthodoxies of their generation and the confrontation of experience and radicalism helps to resolve the conflict in constructive argument. But such a relationship is not egalitarian any more than it is authoritarian. The ideal of the 'community of scholars' implies that, in the humility of scholarship, staff and students belong fundamentally to the same group of peers. But even if there is such an identity of purpose, it is too deeply buried under the different roles which staff and students assume.

"As in an academic context, students want to exploit the experience of the staff, without compromising their independence. They want advice, but on their own terms. They want reassurance without committing themselves to the interpretation of life from which the sense of reassurance arises. They want to test their ideas against experienced opinion, without taking the proof as final. It is difficult to approach a stranger with these demands, even when, like a psychiatric consultant, he is professionally cast in this role; and it is pointless to approach anyone in whom you lack confidence.

Between peers, the need of advice, reassurance, intellectual exploration is reciprocal: if two or three people are in a mood to unburden themselves, the discussion grows spontaneously. But between staff and students it is one-way. Our interviews did not report any instance where staff turned to students with these demands, and I doubt whether students could handle them. I think, then, that serious conversation between staff and students is bound to be more deliberate, and it depends upon the staff's willingness to meet these demands on the students' terms".[i]

It may sound fantastic to a lecturer that his students and his colleagues may actually help him, collectively, giving him a sense of belonging, awareness and a feeling of loyalty and security.

(i) MARRIS P., *The Experience of Higher Education*, pp. 121–2.

But if we take the reverse into account for a moment, the almost universal way in which hate, jealousies and rivalries sap the energies, block the enthusiasm and good ideas of fellow staff and sicken the milieu of education, then one realizes that this cannot be the only, the best possible or indeed the desirable state of affairs.

To summarize point (b): The duties of teachers are confused beyond the point of resolution on the basis now provided.

(c) There is colossal waste of effort and the shortage of teachers is grossly aggravated. Further, the system works according to Parkinson's Law so that however many teachers there are they create the need to teach more "subjects" for which there are then too few teachers (and, of course, too little time). Facing the triple explosion in the world this becomes an increasingly relevant and decisive point.

Educational productivity per teacher is disastrously low.

It is sobering to ponder the pattern of unsuitable staff, in confusion, producing increasingly inadequate education.

III.2.3. Proposals for Separation of Tutorial and Consultant Teacher Functions

From the pattern of self-regulation–co-operation–therapy springs a solution: it suddenly became crystal clear to me that there are two aspects to teaching, two major functions for two kinds of persons: (a) the tutor; (b) the consultant teacher.

(a) The Tutors

The tutorial function is to help the personal development of individuals and the proper working of groups. The tutor is concerned with the means of educreation, the appetite for knowledge and skills, and the resolution of that which gets in the way with therapeutic aids.

The tutor may not even be an expert in any subject except in educreation: thus, whatever the study, he can assist the individuals and the groups to develop effective methods of work, to help to formulate the fertile questions and to understand and integrate conflicting advice from experts. The rest largely takes care of itself.

It must clearly be understood that this goes beyond the kind of thing now experienced under the name "tutorials" (usually a travesty of the intentions, often no more than a frightfully polite or possibly embarrassingly charming sherry party). It is intended to create the vital link between awareness, self-awareness and work.

It should be stressed that as a rule the tutorial staff will, of course, have expertise to pass on also. The type of person really interested in the development of the young, and of society, will normally be engaged in a number of vital activities. The skill is a complex one and remuneration should be reconsidered in terms of the educreational framework.

Tutorial staff, people who have been engaged, and in due course trained, in the art of tutoring, who care for educreation as a vocation, might be engaged on a permanent basis to give the advantages of continuity to a school. And for such staff the sabbatical year is important.

Training teachers for the tutorial function, which is severally strange, is vital. At the moment, those who teach at universities have no training whatever in teaching, and teacher-training colleges have a very narrow approach.[i]

The evolution of the tutorial species will take some time. Happily, talent, attraction and initiative are creating an increasing number of tutor-minded staff spontaneously.

A post-graduate school or department to tutor and teach tutors could be implemented as soon as the opportunity arises. Enlightened experts to do the teaching are available, and the maximum possible advantages could be gained by attaching such a department to an undergraduate school, the head of which wishes to experiment.

(i) PINION F. P., *Educational Values in an Age of Technology*, Oxford 1964, p. 46: "To provide the kind of education needed, we need new courses for teachers at universities and training colleges, and we must be less circumscribed by the subject".

Thus the practical experience could be directly useful. The many techniques propounded in this book would be used, practised, improved, refined, taught, absorbed and new ones invented. The whole would be regarded as a creative experiment and closely and critically examined the whole time so that working difficulties could immediately be diagnosed and remedied.

It is clear that such a course for tutors would include the awareness and group therapeutic endeavours that they in their turn will try to develop with their students. As in psychoanalysis, until you have experienced it, it is difficult and often not safe to practise. Until your own emotions have been sorted out, until you, at least, know what sort of person you are, have become familiar with your strengths and weaknesses and know the ways in which you can help yourself to become healthier, it is not very safe to let you loose on the emotional aid to the problems of others.

(b) *The Consultant Teacher*

There are many ways of passing on all manner of specific expertise and knowledge by what will become consultants in teaching.

Everything in education, and not only in professional education, points to greater use of a greater range of outside people, to a far fuller involvement of the outer world in education and of education in the outer world. The principle of clearly separating (and so powerfully combining) consultant teaching and tutorial teaching, opens up countless possibilities in that direction. It solves the conflict between those who want permanent teachers and those who want temporary appointments: both are valid. It enables schools to be right up to date and make the most of professional advice without absorbing permanently professional involvement which may become of inferior educational quality through the years.

The concept is not impractical: the A.A. School of Architecture 1965 prospectus says that some 1000 visits in the past session from

E

outside showed "a healthy scale of the creative link between an active school and the world around it". (Although their function at the A.A. is not educreational in the main.)[i]

The conflict between academic and practical bias falls away once the students', the new generation's, sharp nose is allowed to smell for relevance and orientate itself within the fields of study. Academicism is only a pest when in authoritarian education the students have to submit to the buzzing of bees in other people's bonnets.

The consultant teacher is like all consultants—best engaged temporarily, from an hour's duration to about three years', perhaps. Every aspect of educreation is orientated towards the search for better, newer things. The capacity for change is built in. It would be ordinary procedure to change consultants and not the great upheaval staff change now represents. A large number of consultant teachers with this very considerable turnover, provides all the freshness and openness in terms of personalities the student might need.

The range of kinds of employment for consultants is great, from the professional who might come in once to add to discussion, free or paid, for an hour or half a day, to the consultant professor who might be appointed for three years to be on tap one day a week; there may be full-time members of staff appointed for a year. The variety is infinite and the flexibility of administration (and let us not forget the whole and only point of administration is to help education) is an important aid to success.

However, even where heads of schools and students have to go begging for consultant tuition, the scope is still considerable. Financially it is not necessarily a matter of providing more funds. If one assumes that the tutorial task can work well with as many as fifteen to twenty students per tutor (particularly once senior student–junior student relationship is fruitfully developed—see school organization, Section III), and we examine the present

(i) I found on my visit in 1965 to the Oslo School of Architecture that "consultant teachers" as described here are used on a considerable scale.

staff–student ratio, it will be seen that, for example in architecture, twenty-five out of thirty schools would be able to use funds now spent on full-time staff, on part-time or temporary consultant staff instead. I am in no way advocating less staff. I am saying that a better use of funds is possible for different kinds of staff even under existing conditions.

Poor teachers are far worse than nothing, and unless the tutorial capacity is there, or exceptional expertise in passing on information, there is little advantage in having a full complement of staff (except for purposes of tidy records). But poor members of staff do act as impediments to growth and enthusiasm. They deaden or poison the atmosphere in an inadmissible way. If my language sounds strong, this is due to the experience of such effects on students.[i]

Whitehead, much more than a generation ago, spoke strongly, too: "We—I am talking of schoolmasters and of university dons —are apt to forget that . . . an unskillful practitioner can easily damage a sensitive organism."[ii] And: "In all education the main cause of failure is staleness."[iii]

As with all the other suggestions made in this book, one can, on the one hand, opportunely and skilfully, introduce the beginnings of this general principle from almost any angle. For example, a student body can find means to bring into the laboratory or studio informally and regularly, the local trade, business and professional people to start fruitful contacts. An isolated member of staff can start something within his sphere, or a head of a school can go as far as co-operation with the administration allows (or perhaps a little further). But this sort of thing is not the full educreational idea. To get the maximum benefit from the help the external world has to offer, students need to have learned the methods of approach that can orientate them, and work must be built around the rich framework of educreation.

(i) At least one British school is purposely not filling one of its permanent posts so that the funds can be used in this sort of way.
(ii) WHITEHEAD A. N., *The Aims of Education*, p. 45.
(iii) Ibid., p. 18.

We can summarize that the fundamental difference between the tutor and the consultant is that the tutor's primary interest is the student, the consultant's, his subject. This is important to note, as the passion for teaching a subject may be vehement also.

It must not be left out of consideration that the integration of society and education would have a two-way effect. I have observed in my experimental work how the professionals, drawn into the consultant teaching network in some of the many possible ways, feel their work suddently enhanced. The attention given, the teaching content, and, doubtless, vanity, make them see their work with fresh vigour. I can in particular say this about practising architects, where it has been acknowledged. A later section (III.9) will give indications on how the general principles above can be used in a school of architecture.

The Robbins Report also suggests that there are teachers whose effective functions differ and that organization should respect and use this opportunity.

"It should also be recognized that teachers differ in their powers and that more attention should be paid to their diversity. There are some first class lecturers who have little gift for intimate teaching and some who are first class in conducting discussion are poor lecturers. The present emphasis on the lecture as a means of instruction is, we believe, stultifying the gifts of some teachers. There are teachers who have a special gift for establishing personal relations with students and might well be given a larger share than others in the work of personal supervision and a smaller share of formal teaching."[i]

The last phrase gets quite near to my recommendation of the tutors on the one hand and the consultant teachers on the other, which, of course, crystallizes the matter.

"If by a 'tutorial system' is meant a system that ensures that the pupil comes into personal contact with his teachers, that he feels he can bring his individual difficulties and problems to them,

(i) Robbins Report, p. 188.

and that his progress is a matter of sympathetic concern to them, we are whole heartedly in favour of a tutorial system."(i)

And again, a little later:

"There are two elements of a tutorial system that we think should be universally established. First, we commend the practice obtaining in many universities of assigning a pupil at entry to a tutor or supervisor of his studies, whom he can consult at any time over his work and, if he wishes, his personal affairs. But we have received evidence that suggests that in some faculties such assignment is a formality and the student actually sees little of his tutor after an initial interview. We consider that regular personal guidance of individual students is one of the most important duties of a university teacher."(ii)

These are unmistakably endorsements not only of different teaching function but of a therapeutic approach. Only one small further step is necessary: to recognize that "guidance" includes therapy or vice versa, and that the onus of initiative lies with the tutor. The recommendation quoted must surely demonstrate to any teacher that more than mere intellectual skills are here involved.

III.2.4. Tutorial and Consultant Professors

The idea of consultant and tutorial staff is a fertile one and many original applications will come from it.

Not only this book but a far wider field of opinion suggests that leadership of departments and schools (not to speak of vice-chancellors) is a unique and vital job at this moment. Radical growth needs opportune channels. Only full-time occupation of exceptional talents will be able to cope with the day-to-day battle and inspire the troops on all levels, once educreational criteria are to be energetically followed and every chance of implementation taken.

At this highest professional level, the distinction between

(i) Robbins Report, p. 186.
(ii) Ibid., p. 188.

tutorial and consultant is crucial. The present state and tendencies are highly unsatisfactory. Taking the architectural profession as an example, with its comparatively short history of about sixty years, we had at the beginning "liberal teaching professors". The outstanding figure, Charles Reilly, was indeed educreationally orientated. The liveness, readiness for change and critical self-analysis of the profession (not particularly marvellous but remarkable compared with all others), is, I believe, due largely to this influence.

However, later, after the 1939–45 war, in a chaotic period of transition, it was thought that the famous of the profession ought to be brought into architectural education, as was the case in medicine, to bring reputation to the schools and to architecture, and heart to the students. The analogy was, however, belated, false and loose.

It is true that architectural education and architecture have, in the public eye, won glamour and reputation as a result of the famous occupying professional chairs. And it is right that, as in medicine, the famous practitioners should be associated with education. But the grave mistake lies in the assumption that there is no difference between a professor of architecture and a professor of architectural education. And this point applies to any field.

Thus, the famous men should (as Bakema in Delft) frequent the schools and stimulate them, galvanize them, fertilize them. But as they hardly ever have more time than, on an average, a full day a week, to spend on the educational aspects of education, this might be the clear limit of their employment as consultant professors. And this approximates to the reality of medical practice, too. Where it does not, medical practice should likewise adopt this realistic attitude.

The German system of what amounts to consultant professors only, professors appointed to various subjects (albeit they have permanent appointments), demonstrates the lack of tutorial staff as vividly, perhaps more vividly and with a longer tradition, than anything in Britain. In Darmstadt, where a real interest in the educational methods and reorganization exists, reactions can clearly be felt.

In Britain, the right idea of bringing practice closer to the schools, carried out the wrong way, has resulted in a weakening of the educational process at the very time we stand in urgent need of powerful development.

The mistake has been an obvious one, the result of a deliberate action, the desperate attempt to improve architectural education by injecting it with famous names and their attraction. But only one or two of the many famous professors have had educational ideas of some substance, and beyond the relatively inconsequential rearranging of courses and the pronouncements of highly generalized and oft-repeated pious hopes of new professors, very little has been contributed to the body of educational ideas. The reason is clear. These men have led, and sometimes still lead, in important professional fields. They cannot, and do not have the time for education as well, let alone educreation. Their appointments as consultant professors would be admirable, with clearly defined duties and times for work with students. But to expect them to inspire by personal contact as well as by their work is plainly asking too much.

The students of today begin to experience the disastrous error. We should take note and try to ameliorate conditions where appointments have been made, and influence the definition of new positions as either tutorial or consultant in the functional manner outlined here.

The professional bodies should clearly recognize the primary need for educational brilliance and enthusiasm in staff. Pointing out their policies and viewpoints to the universities could help greatly. In the creation of new university schools, the opportunity is unique, the responsibility immense, the efforts thoroughly worth while.

Does the architectural profession, like the medical, have to ignore the advice of those who have done the research into the relevant field?

Dr. Abercrombie's advice as I see it, ignored by the medical educationists though gathered for them,[i] leads to the recognition of the tutoring skills as primary, as does my own work done for the design professions.

The professor of educreation, in any subject—as distinguished from the consultant professors in the various specialities—has a supremely important position. His humanity, extent of tolerance and capacity for life, the ability to grow and stay alive, the liberal and really broad scientific approach coupled with enthusiasm, and the desire to spend his time with staff and students—these are the right sort of requirements for such a post.

Our university teaching fabric lacks the whole range of such professors to evolve the needed new teaching environment. This surely must go hand in hand with the Robbins Report scale of expansion. Education lacks direction. Educreation, with tutor-heads of departments and schools, would surely cure this and would bring a distinct flavour to each institution.

If only one professor is possible, it is the tutorial professor, the professor of educreation, who is crucial. For the salaries now offered to the several additional professors, so-called full-time and permanent, for example in architectural departments, it would be possible, and wiser, to engage a larger number of part-time, temporary consultant professors. If university regulations make this impossible, the educational boards of the professions ought to regard it as an extreme priority to persuade the bodies concerned of the wisdom and need of this policy as a matter of the greatest urgency. Perhaps much of this applies particularly to the Architectural School about to move its mobile nature into the rigid frame of a University.

It has been regarded as odd for a long time that lecturers at universities have no teaching-training, no group dynamics tuition, of any kind. It is quite absurd that professors, at a time of change, should not have a profound background in education and clear prophetic views, based on criteria. At a time when we need to regard each innovation as an experiment so that we can glean as

(i) ABERCROMBIE J., *The Anatomy of Judgement.*

much from it as possible, each professor ought to expound in some detail the nature of his hypothesis and the manner of experiment and use of results. This is a central issue of educreation—its inevitable by-product will be to turn out ever more effective students. The educreational experiment is the full-time job of the professor—not the side-line of one or two research fellows.

It is no longer valid to put a set course under way, which continues, year after year, unchanged in this time of unprecedented rate of change. The professor's task to improve and develop courses year by year, month by month, is a strenuous, continuous, task: observing the results of his ideas, ameliorating as the experiment proceeds, as is peculiar to creative experiment, and using his creative genius all the time in the service of educreation. We can recognize in the professor a person who should be particularly skilled in co-operation and the therapeutic approach.

As the staff have therapeutic responsibilities to the students and are helped decisively by the group therapeutic activities of the students themselves, so, in the parallel sense, the head should give the therapeutic leadership to his staff and help to give staff meetings a group therapeutic quality. Here, as with students, abilities and co-operation can be much increased and conflicts resolved—or seen as clearly detrimental.

To summarize: Major transformations in education are currently in progress, or bound to come. Anyone appointed in leading positions in education should therefore be appointed because of his leading ideas in education, apart from his professional or intellectual excellence. Yet this idea has hardly begun to catch on. The rare exceptions in vice-chancellors, and subsequently staff of new universities, are paying rich dividends already.

III.2.5. Staff Appointments Procedure

Many schools are concerned with staff unable to fulfil even the traditional duties the students seek from them. Where engagement is on a permanent basis only special misconduct can allow authorities to give notice (or a transfer to a university in the case of schools of architecture!).

To look at the human side of the picture, we must decide whether it is more important to give some discomfort to an inadequate teacher, unable to see his own lack, or to bedevil fellow staff and, most important, generations of students. The answer is obvious—particularly during a time of full employment, which is likely to continue indefinitely in the construction field. We cannot afford to have the second best at the source. There is no such thing as neutral education. Either you educreate or edukill. Students must defend themselves against inadequate or sick teachers.

The choice of new heads and new members of staffs for existing schools is at the moment often done by selection boards of a very mixed quality.(i) For staff, they include the head of the school, who is sometimes overruled, though he may have definite preference. There is no other member of the staff there, or, God forbid, representative of the people for whom it is all intended—the students. It is a doubtful point of view that students, in their inexperience, cannot usefully contribute. On the contrary, they are sensitive to abilities usually missed by selection boards. They would also ensure less reliance on prearranged appointments. When tutorial staff is differentiated the student can counterbalance in those cases where the professor has considerable outside interests, and it is only natural that these, perhaps rather than the teaching ability, are criteria for choice of additional staff.

Within the context of educreation described in this book it will

(i) The straw-hatted Lady Somebody in Birmingham who was truly horrified because I could not remember the exact ages of my several young children, the gentleman in Belfast who asked me during my interview for a Chair to relate the architecture of Frank Lloyd Wright to the Irish problem, the vice-chancellor in Nottingham who only opened his eyes to offer me a lectureship when I had applied for a readership, the assistant director of education in Nottingham who said that as I had done many things the quality of all of them would obviously be low—these are just some of my own experiences. On the other hand, the enjoyable and enlightened, if unsuccessful, interview for senior research fellow in education at Lancaster University stands out as a pleasant experience.

be seen how the consultant staff arise of more or less spontaneous needs and opportune chances of each school. The students, as much as the staff or head, may be the prime movers in asking for and introducing one or other consultant element for short or longer duration.

Given the prevalence of part-time and temporary teaching, there is no reason why tutors, intended as full-time teachers, should not have trial periods after which students and staff and head could jointly decide whether permanent appointment was indicated. Such a process must be conceived within the framework of educreation—not within the present authoritarian regimes in which students remain the under-privileged, voteless, often voiceless majority.

III.2.6. Learning from Fellow Students

It is with the administratively muted multitude of students, ironically enough, that, given a new attitude to education, we bring in another sort of human teacher, powerful in numbers and influence, beyond the tutor and consultant teacher.

It has long been said that more is learnt from fellow students than from teachers. Where co-operation becomes the matrix of learning and the techniques of working together are taught, this becomes profoundly true. In fact, once a school has reached a certain momentum of educreation (particularly with a five-year course), after a length of time staff may appear remarkably superfluous and even obstructive (in a period of transition) to lively atmosphere.

This particular immense human reservoir of "teaching aids" is the most important untapped source. My experience has made me confident that the idea is entirely and immediately practicable. This, far more than any other factor, can increase productivity in education.

Related to it, but effective beyond it, are the new abilities to learn. Learning to learn, learning to ask questions, to become good at techniques of finding out, and for each person to recognize what are his best ways, all this will make far more efficient use of any teacher.

III.3. TEACHING METHODS AND ASSESSMENT

III.3.1. Examinations—Abominations

One of the general indictments of our educational system as a whole is the dominant place held by examinations; taken for granted, but quite absurd, assessment requirements determine teaching methods. The tail is wagging the dog. And the syllabus of lists of subjects to be covered is the usual example.

Marris's extensive research confirms general experience:

"Examinations unquestionably do great harm, at all levels of education. They alienate the student from his personal interest in the subject he studies, rob him of initiative, and encourage whatever kind of learning is easiest to test, irrespective of its relevance. Original work is discouraged, because it is difficult to mark: original interest, because it upsets the curriculum. The teacher's role is confused with that of assessor, and the student is inhibited from seeking guidance for fear of being judged. Is an impartial, but admittedly imperfect assessment of performance so important as to justify this sacrifice? Even if it compromises objectivity, some more relaxed and continuous evaluation of the student's work, in which his initiative had far more scope, ought to maintain standards of expectation high enough. The compromise seems much less alarming than the risk of so distorting education."[i]

Assessment is almost synonymous with examination and there is little change in sight, in spite of the fact that a vast army of critics have shown examinations to be an inefficient means of assessment and have condemned the extreme emotional stresses they produce artificially, and the horrible aftermath of disillusionment or flat triumph.[ii]

(i) MARRIS P., *Experience of Higher Education*, p. 180.
(ii) The word "examination" makes one feel "funny all over" and hot and cold. It gives instant tummyache, leads to rashes, stops sleep and

Marking most present examination papers is a deadening, boring chore, really an obscene task of dealing with students' excrement, for truly we deal with waste products. This alone— for teachers to be deadened, weighted down and depressed (for the humour of the howler is little compensation) by this time-wasting task—this alone is a strong enough argument for their abolition.

There is an alternative: teach by teaching machines—then the results can automatically come out of the machine that teaches you. I will discuss teaching machines more fully later; suffice to say here that the advantages are that, while it is a teacher's senseless chore it is good that marking is taken from him. But the danger that we get machines which fail *us* and which we fear, instead of our failing and improving the machines, is over-whelming.

Usually after a suicide, or after the wrong examination papers have been given out at Cambridge, or sale of examination paper information causes riots in Paris, or similar spectacle, public attention is drawn to the silly cruelties we inflict year after year. "Final examinations at universities can create such stresses that many candidates fail to do themselves justice. Careers may be at stake, and the more adult one is the more one realizes how critical an examination result may be in labelling one for life."[i]

---

appetite—reactions run the full gamut of psychosomatic possibilities. The sheer hypnotic fear—snake and rabbit variety—was demonstrated for me when in my fourth year at Liverpool University a fine and refined man, Velarde, gave five splendidly inspirational lectures—and then confided that he loathed the idea of setting an examination and marking. So he proposed to give five questions on the five lectures and begged us not to write more than the essentials—five minutes each question, about half-an-hour's total work, he said, for a slow writer. He threatened that long papers would be marked as a sign of failure and as a sign of his hatred for marking. The net result was that I, being a fast writer, was out in 25 minutes. I took the man at his word and indeed passed. But to my astonishment, three hours after the start students were still largely there, re-reading the precious bane.

(i) PINION F. B., *Educational Values in an Age of Technology*, p. 52.

To refine the remarkably crude kind of assessment examinations offer, the custom of marking work throughout a lengthy period is advocated and increasingly adopted. But the absurdity of tail wagging dog remains. The tests, the work to be done is set to allow assessment and marking, and the evil emotional effects are less extreme but prolonged.

To diagnose the reason for the insistence on examinations we have to go beyond teaching to administration or the administrative minds in teachers, which so like the neatness and ease of examination results, of marks, of distinctions, class positions and the like. Maybe the bureaucratic tendency to reduce names to numbers is an important factor. The subject syllabus is at one and the same time the most administratively convenient and educationally restrictive device. It allows you to know exactly where you are—although you have no interest in being there.

It is not relevant to this book to discuss the various merits of assessments within the traditional competitive and authoritarian system. Suffice to say that the outcome—examinations governing course content, examinations which are recognized as inferior means of testing—does not seem a very efficient pattern even in its own context.

It is important to note that once the pattern of education changes to educreation the assessment becomes a far more integrated and organic part of the teaching process and there is certainly no need and no tendency to prefer tasks that are easily markable.

III.3.2. Educreational Assessment

In educreation groups and teachers co-operate towards the individual development of each member of the group. With such strong educational means this (not the passing of examinations), but the rich development of the individual's abilities in the chosen directions is almost invariably reached. And even if, however rarely, they are not, it is not a matter of "failure". Concentrated therapy or the changing of his educational environment becomes, under educreation, something quite different from "retreat under failure", so common today (14%).

Progress and the standard and areas of development arise out of work and work difficulties. They are experienced as part of the process of achieving self-set and group-set aims. Within a framework of awareness and close co-operation, far more reliable, reasonable and useful meanings accrue to the word "assessment" than the daft playing with marks now so seriously and childishly adhered to.

To describe the kind of work that emerges from the interest of the student and the stimulus of his environment is difficult for the variety is great. (Details for one approach are of course given in Section IV.) But the assessment will certainly be concerned with the method of his approach, the relationship of his judgements to the criteria he set himself and the nature of his co-operation and sense and sensibility in his work patterns. For, whereas grading is in itself the purpose of assessing in the competitive system, in educreation assessment is the diagnosis of a person's weak spots so that they may grow strong through awareness and special help; it is largely the diagnosis of emotional blockages in his learning process which directs therapeutic efforts towards clearing them.

III.3.3. The Project

This can be envisaged in terms of what is loosely termed "the project", as a teaching method, and described as suitable for general application at universities by Marris: "The project fulfils, more completely than any other technique of higher education, the aims which, as it seems to me, the traditional emphasis on individual teaching implies. When a student can appropriate his own research problem, it absorbs his interest, and provides a personally meaningful context within which to apply the basic principles of an academic discipline, and to learn the methods of intellectual inquiry. Since the problem has never been tackled before, he shares a more genuine community of purpose with his tutor: however slight the research, either the methods or the results stand a chance of being mutually interesting, and the student can feel he has something to contribute to the relationship. And he will be less likely to feel foolish when he needs advice. The discussions, searching of references, leafing through the pages of journals, could also lead his interest outward to other problems. It students were taught in no other way, their understanding of the processes of intellectual inquiry would, I think, be wider and deeper than it is—though their factual knowledge of their subject might be very patchy."[i]

And this does not mention the interest of the work to fellow students—mutually educating. I have tried "the project" in subjects hitherto taught by lectures. The results were excellent— the patchiness is bound to be there, increasingly, as factual knowledge grows and grows—the project concentrates on methods, and allows practice for the complex skills of intelligent learning itself (as distinguished from other skills).

III.3.4. Amelioration of Examinations

In times of transition it is necessary to act opportunely. Our compulsive ambivalence towards examination is embedded in the very depth of statutes and their eradication will not be a speedy process. So the task of the teacher is to be inventive and make of the so-called examination a test and something positive, something of intrinsic use, something enjoyed and not feared.

"Since there is no question of abolishing the examination system, it should be made as humane and efficient as possible, and it is undesirable to attach very great importance to any one examination."[ii]

(i) MARRIS P., *Experience of Higher Education*, p. 66.
(ii) Kneale Committee Report on Examinations, Oxford 1965.

A student can be asked to write thoughts and ideas that are his, developed from the factual information that has been vital to his studies, which spring from three hours' peace and quiet and preparation for them. The examination can be seen as an integrated part of the year's work, his personal year's work in the field—thinking that leads on, culminates, summarizes the ideas and conclusions and experiences, or uses them to think and theorize further.

When I served on the Board of Architectural Education there was an effort to introduce (for the Part III Finals Examination, taken after seven years' studies and practice) the idea of the use of reference books. In the context this was agreed by most members as a realistic and efficient way of testing a future architect's efficiency—if test we must, which to me shows a despicable lack of confidence in the students, the schools, the offices, born of utterly outworn attitudes.

However, in spite of the agreement on the desirability of the idea, it was rejected outright as impractical. In fact, the meeting had bandied about a few comments for a few minutes instead of tackling, with ingenuity and purpose, the solution of the problem —the usual problem—of how to make the desirable practical.

In the case in point the difficulties are small indeed. But the inertia, the too-muchness of any innovation—beyond expressions of pious hopes or administrative tidiness and convenience—seems to be fairly universal and the first reaction of any executive body.

Beyond the year-by-year assessment, the widespread compulsion to sit examinations even if you are not ready for them (something most Continental universities seem to avoid—you choose the time for your examination) is also contrary—clearly and precisely contrary—to the ideal to which one and all pay lip service: the respect for the individual. The data on variation in development and learning rates is voluminous;[i] the biographies of the world,

---

(i) See for examples proposals in B.A.S.A. Annual Reports, London 1961, 1962, 1963.

no less. The conclusions are clear, the differences are important. Yet the educational system resembles a banking system in its neatness and rigidity. The grants system follows suit. If one has a talented student taking perhaps 10% longer to learn, even if 100 times as profoundly as his fellow, one must "fail him", which often means end of grant, end of career, end of important contribution, so one has to look around for ways out.

I believe that even within present frameworks boards of studies should regard it as one of their chief jobs to recommend such students on extenuating circumstances (pretexts) (for that is a way administration and education committees and senates understand) for additional time—without loss of grants or honour.

It is well known in the architectural profession that a remarkably large proportion of the outstanding practitioners "failed" one year or the other—or sailed perilously near the wind. In twelve years I have perhaps taught six, maybe twelve, exceptionally good students—it depends how you look at it. But every one of those, just because of aspects of his excellence, was subjected to failure or the very near failure of a year. Far sadder is the actual failure and subsequent elimination of perhaps three such students, forced by the crude system and its rigid interpretation by staff.

III.4. RESEARCH

III.4.1. Definitions

Research is a special kind of learning, particularly creative, and with increasingly general relevance. I think that every student (every child), released from the blocking influences of a sick society, uses his mind research-wise as a matter of course and spontaneously. Educreation is concerned with the development of this relationship and with providing the opportunity for its exercise.

To establish this hypothesis that research is a common and not a special phenomenon, a definition of terms is urgent. The pronouncements by Professor Llewellyn-Davies and Peter Cowan[i] do not go to the root of the matter and add to the confusion. The factors of invention, discovery or originality in research have no place, no mention in their analyses.

Clarification comes from the application of the formula of attraction–fusion–liberation. Let us take the chaos of statements on research as a problem. The desire to re-search (look again) to find order, is itself the first part of research (attraction). The insight, hunch that the order may lie in the application of a certain formula is also part of research (fusion). The painstaking work of applying the hunch and investigating whether it is useful, effective or not is also research (liberation).

Let us see more fully the clarification which comes from applying the formula—describing as a pattern what we otherwise do not see that way.

(a) *Attraction*

We tend to ignore the starting points of research, or talk about them in such general terms as to obscure their crucial importance and meaning.

The innate curiosity is a part of the complex relationships of individuals, groups and the environment as a whole. It crystallizes into specific questions; this is the origin of research. They may reflect a sick state or a healthy one. The motive may be ulterior, or clear and straight. And this indicates why the nature of the question is crucial. In fact, in our society, it is likely to need careful consideration.

A society which lays stress on the co-operative responsibility of each person for the welfare of the world, will reap a different and richer crop of research questions than a society, competitively organized, where each person's first concern is to keep up not

(i) COWAN P., Research, *R.I.B.A. Journal*, London, April 1961, p. 212, and LLEWELLYN-DAVIES Lord R., and COWAN P., *R.I.B.A. Journal*, London April 1964, p. 149.

only with the Joneses but also (as they imagine) the Einsteins.[i] Questions, problems require a sort of incubation period before they trigger off the answer-seeking part of the rhythm. This is well described by Koestler[ii] and Gordon.[iii] This applies to individuals or groups.

(b) *Fusion*

Once a question has a fruitful form the whole of the individual or the group, from the most intellectual thought to the most primitive and basic insights and associations, is consciously or unconsciously in the service of the search for a solution.

The attraction is strong. It will not let go—and sometimes persists for years. Then, suddenly—"fusion", "bi-sociation", "eureka", "discovery", "an idea", "invention", call it what you like, the HUNCH arises. At first it is a hunch. It is in the mind's eye. This is an experience more basic than language and mathematical symbolism. But the "mind's eye" can be blind to limitations rather easily. Sometimes the first hunch is associated with certainty, sometimes not.

Whatever the variation, one quality stays the same: "an original combination of parts", a bi-sociation of matrices, an original relationship, has come about. Its fusion is the "act of creation", the central part of any success in research. Einstein said it never came by deduction. How it does come is described, though not fully understood or defined, in Koestler's book[iv] with much authoritative evidence. The suddenness and wholeness of the insight is universal. The process has been described in some detail in *Synectics*.[v] Analogies play a crucial part—Kekule

---

(i) In the main, universities and individuals are concerned with the size and financial grandeur of their research—not particularly with its productivity!
(ii) KOESTLER A., *Act of Creation*.
(iii) GORDON W. J. J., *Synectics*, New York and London 1961.
(iv) KOESTLER A., *Act of Creation*.
(v) GORDON W. J. J., *Synectics*.

literally dreamed up his structural theory of atoms in a "reverie" on a bus,[i] and other accounts of discoveries make a very varied story.

(c) *Liberation*

The hunch is an exciting event and it urges one on to try it out immediately in some situations. Regarding just this third stage, the investigation of the hunch, as the total research, and forgetting the previous two steps, is the common error in much analysis and classification of what is and what is not research. It is in this part of the rhythm that measurement and quantative assessment can (but need not) play an effective part, and only if the first two non-experimental stages are valid.

III.4.2. Confused Thinking

The gigantic waste of money currently taking place in research institutions, the lack of effect of research, is due to the silly notion that research, if it is colossal enough, endowed with computers and large laboratories, can be effective without brilliant hunches— or that the brilliant hunches and the original problem can be forgotten once the "scientific investigation" is under way.[ii]

As we would expect with a common functioning principle, each one of the phases in research as described can again be understood best as following the same rhythmic pattern: attraction–fusion– liberation.

We can now turn to the expositions of Llewellyn-Davies and Cowan, as the best of the traditional exponents, and note the defects: Professor Llewellyn-Davies makes the task of criticism easy. In his usual crystal-clear style he suggests examples of the types of work that should be differentiated from "research" proper,

---

(i) LIBBY WALTER, The Scientific Imagination, *Scientific Monthly*, Vol. XV (1922), pp. 263–70.

(ii) See the pathetic lists of "Research" printed at regular intervals in the *A.J.* as representative of Ph.D. and M.Sc., seeking exercises without reference to question or hunch.

though he gives no reasons for his choice. So he says that the design of a system of building like Clasp is not research but "advanced practice". But this leaves out the brilliant question and solution: the *re*-search of the familiar subsidence problem, the hunch of "hinges" and springs in the structure of buildings, which then led to practical solutions and systems.

The structural experiments of Buckminster Fuller are supposed to be not research but "development work". Again, how can we look at this in isolation from the basic problems and answers on natural economics of structure, etc., with which Fuller began? In fact, the use of this work by Fuller in the research work of bio-chemistry, currently in Cambridge, speaks for the "basic" research nature of his thought. Fuller's work cannot be assessed and used intelligently or developed without knowledge and consideration of its origins.

The Nuffield study is supposed to be "applied research". But it is based as much on basic questions and the brilliant hunch leading to effective survey as the other work mentioned. The survey would lose its meaning without interpretation in terms of its origins. When Professor Llewellyn-Davies tries to "identify" (he does not claim to define) what he really would call "basic" or "pure research", he quotes the work of Penrose on genes which may help us in controlling congenital insanity. I think, if Penrose is like most other creative scientists who have discussed their methods,[i] he will agree that the vital beginning was the question —even though in the first place it could be reduced to "there's more to genes than meets the eye—I am going to find out." In other words, something had significantly been singled out. Subsequently, the manner of looking at such a phenomenon as a gene and actually making useful discoveries, depends on hunches or insights, not on logical deductions or routine alone.

(i) LIBBY WALTER, The Scientific Imagination, *Scientific Monthly*, Vol. XV, pp. 263–70; HADAMARD J., *The Psychology of Invention in the Mathematical Field*, Princetown 1949; SCHWARTZ C. and B., *Moments of Discovery*, New York 1958; PORTERFIELD A. L., *Creative Factors in Scientific Research*, Durham, U.S. 1941, p. 95.

The other identification mark Professor Llewellyn-Davies offers is that basic research is the same as "fundamental knowledge" and so is a part of the fertile "trunk" from which "branches" of applied knowledge spring as "from time to time research throws up an idea". On the contrary, my Lord, ideas should throw up research. To equate "fundamental knowledge" with "basic research" is obviously unwarranted and misleading. At best the former can be a quest for the latter. There is "fundamental knowledge" even where there is no research, for example. But there will be no "research," however much knowledge, without an idea. And, on the other hand, it is just with the fundamental knowledge of one epoch that research sometimes plays havoc, ignores or destroys to arrive at original solutions.

As Koestler says:

"The re-structuring of mental organization effected by the new discovery implies that the creative act has a revolutionary or destructive side. The path of history is strewn with its victims: the discarded isms of art, the epicycles and phlogistons of science."[i]

In other words, things thought incombustible and permanent proved not so. Conversely, unlike fundamental knowledge, a piece of research, however basically intended, can prove to be useless in the intended direction; but one, perhaps technical, aspect of it, what the professor might call "development research", might thrive and blossom and give rise to fundamental insights, and subsequently add to fundamental knowledge. It is not as simple, clear-cut and linear a logic as the Lord Llewellyn-Davies type scientists think.

Similarly, one can show Peter Cowan's analysis is shallow: "Research work itself can best be applied in circumstances where a quantitative result is required. The type of work may vary from high level investigations of a fundamental psychological or physiological nature, via social or statistical survey work, to cost research

(i) KOESTLER A., *The Act of Creation*, p. 658.

and materials testing[i] . . . the important thing to remember is that experimental and quantitative factors must be applied."

On the other hand, "The results of [mere] study will always remain subject to interpretation. The personality of the study worker will enter into the results and this must be allowed for when assessing the work. The quantitative aspect is not covered, and because of the absence of experimental method, most of the observations are unrepeatable under suitably controlled conditions."[ii]

Cowan puts his cards on the table and one sees the game he is playing clearly. It is the poker of the materialist who puts all his stakes on numbers. If it is numbers it is research, even if it is only "materials testing". The vast fields of biological observation and charting are not research?

To make it very obvious: Malinowski's work in the Trobriand Islands, an epoch-making work with a fundamental and profound introduction of a new methodology of research in terms of functional approach to "culture patterns" rather than the comparative approach with variables, in the anthropological field—this was again mere study?

This is laughable. Whether maths and exact repeatability is involved cannot be the criterion. The bloke who watches paint deterioration ("materials testing") over ten years and goes out daily with a microgauge and lens to look and record—without knowledge of what has gone before—is a research worker? Malinowski only a study worker? The point about having to take the subjective influence of the worker into account only where maths are excluded is the dangerously shallow, arrogant attitude of the materialist—shown to be disastrously false in the experiments on experimenters.[iii]

(i) Dr. F. M. Lea, Director of Building Research, Department of Scientific and Industrial Research, in response to the lecture Professor Llewellyn-Davies quoted, made a significant comment: ". . . but please, please, do set your standards high and refuse to be content with collections of data and information masquerading as research".
(ii) COWAN PETER, Research, *R.I.B.A. Journal*, April 1961.
(iii) See page 47 for doubts on quantitative "aspect".

It is relevant to note that after dividing work into "study" if it is "critical investigation", and "research" if it is the "endeavour to discover facts by scientific study" (both oddly taken from a dictionary definition!), the whole of Cowan's paper and the whole of the emphasis in Lord Llewellyn-Davies's later paper is on "research". The pleas for funds for establishments are all directed to "research". So it is more than a mere matter of names. It is singling out one kind of approach, and having done this, as if duty-bound to give credit to each, one of them (not using measurement) is condemned to poverty and ignominity. But this is never actually admitted or explicitly stated.

Yet it is a very serious consideration with far-reaching effects that "research" as a word has a higher academic standing than "study". This influences the kind of work done; it is this that reduces sociology and psychology, for example, to a never-ending quest for respectable—qualitative—repeatable work only because of ulterior motives for "scientific respectability" and funds.[i]

We should ponder:

"The awkward fact, that reason we know is never aware of its hidden assumptions—has been too much for some . . . scientists to admit."[ii]

To define "basic research" and "applied research" as does the U.S. Presidential Research Board, draws a line a little more comprehensible between that which extends the general principles of knowledge and that which examines these new extensions for the purpose of application.

But this, too, is a highly unrealistic definition. It envisages, as does Llewellyn-Davies that there is such a thing as "fundamental knowledge" which will not be changed itself by research. It assumes that people who in fact make basic discoveries are always

---

(i) I feel with Jackson when he writes: "A central plea here is not only the need for more research, but for the support of research which goes beyond the present boundaries of the measurable, accepting the attendant losses but searching for those insights which re-illuminate knowledge".
—(JACKSON B., *Streaming*, p. 130.)

(ii) WHYTE L. L., *The Unconscious Before Freud*, New York 1962.

engaged in a specific quest to extend the general principles of knowledge, which of course is wrong. Many principles have been discovered while a man has done a very detailed piece of what would be called "development research".[i]

The classifications arise out of a rigid, limited rationalism about the sequence of events when a pattern development is in fact taking place. According to the attraction–fusion–liberation formula we can describe the dynamic pattern of research better than by isolating some bits and pieces carried along by it, as Cowan and Llewellyn-Davies attempt.[ii]

But research can fall down in a number of ways: the attraction can be too much to a personal problem of the research worker to be of general relevance (as in the case in much of modern art, for example). The fusion, the hunch, can ignore a decisive point and the theory to be found unworkable or not right for the age. The liberation, the testing and applying of the hunch, might be so removed from the first two phases that it loses much of its research quality and effectiveness.

If the research team lacks those who formulate the brilliant question and have creative hunches, no number of computer-minded white-coats will make up for it. It is less likely that research will suffer decisively from the inaccuracy of the scientific investigation; that, after all, is what our age is good at.[iii] Llewellyn-Davies, urging the architects into the age of technology, is out of date. We have come to the edge of the holocaust with more science and technics—as forecast by Whitehead.[iv] Bio-technics, in the widest Mumfordian sense, is what we need.

Perhaps the most vivid example of ineffective research is in the social sciences.

We have become highly suspicious of "research" which leaves

(i) "A small-scale discovery of little intrinsic scientific or mathematical interest may turn out to be of the greatest social importance—positive or negative".—(BERNAL J. D., *Science Journal*, March 1965.)
(ii) See page 133.
(iii) However, see page 47.
(iv) See page 16.

one with a gigantic "So WHAT?" after great expenditure. Almost every research project undertaken in that field is in that category, and fits Dr. Lea's description of "collections of data".[i]

All this applies particularly to the "research into human settlements". Here we come up against a barrier set up by the methodologies of the social sciences. They insist on work plans that can achieve mathematically recorded results instead of putting first the success of a research project.

III.4.3. Creative Experiment

The "creative experiment" is a phrase coined by the author to describe a method which is more suitable to get useful results. The aim of the experiment, the hunch, is regarded as desirable (as indeed it must be to be tried out). The experiment is within our old hostile environment, and trying to succeed. Part of the success depends on the participation of the people; therefore, the degree to which participation can make the experiment a success is part of the experiment. This is not something that can be exactly repeated or measured. Yet it is most informative, leading to "the discovery of consistent patterns connecting and explaining observed phenomena",[ii] just like Malinowski's functional approach, also disqualified by Cowan's definition.

Thus, the creative experiment has a vital place in the social sciences and education where work is impeded by a lack of effective methods and a branding as "non-scientific" of those that offend the taboos of the academic establishment.

What, then, is the difference between research and learning? The difference is obvious in the name "*re*-search". It is not just search, i.e. looking up the literature, observing, comparing, memorizing or comprehending, but re-search, looking again, at the problem or a phenomenon that challenges the curiosity.

Research is then the activity which springs from original questions or asking an old question with a new emphasis when

(i) Comment on Cowan's paper *R.I.B.A. Journal*, London April 1964.
(ii) MATTHEW Sir R., *R.I.B.A. Journal*.

the scope allows answers. It is a creative activity incorporating art, science, skills and aids.

Two independent sources have similar views. Koestler, in *The Act of Creation*, says at the end of exhaustive reams of evidence:

"Any boy of the sixth form can derive the Pythagoras Theorem, which he has previously learned, as a matter of routine; but to discover it for himself would require a high degree of originality. I hope I have laid sufficient emphasis on the fact that originality must be measured on subjective scales and that any self-taught novelty is a minor bi-sociative (creative) act."

Remarkably parallel are the views of synectics: ". . . the creative process in human beings can be concretely described . . .";
". . . invention in the arts and in science are analogous . . .";
". . . individual process in the creative enterprise enjoys a direct analogy in the group process."

The teaching of the research approach is not intrinsically the difficult thing it sets out to be. It need not be postponed until post-graduate days and it can develop without maturity in the kindergarten. Help by the experienced in the third phase is usually only difficult because of the rigidity so often found in the mature.

"Experts who are inhibited by the image of themselves as professionals, viewing themselves as being above the naive consideration of the commonplace, must enter a conscious didactic phase in order to take advantage of their productive potential."[i]

The general educreational inference of this chapter is this: when we encourage the asking of questions, do not stop the breaking of boundaries of disciplines as defined at the moment, and develop a sense of responsibility, research mindedness will flourish. And I believe that it is this, rather than any lack of funds or lack of research departments, which is at the root of the poverty of our resources in terms of ideas and the fruitlessness

(i) GORDON W. J. J., *Synectics*, p. 117.

without proper orientation of a large measure of scientific investigation.

III.5. TECHNOLOGICAL AND OTHER AIDS

III.5.1. Automated Learning—a Red Herring

Given the desperate situation of education *vis-à-vis* the development of the world, other radical proposals apart from educreation are likely. One that has already been proferred is the Behaviourist concept of the mechanization of the learning process. Teaching machines are to be the means for the quantitative and qualitative increase of learning per schoolmaster, and the idea is in vogue.

I regard this approach as a gigantic red herring. The usefulness of the teaching machine is marginal. And to mistake a red herring for a genuine fish is a very serious mistake if much of our energy is channelled into catching it. Therefore, it is necessary to clarify the water and note what we are looking at. Before we can have a balanced account of technological aids the teaching machine, the behaviourist's contribution, must be shown to be just one of many. It is specially important only because its protagonists are so powerful and that makes it specially dangerous.

The immense persuasive power of stimulus-response of behaviourism lies in its nearness to a genuine appreciation of relationship. Attraction–fusion–liberation is the basic rhythm. The behaviourists disregard the creative, to me crucial, element. But by using the natural rhythm and exploiting it with artificially induced "fusion" they "create", in fact. What they create is a habit—a low form of creation if a very, very common one. But their method is powerful—it's not new but systematic.

The urgency of making education more efficient was seen by the behaviourists. Their view, as put by B. F. Skinner, a most catholic spokesman, reads:

"There are more people in the world than ever before, and a far greater part of them want an education. The demand cannot be met simply by building more schools and training more teachers. Education must become more efficient. To this end, curricula must be revised and simplified, and textbooks and classroom techniques improved. In any other field a demand for increased production would have led at once to the invention of laborsaving capital equipment. Education has reached this stage very late, possibly through a misconception of its task. Thanks to the advent of television, however, the so-called audio-visual aids are being re-examined. Film projectors, television sets, phonographs and tape recorders are finding their way into American schools and colleges.

"Audio-visual aids supplement and may even supplant lectures, demonstrations and textbooks. In doing so, they serve one function of the teacher: They present material to the student and, when successful, make it so clear and interesting that the student learns. There is another function to which they contribute little or nothing. It is best seen in the productive interchange between teacher and student in the small classroom or tutorial situation. Much of that interchange has already been sacrificed in American education in order to teach large numbers of students. There is a real danger that it will be wholly obscured if use of equipment designed simply to present material becomes widespread. The student is becoming more and more a mere passive receiver of instruction."[i]

And so the teaching machine comes to the rescue:

"Psychology's pioneer in automated teaching is S. L. Pressey. Dr. Pressey's first papers present a device, an early version of which he exhibited and discussed at the meetings of the American Psychological Association in 1924 and 1925 . . . Pressey discusses a 'simple apparatus which gives and scores tests—and teaches.' He points out laborsaving devices are quite feasible in education and sees no reason why education should not be run as efficiently as any large-scale undertaking in this country. Rather than stultifying education, such mechanical aids should free the teacher

(i) In LUMSDAINE and GLASER, *Teaching Machines and Programmed Learning, A Source Book*, Washington, 1960.

from unnecessary burdens and leave her free 'for those inspirational and thought-stimulating activities which are, presumably, the real function of the teacher'."[i]

And now for an authoritative description of today's machines:

"Despite great variation in complexity and special features, all of the devices that are currently called 'teaching machines' represent some form of variation on what can be called the tutorial or Socratic method of teaching. That is, they present the individual student with programs of questions and answers, problems to be solved, or exercises to be performed. In addition, however, they always provide some type of automatic feedback or correction to the student so that he is immediately informed of his progress at each step and given a basis for correcting his errors. They thus differ from films, T.V., and most other audio-visual media as ordinarily utilized, because of three important properties.

"First, continuous active student response is required, providing explicit practice and testing of each step of what is to be learned.

"Second, a basis is provided for informing the student with minimal delay whether each response he makes is correct, leading him directly or indirectly to correction of his errors.

"Third, the student proceeds on an individual basis at his own rate—faster students romping through an instructional sequence very rapidly, slower students being tutored as slowly as necessary, with indefinite patience to meet their special needs.

"The devices thus represent a way of providing a preprogrammed study-practice combination which simulates, in partially or fully automated fashion, the functions of a private tutor in recitation and practice, with immediate correction of errors and feedback to the student."[ii]

Programming differs in some ways. In Professor Skinner's programming, as one would expect, frequent regular reinforcement is crucial. The steps taken are so tiny, the answers so

(i) In Lumsdaine and Glaser, *Teaching Machines and Programmed Learning, A Source Book*, Washington, 1960, p. 23.

(ii) Lumsdaine and Glaser, *Teaching Machines and Programmed Learning*, p. 5.

obvious that 95% of them should be right the first time of trying. This is the reward (reinforcement) which theoretically gives the student the motive to proceed. Other psychologists give larger chunks at a time and spend more care on the procedures for helping those who have given the wrong response.

At the University of Sheffield, England,[i] the student moves along the main route and can press a button for extra information when he gets stuck. Professor Kay[ii] stresses that programme construction demands "great labour and skill" and co-operation between teaching and subject expert.[iii] The evaluation of any experiment should be through students reactions.[iv]

But there are grave, fundamental and decisive weaknesses in teaching methods based on mechanistic theory and tried mainly in the behaviour of uncomfortable rats in mazes, or harnessed famished pigeons. The criticisms again first, as they come from the authoritative source:

"The traditional reinforcers in psychological experimentation have been food, water, and electric shock. There is good reason for their use: all animals will avoid electric shock, hungry or thirsty animals will work for food or water, and it is relatively simple to control the degree of motivation by varying hours of deprivation or intensity of shock. Since it is unethical to shock, starve, or dehydrate children (BERG, 1954), other reinforcers have to be used with teaching devices. Skinner has suggested that explanatory and manipulative activities are reinforcing enough to keep a student at work with a device (SKINNER, 1954). Recent experimental studies suggest that this is so (WOODWORTH and SCHLOSBERG, 685, 1954), but it has also been found that an

(i) £13,000 has been granted by the Government to Sheffield University Department of Education for research into the use of teaching machines.
(ii) KAY H., Machines for Teaching, lecture at B.A.S.A. Conference, reported in B.A.S.A. Report, London 1963.
(iii) Another example of tutorial and consultant functions distinguished.
(iv) It has been found that to formulate a "normal lecture" into a "programme" gets as a useful check technique to show whether steps, as explained usually, have the precise logical sequence right in some subjects.

CHAPTER ONE   GERMANIUM

Semiconductors

1   Materials which have a .... (low/high?) resistance to electrical
    current flow are called 'conductors'. Materials which have a ....   low
    resistance are called 'insulators'.   high
    (Remember low resistance = high conductivity.)

2   Copper permits a large current flow so it is classified as a ....   conductor

3   Glass and rubber have a high resistance so they are classified as ....   insulators

4   Materials which are neither good conductors nor good insulators are
    called 'semiconductors'. The element germanium, like silicon, is in its pure
    state neither a good conductor nor a good insulator. Germanium is there-
    fore a ....   semiconductor

5   One of the most useful semiconductor devices is the transistor. The ele-
    ment g........................... is extremely important in the manufacture of transistors
    and other semiconductor devices.   germanium

6   Now it is a characteristic of pure germanium and all semiconductors that
    their resistance can be lowered quite considerably by heating the material.
    If the temperature is increased the resistance will be ....   lowered/decreased

7   The higher the temperature of germanium the .... will be its
    resistance.   lower

8   When germanium is used for making transistors special types of impurities
    are added. This also can cause its resistance to decrease. Transistor ger-
    manium has a .... resistance than the pure material.   lower

9   So the two important variables affecting the resistance (conductivity) of
    germanium are *(a)* t...........................,   temperature
                  (b) i...........................,   impurity

Sources and Refining of Germanium

10 In Great Britain germanium can be obtained in the oxide form from flue
    ash resulting from burning Northumberland coal. Oxide extracted german-
    ium contains many impurities and further refining is necessary to obtain
    the necessary degree of ....   purity
    Look at Diagram 1.

11 Diagram 1 shows you a method of zone .... of ....,   refining
    germanium

FIG. 7.   First page of nineteen (actual size $11\frac{3}{4} \times 8\frac{1}{4}$ in., A4 size) of
a programmed book on Semiconductor Devices, programmed for
Mullard Educational Services, London, by Educational Systems
Limited, London 1964. This is programmed learning: page after
page, "frame after frame", amassing knowledge in tiny, perfectly
controlled steps. Many grown-up people find it terribly off-putting.
The backers will say that it is because they have not been conditioned
to this type of learning. My reply is that this is exactly where the
great danger lies: that we condition children to learn in this way,
which then excludes or makes less effective other far more vital ways.

organism's 'curiosity' becomes satiated by prolonged exposure to novel situations (WOODWORTH and SCHLOSBERG, 671, 1954). Under such circumstances, manipulation and exploration no longer provide adequate reinforcement. To make exploratory activities reinforcing again the organism has to be removed for a period of time from the formerly novel situation. This restores the effectiveness of reinforcement.[i]

"Any teaching device used almost continuously in the class-room would face the same problem of satiation. Unfortunately, none of the authors reviewed deal with this problem. One method of avoiding satiation would be to mete out reinforcement in small doses. Another method would be to have alternative reinforcers available.

"Although no author treats in detail the problem of what alternative reinforcers might be used, Skinner suggests several: social approval, desired activities, and as a last resort, aversive stimulation (SKINNER, 1954). By including a candy delivery attachment on his device, Pressey (1926) indicates belief that the presenting of sweets can be reinforcing. All the above events, and many more, can be made contingent upon a student's perfor-mance with the teaching device. Whether these events will serve as satisfactory reinforcers will not be known until they are tried (BIJOU, 1955)."[ii]

It emerges clearly that the teaching machine enthusiasts merely wish to do better the same things that are done today—the teaching of subjects and lessons according to rigid syllabus and curriculum.

"Stimulated by the apparent potential for educational practice that 'programmed learning' and 'automated teaching' methods offer, a number of smaller colleges are in the midst of experiment-ing with radical curriculum changes—not so much as to subject-matter content, but with respect to the teaching of it."[iii]

The programmed learning can, of course, be written down in

(i) Incredible how a piece of really common observation can sound pompous once the result of a great big piece of "scientific research".
(ii) LUMSDAINE and GLASER, *Teaching Machines and Programmed Learning*, p. 124.   (iii) Ibid., p. 29.

a book, page by page. For 3*s*. 6*d*. you cany buy from Mullard Educational Service a "programmed book on semiconductor devices," and note exactly what is involved.[i] And the only reason for needing a machine rather than a book . . .?

"Glaser, Homme and Evans (1959) employ response-and-correction sequences provided by a special, non-conventional form of 'programmed' question-and-answer book, in which the answer to each question is always given on the following page. These devices are especially attractive in terms of cost, but they lack some of the features of stimulus control, and perhaps some of the fun of learning and being quizzed by a semi-automatic 'gadget' or device—which is part of the appeal that slightly more complex devices seem to have for students. Also, they do not have the self-scoring features that are capable of relieving the teacher of the drudgery of quiz-scoring; and since the answer appears on the succeeding page in each case, they are not cheat-proof even as practice devices."[ii]

No other advantages! And on this rather weak reasoning of why we should have enormously expensive machines rather than cheap, handy books (even if we believe in programmed learning) the process goes on. (How can they pretend that the machine rather than the book is a reasonable alternative for education in the underdeveloped countries?)

It is typical of much educational thought that not the motive for cheating but the cheating is to be tackled—one might add, by spending in total in the world, hundreds of millions of pounds on teaching machines instead of a minute percentage on programmed books! In a country like America the vested interest of those who make such machines is bound to be an extremely influential factor.

"Technology never sits still. The extrapolations given in the last section are immediate. What of those that can be made for a time slightly farther into the future? I see several developments. First it is reasonable to expect that teaching machine development

(i) Address: Mullard House, Torrington Place, London W.C.1.
(ii) LUMSDAINE and GLASER, *Teaching Machines and Programmed Learning*, p. 12.

will move from verbal-Socratic-Skinner type programming to audio-visual-branching type programming. That is, the machines will present, based upon student pretests, conceptual content using films, slides, filmstrips, tapes and/or video tape as the medium (cf. RAMO, 1957). The presentation sequences will be longer and the student will be given an opportunity to select additional sequences for further explanation if the machine, through testing, informs him that he needs it. Records, of course, will be maintained instantaneously by miniaturized computers."[i]

Let us repeat: ". . . the machine, through testing, informs him . . .". The teaching of answers perfected, and perfect records. Educreation teaches how to ask questions and none of the above relates in any way to the real world. Just how traditional the "future" is emerges from the last sentence of the quotation; records, i.e. marks may cost more to get than the teaching machine proper!

In contrast to the common tendency to enrich the academic by bringing in the real world, automated learning seems, significantly, to ignore the possibilities altogether.

"Successful transfer of training from the teaching device to 'real' problems is the ultimate criterion of a teaching device's effectiveness. Yet Pressey [the inventor of them] is the only author to even mention transfer as an area for research."[ii]

Anti-creative education, whatever its avowed intentions may be, emerges from the following description:

"In a 1957 article Simon Ramo, a distinguished electronics engineer and designer of missiles, speculates about the schools of the future. His concern is that, given the rate of present technological and scientific advances, education will not be able to keep up with the pace of the new technical society; and he feels that it is the obligation of individuals who are engaged in engineering to apply themselves to help the process of education. He pictures a high school of the future in which the student upon

(i) LUMSDAINE and GLASER, *Teaching Machines and Programmed Learning*, p. 390.
(ii) Ibid., p. 125.

completion of registration, receives a specially stamped small plate (like a charge-plate) that identifies him and his course of study. Introduction of this plate into a machine makes available the entire record and progress of the student; it also presents to the student his program for the coming term.[i]

"A typical school day consists of a number of sessions, some of which are spent in rooms with other students and a teacher and some of which are spent with a machine. Sometimes a human operator is present with the machine and sometimes not. After a short period with a human teacher and after a motion-picture lecture, the student goes to the machine room. The student places his identification plate in a slot, his attendance is recorded, and the machine is connected with the master records machine. The machine then proceeds to tutor the student. Some machines present questions of the multiple-choice type. The progress of the student is then recorded by a master scheduling device. This sets the student up for other machines which are adjusted to his special needs and teaches him in Socratic-like question-and-answer fashion. Information from weeks of machine operation then form a record which the teacher uses to determine his further course of study. 'Ultimately,' writes Ramo, 'with the proper co-operation between experts in education, expert teachers, experts (in specific subject matters), and experts in engineering these automatic systems, we can evolve that high level of match between the human teacher and the machine that we seek in that improved high school'."[ii]

The rarefied, seductively lush treatment promised for teachers must be set side by side with the less charming idea that they will be very much in the service of the programmed machines (and the manufacturers), to feed them adequately and to treat their pupils with respect.

"The high school becomes partially transformed into a center run by administrators and clerks, with a minimum of the routine assigned to the teaching staff. The teaching staff is elevated to a role that uses the highest intelligence and skills. A smaller number of teachers make possible the education of a larger number of pupils. The creation of education material moves partially out into industry, which goes into the education business in partnership with the educators."[i]

". . . when this close partnership comes about it would be desirable if the science of psychology could offer technical assistance. Indeed, selling instructional aids and materials to our school systems is already a major business enterprise. The industries concerned should seriously consider the increased sponsorship of research in learning and teaching."[ii]

Big business rears its ugly head. Are we to have inferior teaching, like dangerous cars, to satisfy "the market"—or, rather, create it? The potential danger of teaching-machine selling combined with sponsored research at U.S. universities[iii] is truly frightening—and what the U.S. does today the rest tends to do tomorrow.

There is no flavour of humility about the teaching machine. And while the children are not taught, at the same time, to look critically at each programme and what it teaches, as they might at a textbook or a film, we are perilously near to very dangerous, powerful things. Even when critical views are encouraged the fact that the programme, unlike the book, can never be seen as a whole makes critical appraisal much more complex and virtually impossible.

In the final resort, even within a democratic framework the danger of the teaching machine or the programmed book, if used as a constant aid, and not the occasional one, is that it will set up a habit of learning which is anti-creative. For though the behaviourists may argue that if they reinforce "creative behaviour" they will stimulate it, and get creative response, this is just not true. Monkeys, painting with verve and enjoyment, will do less once rewarded or reinforced (they then concentrate on the new

(i) LUMSDAINE and GLASER, *Teaching Machines and Programmed Learning*,
    27 and 28.   (ii) Ibid.
(iii) For a description see GOODMAN P., *Community of Scholars*.

pleasure of eating). The creative is the result not of reward but of far more complex and richer relationships.

Immediately the behaviourists leap into the breach:

". . . the work in England of Ashby, Pask and others with teaching machines based on the design concepts of biological computers will affect the technology of the present teaching machine . . . Pask has already produced a machine which, in training key punch operators, actually senses the characteristics of the student as he works and automatically adjusts the program of the machine to the individual needs of the student. This is a pure transaction, and Pask (1958a) maintains he can develop such a machine to teach decision making with present hardware and know-how."[i]

But now we have turned full circle: the machine is so complex so expensive (think of the maintenance!), and so difficult to feed with software that we come to the conclusion that human teachers might be trained far more quickly, more effectively and more cheaply.

The crisis the machines were meant to meet cannot be met by such expensive hardware. We are left with the technologists' bravado: "Look! It's almost like a man!" The tragedy of it all is just this—that what we have neglected is to make the most of man, and that we continue to neglect ourselves while toying with machines like us. This, above all, is the danger, the red herring quality of the teaching machine; it lures our efforts and our attention away from our prime and fundamental problem: people.[ii]

(i) LUMSDAINE and GLASER, *Teaching Machines and Programmed Learning*, p. 390.

(ii) PINION F. B., *Educational Values in an Age of Technology*, p. 38: "It is unfortunate that the term 'teaching machine' has been used so often in connexion with the 'programme' method of learning. The machine has been used a great deal in the U.S.A., but one must question how long it can be effective without a teacher. Intelligent students can make steady progress with this 'help yourself' technique but for many the process is likely to be still and tedious. Some types of machines may stimulate guesswork. In general the method does not seem likely to serve the imagination as will good teaching; it is most suited to deductive work,

The Behaviourists' education throws us right off the therapeutic approach.

III.5.2. Classification of All Aids

Having, I hope, diagnosed and disarmed the disproportionately loud voice and large claims of teaching machine addicts, we can proceed to deal with technological aids in a more balanced manner and from an educreational point of view.

My own classification of aids in education is designed to show their applicability and the basic similarity of all aids, from the primitive to the complex, from barely to highly technological.[i]

(a) *Aids to expression* (communication): symbolism, language, e.g. mathematics and braille, morse code, all writing and drawing implements, typewriters, drawing projections, printing machines, book-production, maps, charts, photography, filming, tape-recording, microphone and loudspeakers, postal services, telephone, radio, and television.

(b) *Aids to senses* (clarification, magnification, sensitivity): lenses, filters, microscope, telescope, response indicators of photocells and other electrical measurement, i.e. thermometer, thermocouple, wind tunnel, ripple tanks, heliodon, all means of measurement, microgauges, chemical determining, e.g. litmus.

(c) *Aids to memory* (recording, availability): many of the aids to expression, and micro-film and indexing.

(d) *Aids to skills* (calculating, assessing, interpolation, extrapolation, abstraction): calculating machines, computers, models of all kinds (concrete and abstract), counting devices, metronome,

(i) PORTER D., in LUMSDAINE and GLASER's book, tabulates teaching aids and devices according to "stimulus devices", "response devices" and "stimulus–response devices" in a behaviourist framework, which I find extremely limited and misleading in use.

---

e.g. in mathematics and science. An alternation of teaching with programs of carefully scheduled work is clearly desirable. The most valuable contribution which the 'machine' or 'programme' teaching can make to education will probably derive from the evidence it brings to light on inconsecutiveness and points of misunderstanding in conventional courses and text books".

abacus, scales, all manner of laboratory apparatus (language labs. as well as physical and chemical).

(e) *Aids to experience* (simulated and second hand): workshops, laboratories, films, television, books, tapes, wireless, experience simulators, i.e. mock-up models.

(f) *Aids to learning knowledge*: television, radio, books, tapes, teaching machines, programmed books, sleep-learning, wall charts, maps.

(g) *Aids to the design process* : all aids into which one channels information or ideas or spontaneous imaginative action, and which responds so that further action is elicited by the response of the aid; anything from pencil and paper to a Pask-type computer, which allows discourse and activates relationship (see also IV.8).

The comprehension and evolution of any aid will be well served by applying the formula attraction–fusion–liberation. Though it is not likely that any aid will always go with any one of the beats, in particular application, this allows one to see their basic function and assess its best use.

III.5.3. The Rational and Early Use of Aids

My approach to mechanical aids is twofold: (a) I am concerned with making the student aware of the existence of technological aids and give opportunity to learn the skill in their use to prepare for the real world. (b) I also see the direct use of technological aids as teaching aids. With regard to the first, education has hardly begun to think rationally about them.

Traditionally, the use of aids is left until very late in education. This seems plain nonsense born of Victorian prejudice and results in a very reluctant, clumsy approach later on.

I have seen my five-year-old tape her own voice and play it back; my three-year-old son has managed record after pop record on a standard automatic three-speed radiogram for about fifteen months now, without breaking it, and gaining immeasurable joy and independence.

I have seen all my children engrossed in the magic of hitting typewriter keys and getting letters and remembering which, from when about two years old. (For the stimulus-response school this is a walk-over!) I have seen five-year-olds manage to phone up their friends—and architectural students frightened, put off in some vague way, from making phone calls. The introduction of aids can and should come early. (Students persuaded to use the phone as a quick means of tapping sources soon reap decisive benefits.)

It is wrong to leave the use of slide-rule and simple calculating machine until so late, when it is the very thing children need to use, if they use anything at all. Basic, useful mathematics and the principles of handwriting and mental arithmetic, need not be dropped but can be taught on a much more rational footing— many examples of which are now being developed, and many of which use simple and effective aids.[i]

To take a specific example of a one-sided outlook: it is extra-ordinary that in an age where letter writing and essay writing (why this special art form always puzzles me) are sometimes mentioned as skills not properly learned, that the use of the telephone is ignored. In a field like architecture this is such a brake to learning, to gleaning information quickly, that not to perfect the proper use of the phone is very silly. I have found no school that thinks that a student ought to have a phone available to use as part of his course work. I know we are so afraid of allowing phones for students—or even staff!—because of possible use for private purposes.

There is no solution if staff cannot be trusted to spend money well, even if it involves their persons sometimes. But with the student telephone the cure is quite simple: if we allow a certain amount of money for each student for phone calls per term, then not only is the authority safeguarded against hour-long calls to uncle in Brazil (which can be detected anyway) but the manage-

(i) Note, for example, SKEMP R. R., *Understanding Mathematics*, London 1964, and the Leicestershire techniques explained in *The Observer*, June 7, 1964, by Caroline Nicholson.

ment side. To make each call efficiently and use it to the full, would really become part of the exercise. To get the most out of each conversation would become a worthwhile skill for the student to practise and assess as part of his work. Simpler still provide a bank of telephone stalls in the studio.

The artificial divisions in our thinking about aids is becoming obvious:

"Books, blackboards, pencils, and paper have been so long a part of teaching that they are accepted, perhaps, as essential to the teaching-learning process. Newer types of mechanical teaching devices, however, have not been accepted as so essential. They tend to be thought of as ancillary to the teaching situation.

". . . conventional classroom paraphernalia and the newer optical, electronic, and electro-mechanical types of device actually have the same basic function: they provide the manipulanda and the discriminanda upon which learning is based. Therefore, mechanical devices should not be placed in a special category but should be judged in the same manner as other teaching devices, in terms of their effectiveness."[i]

But even re-examination of the very simplest aids is very much overdue. Just as hypnotized by the black and chrome of the teaching machines, we forget that people might become far more efficient, so we forget also that textbooks and the use of writing and drawing are aids that can become infinitely more productive, if we develop them on an educreational basis.

The use of drawing, for example, is introduced as a means of presenting work to juries or others. Very advanced schools will even let their students experiment with throwing various media at some base and getting real thrills and releases from this exercise.

But to learn to regard the image produced on the paper as an entity that is talking back at its originator, that is the most important and basic aspect which is not taught. Knowing that our concepts are always only partial when in our "mind's eye", to transmit these "half-baked" ideas on to paper allows the

---

(i) LUMSDAINE and GLASER, *Teaching Machines and Programmed Learning.*

"baking" process to continue. It allows the eye to note new aspects, see new combinations and possibilities that the imagination did not conjure up by itself. This is, of course, what is done much of the time in designing, but to make the student and staff conscious of it opens up a new range of possibilities. And others are described in later contexts.

At the moment, the student looks upon drawing or writing as committing himself to paper, as a dangerous procedure of possibly committing himself to something that shows his weaknesses, which will be condemned, marked by teachers, often ridiculed with the sarcasm so easy and frequent a satisfaction for inferior teachers.

What is put on paper is too often wastefully and compulsively neat (conditioned by schooling) or without specific intellectual discipline and intent (not meant to be taken seriously or as a commitment). We have much to learn and to teach about the use of pencil and paper. Similarly, textbooks as aids await much imaginative development.

III.5.4. "Co-bo" and Other Fresh Ideas

The finalized textbook as we now know it will change into the open-ended phenomenon that allows and invites the students' participation:[i] keeping the book up to date, adding comments, criticisms and illustrations.

To face a textbook, which gives the space on each page, or every other page, for the student's contribution or comments, is a realistic idea that will catch on as educreational concepts are put to work. A small beginning has been made: the publishers of this book were persuaded to leave at the end of each section of my textbook *Planning for Man and Motor*, empty pages for the above purposes. It is hoped to do the same for this book.

(i) "To initiate the kind of change sought a reformation of text books is necessary; freedom and originality in teaching are hampered by the conservatism of text books".—(PINION F. B., *Educational Values in an Age of Technology*, p. 46.)

Such a book becomes an exciting work tool, has a much longer range of use, presents a challenge and a sense of belonging, and invites thought. It becomes a record of development—more so than any detached, loose-leaf file would. We have not yet begun to think creatively about the form of books, which transcend the programmed textbooks and fulfil many more functions. I suggest as a name for this phenomenon, "Cobo"—contribution book. The creative and critical attitude to such books will gradually develop from the artificial inhibiting respect we have for the "printed work".

The use of more sophisticated aids by the students should be encouraged, or at least allowed and helped. An architectural student showed a film to his final examiners. He was able to demonstrate, having cleverly filmed a combination of a quarter full-size scale mock-up model and diagrams, how a movable theatre was designed, transported and erected. This has been shown in many places as a major achievement and breakthrough in architectural education presentation and communication. But the external examiners merely regarded it as a gimmick.

The use of more sophisticated aids to learning, such as films and tapes, is in a chaotic position. At the moment, the makers of the technical paraphernalia have completely outstripped those who might design the proper use of it—the films, the programmes for the teaching machines; all these are in a crude stage and scarce.

The poor quality of much of the material makes people militate against it, or merely keeps them ignorant of the potential. But once one has seen the possibilities explored in just one brilliant instructional film; the imagination boggles at the unfulfilled opportunities. I am not suggesting that film should take the place of direct experience. But, just as one must take much of knowledge second hand, so experience can be presented in a second-hand manner on countless elusive topics.

It merits the best backing it can be given. In natural history, in history by old newsreels, in science, in medicine; countless other applications cry out for development. The best one has seen it breathtakingly exciting, instructive and an excellent extension of one's direct experience.

The availability of films to students, individuals or small working groups (as the records to my two-year-old son), when and where they are relevant, just like the books in the reference library, is the type of use which would be educreational—not the herding of classes, on beautiful days, into dark rooms to see what is relevant to some of them, perhaps.

We could extend the discussion and illustrate many more implications. But the principle has been demonstrated and I am really far from competent to describe the ranges of possibilities in any of the fields. I suffer acutely from having been brought up without aids. I did useless drawings during my first term at a school of architecture instead of learning to use a typewriter properly, for example. It took me quite a time to lose my loathing of phoning. The widespread malady; my lack of familiarity with knobs and what's behind them is very limiting. And I feel slightly guilty if I learn with great pleasure from a thoroughly fascinating film.

To summarize—some fundamental principles to help proper judgement:

(a) Where direct experience is possible, teaching by aid is second best.

(b) Where standard class and subject teaching occur, the replacement of the lecture or teacher by superior "consultant" programmes or films or tapes are possible and desirable.

(c) Teaching aids can usefully replace anything but the authoritarian-type personal contact in transition stage, so increasing the kind of personal contact in those ways which are most valuable in education.

(d) Teaching aids should be such that the students can themselves decide on their use, and that their use is voluntary. In other words, there is the profoundest difference between educational and educreational use.

III.6. THE PLACE

A discussion about the physical environment for education involves not only the buildings but also their use. The architecture should maximize the opportunities for relevant activities, but one and the same halls of residence for example is quite a different place if mixed instead of monastic.

We need to have a clear view of this complex matter to be able to assess the many new ideas and innovations in the context of the educreational pattern.

III.6.1. Residential Needs of Students

Educreation endorses and extends a student's right to privacy. He is often allowed his own room, but it can rarely become "his room": the matron-marshalled staff make so sure that this space is clean, tidy, dusted, polished, (even if he hates the stench of the polish), that he has no key to it, and so cannot be sure of privacy. Any matron will tell you that anything else is quite impracticable and, anyway, "it's for the good of the student's health and hygiene"; and "there must be order". This is the kind of argument which starts from the administrative angle and so determines education! Topsy-turvy, but standard.

The other way is to assess the needs of the student and administer accordingly. This means an entire change of the usual administrative attitude. But is exactly what is desirable, what we need and expect. It may be difficult, but that is no argument against its desirability.

What are the needs of the student?

(a) I say that a student ought at least to be able to choose whether he is looked after by bursars or matrons and their minions or not. Many students would prefer to put out their dirty linen themselves and to dust when they see fit, and perhaps choose the kind of polish they like. They could then have keys for their rooms if they desire. The limit of tolerance could come from nuisance to fellow students; when the smell of a room or a student became obnoxious the therapeutic attitude becomes active to alleviate the nuisance.

It is therapeutically of value for a student to live in a room that some adults may consider revolting, if he does so out of choice. He should experience the disadvantage of a pig-sty, find out how it comes about, learn the economy of order if he can get the chance.

Students develop. The fresher lives out his revolt against his middle-class routines by not having a bath; letting his hair grow; the dust settle; the paintpots mix with the teacups. He develops into the person who has no need of this kind of protest and can see the advantages of creating his own kind of order—neither middle class nor compulsive, constant revolt. With students surrounding him who have been allowed to go through this process, the transformation would be greatly helped.

(b) I say further that a student ought to be able to decorate and help furnish his own room, if he wishes. Today, architects plan rooms so that the decor is as permanent as possible, to minimize, very properly, the maintenance bills. Once the student can decorate his own room, and a very large proportion of people wish to decorate new quarters they occupy, whatever their age and nature, capital expenditure on building would drop and so would maintenance cost, even if the paint and materials are supplied and regarded as part of the student's education, design and handyman-wise.

An example is the student who moved in next door (where I had let a large Victorian house to a more or less co-operating group of young friends and students) and fulfilled his long-lived desire for a shiny black ceiling. Appalled at the result, he was glad he could move into another room (leaving the black ceiling) and has learnt a lesson and created an object lesson for many others.

Awareness of environment is important beyond the design professions. The richness of environment would be much increased if a room was really a student's own, and so, a valuable form of artistic expression.

(c) Now one step further. Imagine a structural concrete frame of a building with some floors, walls and services and the communal service accommodation (bathrooms, etc.) ready. Imagine a yard full of building materials and/or a store with all the pieces of a pre-fabricated system, a kit of parts, that each individual student, who wishes, can compose and build and erect, in any of many ways, in the space allotted to him on the structural frame. While the students are building they could sleep in temporary dormitories, very densely if necessary, in a pioneering spirit. Students would say before coming up whether or not they wanted their rooms ready built.[i]

Let us think on: if, instead of the normal forms of colleges, with staircase accesses or tall towers now becoming fashionable (but a very inferior way of living) we think of the deck principle, of streets in the air, as at Park Hill, Sheffield, a number of things fall into place: the transport of the building materials; the sheltered, informal meeting grounds so sadly missing outside the rooms of students are there (corridors are deadly); the decks also form the means of achieving high density, often desirable, without the inhumanity and loneliness that high blocks lead to, even if there is a common room every fourth floor. The decks could, of course, provide sheltered links with the teaching blocks at various levels.

The idea of a student creating his own environment more or less (groups could give individuality to certain areas of deck) is educationally desirable, entirely practicable (if the architect is properly briefed) and also represents a financial saving. What are we waiting for? Only the strength to shift inertia.

The vision of gay decks, with all the frivolity in keeping and unified by the strong structural frame and the kit of parts, is such a relief after a visit to any of the pompous, sophisticated or rusticated halls now proliferating in many cities with depressing sameness—lamely aping luxury hotels or Cambridge medieval.

(i) In Göteborg there is a structure as here described, but not student rooms, ordinary prefabricated timber dwellings are built on the floors.

Large Victorian houses bought and given over to groups of students and responsible relaxed staff are an excellent temporary solution—if treated in the spirit described. I have some experience with one of these. The small number of people demands a special co-operative skill and the help of a tutor to overcome the internal difficulties that are bound to arise sooner or later (society being sick).

III.6.2. Teaching and Learning Accommodation

In the teaching accommodation, division between departments need not be so rigid. The desired breakdown of department borders, the aim to allow students to partake of a much wider range and choice of subjects and tasks (according to their relevance to the student), this should reflect in the architecture.

In primary schools, a brand-new approach to building is leading to educreational environment; we can quote to show that in principle the same applies in any kind of education:

". . . the teaching rooms must be planned to accommodate a wide range of activities, often carried out simultaneously by small groups . . .".

". . . frequently the children will come together for a story or a song (lecture, etc.)."

". . . rearranging standard desks . . . improvised large display areas form part of the highly flexible environment . . ."[i]

It is obvious that laboratories, machine shops, atomic plant and the like must have very special accommodation. But even here the need to keep the facilities so very strictly apart is just not necessary. One can either begin, as shown before, and dictate with rigid administrative preferences, or one can adminster to fulfil as many of the educational needs as is possible, regarding administration as a service.

". . . there seemed to be a fruitful blurring of the traditional sub-divisions in schools. There would be a mixing of ages in

(i) KAY and MEDD, A New Approach to Primary School Design, *A.J.*, February 17, 1965.

'family' groups, and more coming and going between adjacent classes—in fact, a general 'open doors' policy, with children being free to move around the school."[i]

Most of the rooms now found at universities are one-use spaces, permanently sub-divided in such ways that never, never allow for improvisations beyond moving a chair or table. One hopes that the research undertaken for the enlightened vice-chancellor of Lancaster University[ii] on space requirements based on teaching techniques will give the architects, within their splendid master plan,[iii] the scope and chance to give us a new vision.

III.6.3. Social and Sexual Basic Needs

The hall of residence is taken too much for granted as a good, and the only good, solution for accommodation of students, as the image of the ancient colleges. To quote from Marris's research:

There is discussion whether the concept of mixing students from various departments in colleges or halls of residence really has the effect desired: to give them that broader outlook in association that they would otherwise lack.

"In the residential planning of universities, formal halls are, I think, likely to increase the social distance between staff and students, because they tend to emphasize the hierarchy of authority, rather than the community of interest. They can provide an opportunity to meet, but since it is seldom spontaneous, it leads most often only to a stiff exchange of forced conversation . . .".[iv]

". . . a wholly collegiate pattern has drawbacks, because it reinforces the sense of artificial isolation; and again robs the

---

(i) KAY and MEDD, A New Approach to Primary School Design, *A.J.* February 17, 1965.
(ii) C. F. CARTER.
(iii) BRIDGEWATER, SHEPHEARD and EPSTEIN.
(iv) MARRIS P., *The Experience of Further Education*, p. 181.

students of initiative in determining their pattern of association."[i]

"But ambiguity of the evidence I have discussed suggests that
halls of residence should be re-examined before we assume that
they can achieve in practice what their advocates intend. Does
living in the same building and eating at the same table in itself
promote any but the most trivial relationships? The image of a
determined warden, forearmed with stimulating talk, bearing
down on two mute students as they spoon their brown windsor
is doubtfully reassuring. Relationships develop most naturally
when people already share an interest in common: in an academic
community, will they not get to know each other most easily
through the subjects they study?"[ii]

"The relationship will develop most naturally from work, and
the social amenities of a department can therefore promote
the relationship more effectively than a hall. It matters less
where people meet to dine than where they drink coffee together.
If each department were equipped with a coffee lounge, and
informal study-rooms, where staff and students could continue a
topic raised in a lecture or seminar, and discover each other's
interests and experience, it would do more to break down reserve
than the best endeavours of a conscientious hall warden."[iii]

The dynamic participating approach to residential accommodation of educreation ensures that the generally desired social
advantages accrue from living together.

Beyond the mixing of age groups, the mixing of tutors and
students, there is the question of the mixing of the sexes. Anything but free mixing must be seen as a monstrous deformity of
social structure, even if inherited in our culture pattern.

We now have research to show what those who studied after
the war knew from direct experience:

"Frustration and emotional anxiety are more distracting than
studying in an overcrowded flat, even with baby crying and

(i) MARRIS P., *The Experience of Further Education*, p. 182.
(ii) Ibid., p. 89.
(iii) Ibid., p. 181.

nappies drying among the textbooks. And to be engaged is less distracting than an uncertain attachment.

"Emotional security seems, then, to release energy and provide a sense of purpose. Examination results bear this out. The married and engaged student did consistently better . . .".[i]

Dr. Nicholas Malleson wrote:

". . . American university teachers say that their married and engaged students are to be depended upon to be the most diligent, they are not distracted by the need to go out hunting for a partner."[ii]

Once we have established that heterosexual associations of the married and engaged kind are not a bad thing for study (it cannot but be regarded as a wonderful thing otherwise—or have you forgotten?) we come to the question of informal relationships.

Let us recapitulate: the therapeutic approach increases the capacity of individuals and groups. They are able to work, enjoy and co-operate with this influence beyond the levels normal in traditional compulsive–competitive–moralistic educational environment.

This affects matters profoundly, whether we discuss the "new approach to primary school design" or university living accommodation. The therapeutic approach creates the therapeutic milieu. This means that the various groups living and working together help each other in personality development.

If we take a fresh primary school class, it means that the working peace and co-operation establishes itself with the guidance of the teacher and follows after the anti-social outlets, particularly at first.

Children must try out whether this freedom is not just sham and will, necessarily, go "too far". If, instead of being punished their actions are explained to them with a reassurance that they are appreciated and needed in the group, then soon an atmosphere develops which passes on just this kind of enlightened

(i) MARRIS P., *The Experience of Higher Education*, p. 150.
(ii) Quoted in *The Experience of Higher Education*, p. 151,

behaviour. Six-year-olds can adopt the therapeutic approach just as they now adopt the moralistic one.

A similar thing happens among students. If, for example, sexual bravado is dispelled by a proper tutorial approach, as outlined under the chapter dealing with freshers—putting the accent on quality and the tenderness of feelings, rather than competitive sadism on the one hand and the fear of God on the other—then a mixed hall of residence becomes quite a different idea from the one burning in the minds of those who can see, in mixing virile man and woman, only indiscriminate temptation, in the image of their own experiences, their own imaginations, formed by the traditional educational zoos, where the separate caging of male and female, scientist and artist, fresher and senior, tutor and student, is the criterion of accommodation.

In considering proposals, it is always best to check back before loudly expressing one's disgust, moral indignation, or approval, whether one's judgement is based on the lack of capacity of one's own memories and imagination, or whether one has genuinely assessed the ideas in terms of the other factors that would decisively influence it.

It is a pity that our puritanism so compulsively and narrowly focuses on the fears of sex (our fears of pleasure, of course) that we cannot see the advantages of a more relaxed attitude.

It is in this field of the deepest pleasure that the emotional plague is most virulent, that the hidden hatred and fear of life in oneself is projected onto those capable of it.

As young people who wish to have intercourse have had ample privacy and facilities since the advent of the motor car, there is no logical point in the belief that accommodation in mixed halls or houses will have any effect at all. But the daily interplay with many of the opposite sex, getting to know them in many ways and many different kinds of relationships, has a far more fundamental function than furthering or stopping sexual intercourse. But even within that limited field it will allow an intelligent attitude to grow leisurely. The Anglo-Saxons are perhaps the only ones left to enforce separation of men and women during a period of their lives when there is tremendous therapeutic and co-operative potential.

In Swedish mixed students' hotels, the impersonal atmosphere is permissive and the regulations are merely functional. Once a girl has a child she must leave (not the university but the hotel) as the accommodation is deemed wrong. No moral overtones.

But a more positive attitude is possible: it is my experience that to have the young married couples with babies mixed with students in residential accommodation would be a positive help all round. There is a great deal of labour for cuddling the baby when the mother is tired, baby-sitting ceases to be a problem, the atmosphere is very stimulating for the young child. From the student's point of view a whole new world is opened up: childbirth, more likely than not natural childbirth among such a student population, has its mystery removed. Nappy changing becomes a matter of course, chore and skill, and not only a silly joke.

The very nature of the very young baby becomes something real. And this is badly needed to reform our callous inheritance *vis-à-vis* the very young. I feel that to have pregnant mothers, and babies, as part of the student environment would enrich it. The newly-weds' emotional problems would, in a therapeutically orientated establishment, get a far better kind of help than that now offered, often clumsily and moralistically, by marriage guidance councils, or worse, none in a lonely flat.

For students to see, under their very eyes, the dynamic task of working on the problems that arise when two intend to form a closely knitted team, could only do a great deal of good.

If the married couple have a lot to gain, and to contribute, as part of the student's environment, it is all the more so with the unmarried mother and her child. The child is in need of more affection than one person can give. The sense of belonging to a "college" could be great. We have begun to think here in terms of social units, which exist in some countries and in some social contexts, which share responsibilities which normally reside narrowly in the family. The mother also needs the feeling of belonging and the emotional support. What is more, the possibility of finding another mate is greater than if thrown out. It is really the only human thing, the only economic thing.

To make girls retire from a course or from a university because they are pregnant is, in the twentieth century, moralism gone mad. Not to sell contraceptives in students' unions (though cigarettes and alcohol) is hypocrisy, dangerous hypocrisy. It might be shattering, I think, to find out how many pregnancies are due to the non-availability of contraceptives at specific times and places.

However much of a moralist you are, if you are any sort of a realist as well, you must see that you cannot stem the occurrence of sexual intercourse. Your only chance is to hope that the "moral" student might abstain because he wants to; he does not envy those who have intercourse, because, to him, a certain quality he demands is lacking. Contrary to belief, all is not over once a person has had intercourse. Young people do not then throw themselves into an endless debauched sex-life. On the contrary, if the first intercourse is just experiment or bravado it is often a shock and a disappointment. And many young people then refrain from repeating the experience until the real deep feelings of a genuine love relationship overcome their previous experience. Each sexual relationship requires a dynamic therapeutic attitude to sustain its growth, in or out of marriage.

The university cannot continue in the "Noddy-land" that Cedric Price sees and *Punch* endorses. It will increasingly become part of the real world and benefit from this. To quote Marris:

"The setting of a modern university should, I think, be dense, urban, informal: a network of interlocking teaching rooms, coffee bars, laboratories, restaurants, libraries, study bedrooms, theatres, shops—a street market of ideas rather than a cloister for their sanctification—and integrated with the towns and cities which house them. We site universities in parks, as if ideas, like wild game, should only roam free in protective seclusion."[i]

---

[i] MARRIS P., *The Experience of Higher Education*, p. 182.

But even if in a park, and that can be pleasant, there is no need to "roam free".

If we have the two kinds of teaching personnel, tutorial and consultant, then the concept of the latter will create functional avenues galore to bring town to gown. This should do more to integrate universities with real life than the mere siting or the mere sending out into the world of students for a while. The latter does not resolve the dichotomy of university and outside world, it merely burdens the student with it; he cannot resolve it on his own. The 'consultant' staff idea would tackle the problem of the rigid division more fundamentally and many growing contacts would emerge from it.

Marris has this idea:

"If men and women could return from the professions, industry or the civil service to teach and study a year or two at universities, if university teachers taught for a while in schools, and schoolteachers in university, they would through their own experience achieve the detachment of academic life, without impairing its autonomy".[i]

III.7. ADMINISTRATION

III.7.1. The Retarding Effect of Mal-administration

Administration, the arrangements to allow a given activity to run smoothly, has in education (as well as in other realms) taken on a different, ominously powerful position. Instead of serving activities it now governs them. It is absurd that the nature of activities can often be best understood as a function of the smoothness of administration. We have administrative techniques which may be rational for a stable society (e.g. ancient Egypt). But they are particularly harmful at a time of rapid change. Education needs to evolve, and administration gets in the way.

It is truly a powerful bastion against progress, and wearing it down, overcoming the immense inertia bound up in its big, stiff body is no small task. But it must be done.

(i) MARRIS P., *The Experience of Higher Education,* p. 183.

If the case is clearly demonstrated each time, the kernel of the situation isolated, progress will be made. We must avoid making a scapegoat of this or that official and the odious tasks he may have to carry out, caught as a cog in the inexorable machinery. That administration, as we know it, "breeds" and attracts particularly objectionable people who are aggressively resistant to change is also true. So are the tendencies described by Parkinson.[i] The work has been done to show, albeit in a different context, that "The Management of Innovation"[ii] is a special democratic technique.

A few examples will give a clear indication of what is involved, how progress is stemmed by administration—theoretically there to foster it. If many of the shrewdest educationists have recognized and said that a first step is to adapt society to fit the child, rather than vice versa, then this applies with particular poignance to educational administration. It is the rare experience of the truly, actively, imaginatively helpful administration that opens one's eyes, and the revelation of what administration might do for education is wonderful.

The retarding effects of the administration in education can be divided in four broad categories:

(a) Threatening progressive staff.
(b) Stifling imaginative activities.
(c) Endorsing the accent on examinations.
(d) Authoritarian big-business methods of management.

(a) Threatening staff

My own personal experience of this kind of phenomenon is interesting. A lecture I gave to the British Architectural Students' Association at Nottingham was based largely on Paul Goodman's Community of Scholars. Thus I spoke of "the dead hand of administration", and was reported in the local press. The most delightful irony was that the "the dead hand" moved as might

(i) PARKINSON C. N., *Parkinson's Law*, London 1958.
(ii) BURNS and STALKER, *Management of Innovation*, London 1961.

have been predicted, and I was asked in a letter with a threatening tone, sent by the Director of Education, Mr. Jackson, "What do you mean by this?"

It was the same Director of Education when I was disallowed leave of absence, three days before leaving on a world lecture tour "with or without pay", for a fortnight before Easter vacation, for which I had, as a formality, asked the usual consent in good time, arranged and backed for months with the help of the Head of the School of Architecture and the Principal of the College of Art.

Now the crucial issue is that without any valid or given reason, and contrary to the advice and wish of all those concerned with the teaching and learning aspect, administration tried to stop a most valuable and valued educational venture which had taken great energy and initiative to prepare.

This, of course, is only one rather vivid example of the kind of thing that goes on all the time and of which I heard continuously during my twelve years of teaching. As this happened to me I can be sure of all the facts involved.

(b) Stifling of imaginative actions

Perhaps the experience of Mackenzie, who has for some time tried hard to reform his school in a very mild and effective way, is a good example. Having found that officials dare not take any risks in giving permission for ventures which are obviously a fine thing, even from the official point of view, he says:

". . . this example does indicate a lack of wisdom in society, an inability to make the machinery of administration do what administration wants it to do."[i]

". . . What our comfortable welfare society is up against is the need for an administrative system in which people will not be penalised for taking imaginative decisions which may involve risks."[ii]

My own experience of this kind of thing is quite amusing:

(i) MACKENZIE R. F., *A Question of Living*, p. 94.
(ii) Ibid., p. 95.

for administrative reasons, all spontaneity is precluded in student visits as a fortnight's notice must be given to the Director of Education. This is apparently so that any inspector looking around can be sure to find a "class". On this occasion, not only had my colleague and I arranged a joint "criticism" with the Leicester School of Architecture at short notice, but we wished to take a great many models and some sixteen students to Leicester also. Knowing the likelihood of a refusal of transport for the models, we took the risks (for the umpteenth time in years) that the administrators would not, and transported models and students in our own vans to Leicester, saving the Education Committee a dozen pounds or more.

The task was successfully completed and, on my advice, we both put in for the third-class rail return fare, which was the usual and only travel expense allowed.

However, since the last time I had done this a "senior administrative officer" (office right next to the Principal) had arrived. My colleague, then new on the staff, had a phone call from the said officer that his claiming of a third-class return fare on that day (7s. 6d. or so) was a very wicked thing to have done as the administrative officer had found out there was a cheap day-return fare on that day for about 3s.!

I had given the advice in good faith and was furious. I went straight to the Principal and said that on the one hand what I had done I had done in good faith and, on the other, that I did not wish to have my name on record for having made false claims, when in fact I had saved the Education Committee a lot of money and we had broken new ground, educationally speaking.

The Principal was sympathetic; he felt with us. "But you know," he said, "I am powerless. I will tell you that when I lost the receipt for the fees of the conference which I attended last summer I was refused the refund." (The Principal!) Nothing could be done, he said. In the face of administrators he was powerless.

In countless details administration hinders where it is meant to help. A particularly fine architectural model worth many hundred pounds was worthy of storing. I asked for a few large sheets of tissue paper, and they were refused!

The saddest aspect of this particular retarding influence by administration does not lie in the relatively few cases which occur but in the countless good ideas and desires for initiative which are never developed beyond a first thought because of the knowledge of the complications and senseless opposition by administration, which would result in wasted effort. And the administrative-minded senior lecturers or vice-principals or professors are worst of all in this.

Goodman warns us that:

". . . the peculiar disease of modern administration is that it replaces in a formal and functionless way, the community of scholars itself."[i]

I learned a rule from Dennis Chapman: that institutions are normally organized for the convenience of the staff who run them and not for those who use them. This is abundantly true in education.[ii]

Whether you are in England or America, it seems that in spite of all the talk of the importance of, for example, enthusiasm, whether hundreds of people, or sometimes just a few, carry on a vital stage of a discussion on a project or a problem, depends on the caretaker and whether he can be paid overtime or other arrangements made. There to serve, his inflexibility determines the end of important work, sometimes for hundreds, for the convenience of a tidy administration.

My favourite example is of the Festival Concert Hall in London. Having read in the paper how the roof would give romantic delight with views of the Thames aglow, after the concert, I hastened to enjoy. I was met by the barrier of the attendant's arms. "But I want to enjoy the view; it said so in the paper," I uttered. "Oh, none of that," he admonished. "I've got to catch my bus."

(i) GOODMAN P., *Community of Scholars*, New York 1962.
(ii) At this moment I find that the same applies to first-class liners.

The administrative set-up of universities, although their independence from politics is generally admired and is good, is incredibly clumsy. The immense difficulties involved in changing courses, almost like changing the laws of states, are just not right for the rapid rate of change of days of creative experiment. The definitions and restrictions are plainly laughable in our age, and have sad implications for the "community of scholars".

Departmental power politics, academic snobbism, the arbitrary way degrees, especially higher degrees, are given, regulations with regard to students' behaviour—all these things are tied up with an administrative outlook which rests on welters of traditions and demands recasting in terms of rational criteria. The first step is to recognize the need for this and to agree on the criteria. Those outlined in this book might do.

Most of the experiments carried out at the Nottingham School of Architecture in course changes, recorded in this book, could be carried out just because it was not part of the more restrictive framework of a university. Those of us who have long argued for the inclusion of schools of architecture in universities have usually forgotten this and other important negative aspects which exist but which could, and ought to be, changed in universities. The whole vast examination structure is the most influential and tragic example of this.

"The examination system in Britain is both a result of an ineffectual cultural education and the cause of the continuation of this education—a vicious circle."[i]

And useful only to administrative minds, one might add. The administrative element within actual examinations makes things worse:

". . . examination papers have placed too much emphasis on knowledge which is markable . . ."[ii]

The mark recording teaching machine in the administrator's ideal is caught within the administrative set-up. The individuals cannot act with initiative.

(i) MACKENZIE R. F., *A Question of Living*, p. 41.
(ii) PINION F. P., *Educational Values in an Age of Technology*, p. 75.

"Pupils go for forty minutes to one room for history (and there history begins and ends) and to another room for geography, and another for English, and another for mathematics. For the administrator, this is tidy and convenient; but administrators have to learn that education is not made for them but they for education. The shock of the remaking of education may cause them some severe headaches, but although the administrators (like most people whose job is to pigeon-hole and tape) dislike change since that means more work sorting out their files again, many of them are able people and, once shaken out of their rut, would co-operate vigorously."[i]

Mackenzie's optimism is commendable.

Paul Goodman has treated this subject thoroughly. He has shown the disastrous effect on the educational atmosphere of the American management system, with its presidents running universities "like banks", the hiring and firing by those who have as their goal a smoothly running business machine, interested chiefly in aggrandizement and smooth, smooth running. He gives many examples. Describing the more extreme influence of administration at American universities, he paints a relevant warning notice to those who so often and blindly follow U.S. footsteps. Goodman's outstanding observations are:

"My argument . . . is a simple one . . . the personal relations [in colleges and universities] have come less and less to consist in growing up, in the meeting of veterans and students, in teaching and learning, and more and more in every kind of communication, policing, regulation and motivation that is relevant to administration. The community of scholars is replaced by a community of administrators and scholars with administrative mentalities . . .".[ii]

"Modern administration isolates the individuals, the groups, and the studies and, by standardizing and co-ordinating them reconstructs a social machine.

(i) MACKENZIE R. F., *A Question of Living*, p. 140.
(ii) GOODMAN P., *The Community of Scholars*, p. 74.

"The machine has no educative use, but it occupies the time of the students . . . it pays the salaries of scholars, and it manufactures licences and marketable skills. Yet these are not its purposes. Like the American economy itself, the system of universities is really a machine for its own sake, to run and produce brand goods for selling and buying. Utility is incidental. More revolutionary products like free spirit, individual identity, vocation, community, the advancement of humanity are rather disapproved. But frictionless and rapid running is esteemed."[i]

And mechanization of administration highlights its nature, to quote Goodman again:

"The machines have strong personalities . . . At one college, the teachers were told to drop the plusses and minuses from their A's and B's because the machine would not score them. But at another college, the teachers were told to add plusses and minuses because their machine could score them, and presumably it was necessary to put capital investment to maximum use. What we need is a machine that declines to grade, and then we shall win the battle against grading."[ii]

Letters being sent to every member of staff because the new machine makes it cheaper to send everything to everybody, disregarding the appalling waste of time and energy, is another of Goodman's examples.

III.7.2. Work Democratic Management

The unfortunate parallel between industry and education, as vividly shown in some detail by Goodman, has a positive aspect in another comparison. It lies in the relevance of the management methods found to be effective and recommended by Burns and Stalker in their book *The Management of Innovation*, a book on their study of industrial concerns as communities of people at work. Their findings are important for systems that have to cope with innovation. Now education is certainly of this kind. And as

(i) GOODMAN P., *The Community of Scholars*, p. 63.
(ii) Ibid., p. 94.

K. G. Collier, Principal of Bede College, Durham, said in a letter to *The Guardian* on education (November 1964): ". . . we need to realize the importance of a flexible and non-hierarchical authority structure in facilitating adaptation."

It is as well to quote at some length from the Burns and Stalker book. It mirrors in the two kinds of administration it describes, vital differences similar to those between education and educreation.

"As an acceleration of the rate of change requires a change in the system of managements, so does it force the individual into a new relationship with his work."[i]

And if the requirement is not satisfied the innovations result in "a pathological adjustment of the individual—and, eventually, the concern—to the conditions of change. If one adopts the view that an increased rate of technical progress [in industry] is healthy, or necessary, or desirable, then resistance is indeed pathological."

How this pathological behaviour invokes many kinds of rationalization is described. Burns and Stalker make it clear that a "resistance to change is a Defence for the Self". In our interpretation it is a matter of defence against too much life and growth in organisms fearful of both, and of the anxiety arising from their threat. The different involvement in the two approaches to management is described:

"The shift from mechanistic to organic procedures, therefore, makes considerable demands on individual members of an organization. In general terms, they are required to surrender the safe determinacy of a contractual relationship with the firm for one in which their obligations are far less limited, to replace a view of the firm as an impersonal, immutable boss by one which regards it as something kept in being by the sustained, creative activity of themselves and other members, to cease being 'nine-to-fivers' and turn 'professionals' . . .[ii]

(i) BURNS and STALKER, *The Management of Innovation*, p. 236.
(ii) Ibid., p. 234.

G

". . . the individual . . . is more implicated as a person, more committed, more involved . . . .

"The growth of importance of the occupational self implies a closer identification of the whole person with work, the centre of gravity shifts significantly away from the family and the outside world towards his working life. The notion of subordination itself becomes less tolerable and is often rejected, or set aside by collusion between the members of the organization. Yet, at the same time, his closer incorporation in the system involves a loss of personal autonomy. Not only is the life he leads and its emotional and intellectual content more contingent on his participation in the working organization; he is drawn more frequently and more closely into personal relationships with the other members of the organization. He is no longer left to get on with the job himself."[i]

"If conditions are unstable, a mechanistic system becomes extravagant in numbers of persons employed [due to growth of intermediaries and interpreters] each with his limited commitment to the working organization.

"Visible power, seniority, and the pressure towards limiting commitments and mechanizing the working organization all focus on the managing director. In the last resort, in the modern industrial concern, it is for him to define the situation—the organizational structure and degree of commitment—of all others."[ii]

And so often in the modern educational concern also. Read "educational" for "industrial" in the next quotation:

"There is much evidence to suggest that the optimal use of human resources in industrial organizations requires a different set of conditions, assumptions, and skills from those traditionally present in industry. Over the past twenty-five years, some new orientations have emerged from organizational experiments, observations and inventions. The new orientations depart radically from doctrines associated with 'Scientific Management' and traditional bureaucratic patterns.

(i) BURNS and STALKER, *The Management of Innovation*, p. 234.
(ii) Ibid., 210.

The central emphasis in this development are as follows:

1. Wide participation in decision making, rather than centralized decision making.

2. The face-to-face group, rather than the individual, as the basic unit of organization.

3. Mutual confidence, rather than authority, as the integrative force in organization.

4. The supervisor as the agent for maintaining intragroup and intergroup communication, rather than as the agent of higher authority.

5. Growth of members of the organization to greater responsibility, rather than external control of the member's performance or their tasks."[i]

At the roots of the trouble lies the permanence of the administrator. In national government, in the government of professional institutes and in education, the permanence and power of the administrators give them a position far more influential than democracy warrants, and which it keeps from the technical officers and the democratically selected officers and committees (the teachers are one of these) who actually do, or should do, the productive work.[ii]

Among those who make the decisions at high levels of influence and government, those that are called in to prepare the white papers, there needs to be a realization that a whole way of life, deeply entrenched in their training, must be modified before

(i) BURNS and STALKER, *The Management of Innovation*, p. 125. See also SHEPARD H. A., Superiors and Subordinates in Research, Paper 12 of the Symposium on the Direction of Research Establishments, H.M.S.O. Department of Scientific and Industrial Research, 1956.

(ii) I liked the following example: the Under-Secretary of the Board of Architectural Education had too much work and wanted to change monthly meetings of the board to bi-monthly. The Board, after discussion, voted for monthly meetings: there was too much to do, yes, but the Under-Secretary's work might be spread on to members of the board. So, from then on, a card from the Under-Secretary cancelled every other meeting! (No doubt with the understandable agreement of the chairman.)

a democracy can take its next effective step, relevant now that the masses are really able to read, write, watch television and participate in the privileges of education. Fear of authority is fading, as is fear of freedom. The initiative, the momentum society must have to wrench itself from the path to destruction, is feasible now.

"Work democracy,"[i] the spontaneous change of leadership according to ability, described in great detail by Wilhelm Reich as early as 1939, is discovered by the right answer for administrating "unstable groups", developing groups, by Burns and Stalker a quarter of a century later:

"One important corollary to be attached to this account is that while organic systems are not hierarchic in the same sense as are mechanistic, they remain stratified. Positions are differentiated according to seniority—i.e., greater expertise. The lead in joint decisions is frequently taken by seniors, but it is an essential presumption of the organic system that the lead i.e. 'authority,' is taken by whoever shows himself most informed and capable, i.e., the 'best authority.' The location of authority is settled by consensus . . . ."[ii]

This has crucial application to education. It is a basis for educreation, an administrative system that allows for imagination and initiative and is designed to grow and change, through needs.

III.8. IMPLEMENTATION

III.8.1. Primary and Secondary Truths

In this, as in any book of ideas and recommendations, the crux of the matter is implementation. One must safeguard against the classic, age-old objection that "it's all very fine, but, you know, impracticable, today certainly".

An understanding and analysis of this "yes but no" reaction

(i) REICH W., Die Natürliche Organisation der Arbeit, Arbeitsdemokratie, Oslo 1939. Also *Weitere Probleme der Arbeitsdemokratie*, Oslo 1941 (manuscript only).
(ii) BURNS and STALKER, *The Management of Innovation*, p. 122.

can usefully help towards effective action.[i] It is a good beginning for those who wish to overcome difficulties. It is also a guide to danger for those who might rush in, pushing freedom too hard,[ii] unaware of the terror it has for those who have lived their lives in chains, and how preposterous and pitiless their opposition is.

Central to educreation and this book is the therapeutic approach. As explained at some length, this implies a state of sickness which can be improved towards more healthy performance of the total individual as part of the larger groups and of the organism of society generally.

This entails the supposition that we know, adequately to distinguish what is healthy and what is not, in emotional as well as in physical and mental behaviour. And the neurotic state, as Chapter II.1 demonstrates, has been severally diagnosed as the general state of men and women in our societies.

So statements which describe the behaviour or predict the behaviour of people in our society, are statements true of sick people and sick groups.[iii]

This is the meaning of "secondary truths". "Primary truths", on the other hand, statements which describe or predict, healthy behaviour of human beings. (Untruths are plain lies, falsified facts. And there are also mistakes which can be untruths.)

For example, it is true of little boys that they are sadistic if brought up in the normal repressed society.

This is a secondary truth, because little boys brought up in a self-regulated way are not sadistic and are healthier, by biological, psychological, sociological standards. The truth, then, is that little boys are not sadistic. To be effective the truth ('that little boys are not sadistic') must include the countertruth(s), i.e.

(i) The analysis advanced was first made clear by Reich in *The Murder of Christ*. He used the names "truth", "countertruth" and "untruths" for lies. I regard it one of his many invaluable contributions to a science of life.

(ii) REICH W., *The Murder of Christ*, Maine, U.S.A. 1953, and *Listen Little Man*, New York 1949.

(iii) This includes most of sociology and social psychology and much of psychology of learning and development theory.

"unless they are forbidden to masturbate or prohibited other healthy energetic outlets, then they will become sadistic".

Experienced people often understand this intuitively. Jackson,[i] for example, suggests that streaming should not just be abolished, mechanically, as if this would automatically bring into being something better. He knows that the teaching techniques in unstreamed schools are different and that unless this is acted upon, and the capacity to this is likely to be largely lacking, merely to unstream schools is not necessarily good. But he does plead for encouragement and for information of the alternative of unstreamed schools to be made available, and experiment supported.

Young people often read of really, and obviously, good ideas. They puzzle and try to comprehend why these ideas are not accepted and acted upon. The response of their elders—that this or that political system is to blame, this or that person's ill-will, or, most depressing, that this is "just human nature"—produce a cynical attitude.

Age brings cynicism—another countertruth—describing the sick attitude that springs from inability to comprehend. But given comprehension, cynicism—does not take over, hope—a sign of health—does not disappear. So the truth is that man stays hopeful . . . unless his elders educate cynicism.

Let us take another example: I say students will work without the threat of examinations. Another person says students will not. Now unless I qualify that I mean within an educreational orientation, at least, which can differ widely from today's method and syllabus, my truth will prove not false but inapplicable. My opponent will be able to demonstrate by any class in any technical college, for example, that, if they are told that examinations will cease, and nothing else, this would hinder their progress. The students are likely to attend less lectures, do less homework and all the other currently used methods orientated towards examinations.

(i) JACKSON B., *Streaming, An Education System in Miniature.*

This problem arises not only in technical colleges. In its recent period of changes the Bartlett School of Architecture has set examinations in sociology specifically because, so the lecturer John Madge says, it is this that makes the students recognize "its importance".

This may be regarded as defeatist, and I regarded it that way in that situation; or it may be regarded as a shrewd consideration of a secondary truth, that these students can only be persuaded to attend by pressure and habitually regard those things not associated with examinations as less important and a waste of time.

Some examples of truths, secondary truths and untruths:

Truth	Secondary truth	Untruth
Babies cry to show discomfort.	(Given insensitive mothers), babies cry a lot.	Babies cry to exercise their lungs.
Children long to learn.	(Given arbitrary syllabus), you have to set exams to make sure children learn.	Children will learn only if you make them.
Students have the capacity to regulate the rate of their progress and the ability to study from books.	(Given set degree courses), lecture courses are valuable in keeping the students up to scratch.	Students won't ever learn unless you make them take notes and you ram it down their throats.
Teachers are fallible; to know their area of ignorance gives confidence to the student.	(Given an authoritarian set-up), teachers must show a façade of superior behaviour and knowledge.	Teachers know more than students.
Co-operation is the rational and effective behaviour of a group.	(In sadistic-masochistic society), competition is the way to spur people on.	Competition is the only way to get good work.
By removal of emotional blockages the intelligence and creative capacity of a student may rise dramatically.	(Given a "stream" system of marking), "we can tell when they start how they'll do."	Once a dullard always a dullard.

The reason why people do not act on good suggestions is that they have not got the capacity. It is a very pathetic phenomenon, like the drowning man too weak to lift his hand to reach the lifebelt.

This lack of capacity is a major aspect of the sickness of society and the difficulties of implementation of any good idea. Our hope lies in becoming aware of it through the creative element in life which throws up fresh convulsions of energy all the time. The "armoured character structure", as Reich, and others after him,[i] have explained, draws that energy into destructive channels, and fixes the incapacity to use the good ideas which might help one to emerge from obvious plights. Reich called this "The Trap:"[ii] an important secondary truth.

III.8.2. Implications and Dangers

The idealist, unaware and uncomprehending, seethes with enthusiasm for his genuinely, obviously good ideas. He bullies and badgers people, for their own good, to adopt his innovations. But they will not, they cannot, they dare not, and they have to destroy him or adequately protect themselves. (The central theme of *The Murder of Christ*.) The idealist is applying truths, indiscriminately, primary truths, where secondary truths apply.

Take the teacher like D. H. Lawrence who feels and knows that the right way to treat children in education is not to coerce them. Read, then, how this idealist fares when he tries to put his idea into operation . . . he cannot, is driven to near despair, and has to adopt society's conventional techniques in the end, though he still feels they are wrong. Why?

Lawrence adopted the techniques based on truths, primary truths, in a situation where secondary truths applied. Even if his guts told him this was not all, his brain found no way out.

And this is where Reich's concepts are vital: the therapeutic attitude is the introduction of primary truth with a full knowledge

(i) FROMM E., *The Fear of Freedom*, London 1954.
(ii) REICH W., *The Murder of Christ*, Maine, U.S. 1953.

of the resistance of those who behave according to secondary truths, and stems from the desire to help them escape from "the trap".

In other words, had Lawrence (and many teachers after him) realized the inevitable explosion he would get from taking the lid of authority off his pupils, had he realized that repression keeps the explosive forces continually replenished under, he would have been circumspect in the application of the principles which can be applied without any difficulty to reasonably healthy children where a modicum of freedom and self-regulation is generally encouraged by more than one person.

Introducing healthy living (it is a truism to state in our society) is therapy, and this involves art, science and skill; the primary skill of the tutor teacher, and the tutor teachers of the tutor teachers.

To maximize the capacity for health and freedom for any individual, any institute, any superior or participant, therapeutic opportunism is the right approach. And maximizing then means doing as much as you can, with whoever it is most effective, whenever possible, and in the best possible circumstances.

Moralistic blaming never helps. The positive alternative to the blaming attitude is to discern the pattern of an unhealthy situation and then alleviate it skilfully with the therapeutic approach; to increase the capacity of each person by building up confidence and security to enable recognition of, and possible giving way to, their weakness. This is the basic strategy of "living out", "living through" emerging healthier, with greater capacity for the next therapeutic crisis.

Groups have a special place in this, but fundamentally, if secure enough, awareness, with outside help, can lead to overcoming anxiety bit by bit to allow re-activation of dead areas and redirection of blocked energies from secondary, back into their primary paths.

Sometimes opposition to help is bitter; the person, beyond approach, turns viciously against specific people or manifestation of life. People so diseased have been diagnosed as suffering from the "emotional plague" by Reich. With such people strength is the only effective weapon. This is a countertruth, of course. This is a secondary weapon, to combat a secondary phenomenon, recognized as such and used knowingly and rarely only in irrevocable and very dangerous situations. To recognize the plague (and aspects of it are, of course, in all of us)[i] allows one to realize where the Christian ideal of turning the other cheek is a useful truth and where it merely feeds a diseased condition, as clinical diagnosis can clearly show, and has shown.

Take a group of students. Take an average school today where some of the staff are pro-life and pro-self-regulation and others are not. To explain to this group of students just this very problem and situation is a first invaluable step. Given the therapeutic attitude to diagnosis evolving social patterns, this can be done without blaming or condemning any colleague.

The student usually understands the situation and is attracted to the change offered to his personality and his attitude to learning. My experience tells me he even overcomes the considerable obstacle of the other teacher's neuroses and sometimes even emotional plague. There is the odd student who cannot take the extra life over and on top of the anxiety already normal to most students in the turmoil of universities. Such students may display emotional plague attacks which can seriously menace the livelihood of teachers, particularly in establishments where, for example, the head is anti-life. To guard against such emotional plague in the students is essential, but not obvious to the idealist who naïvely believes that students are bound to be on his "side".[ii]

Working with one's colleagues the same non-blame creative

(i) For really strong meat on this point read Reich's *Listen Little Man*, with brilliant cartoons by William Steig, of New Yorker fame. This concept explains how a nation which has its plague tendencies constantly activated arrives at nazisms and fascisms of every kind.

(ii) For a classic "pupil-betrayal" see WILLS P. W., *Homer Lane, a Biography*, London 1964.

and therapeutic attitude is more difficult but still fruitful.[i] One respects the position where a person is pressed to take or do more than he can stand in terms of new ideas or enthusiasm—or just life. To formulate and introduce, invite participation or leave well alone—accordingly, will avoid much unnecessary struggle, strife and useless unpleasantness.

But again, with the plagued reaction of colleagues, one must expect no mercy, and one will have to show the maximum of strength.

The response to the proposals made in this book can, to be rational, be one of two only. Either there is disagreement with the general theory and my criteria, in which case it behoves the objector to produce his evidence as fully as I have given mine. Or it is merely a matter of capacity, opportunism and judgement of skill how, where and when the proposals are carried into action. Such action is always a creative experiment; the experimenters are a crucial part of the experiment, and the exceptional person is a vital need. No partial comparison of results with other kinds of education have much relevance. If the experiment is ineffective it is because of too great adverse conditions, or lack of capacity of the participant.

The probability of each creative experiment going according to broad plan, according to the hypothesis, is too well established by previous experience to be questionable.

III.9. SUMMARY OF CHANGES TOWARDS EDUCREATION

From what is, by and large, a nineteenth-century educational system the following fundamental reorientations aim at the ends

(i) In industrial management the same problem of introducing "work democracy" while authoritarian traditions still reign: ". . . the two forms of system (the mechanistic and the organic) represent polarity, not a dichotomy; there are, as we have tried to show, intermediate stages between the extremities empirically known to us. Also, the relation of one form to the other is elastic, so that a concern oscillating between relative stability and relative change may also oscillate between the two forms. A concern may (and frequently does) operate with a management system which includes both types".—(BURNS and STALKER, *The Management of Innovation*, p. 122.)

described in the next few pages. They represent fifteen criteria by which to judge whether innovations represent progress.

They define and describe educreation as the specific orientation of education relevant and right for the twentieth century. They denote the practical application in principle, and suggest or imply the integrated elements within the pattern of self-regulation–co-operation–therapy.[i]

1. The key to order should be: self-regulation instead of traditional discipline imposed by "authority". This should liberate maximum energies for learning. Learning is then born of the wish to learn.

2. Co-operation should be the modus operandus replacing prize-and-failure orientated competition. This uses the teaching function and capacity of each student to the full, helping staff shortages decisively and raising the degree of involvement for students in education.

3. Interest born of pupil or teacher should regulate contents of education not the set syllabus. This should raise both quality and quantity of learning by aligning to individual talents and provides spontaneously for the "diversification" now asked for on all sides.

4. Functional continuous assessment of skills (of which memorizing is only a small special part) should replace sterile examinations. Live thought and action should replace dead knowledge. Time and energy now used in "swotting" and harnessed by fear can then be used to much better effect.

5. The relaxed organization of many activities in various spaces, for very varied lengths of time, with and without teachers, in groups or alone, should replace rigid hour-by-hour—time-table—classroom teaching. This then should allow for a more opportunist use of creative talent, personal rhythm and the periodic great momentums of enthusiasm.

(i) The 1965 International Students Conference Resolution in Stockholm included "self-regulation—co-operation consulting attitude" as one of its policies for architectural education. Educreation had made its impact.

6. A very full and significant use of aids—typewriters, slide rules, etc.—now forbidden and shunned in early years should facilitate learning, the solving of technical problems, communication and storing of knowledge. This will release energy from fruitless chores and generate and develop the right balanced attitude of mind in an age of technological aids, recognizing early that the machine is servant not master.

7. A broader concept—far more learning from direct experience, participation and observation of real-life situations—should emerge from our school-centred education. The strict division between school and holiday will then disappear. This will allow use of good weather for health-giving activities—and a combination of theory and practice in reality—and intellectual abstraction missing in modern upbringing.

8. The concept of teacher should clarify into two major functions: (a) That of the tutor involved with the methods of work; with the emotional development; and with the therapy and integration of the personality of the student. (b) That of the consultant teacher—the person expert in a field; or at teaching a subject; or creating interest in a subject.

This should decisively improve the vital emotional content of education on the one hand, and on the other, allow for the introduction of far more experts interested in their subjects, able to teach them, but averse to close personal contact.

9. Education should be orientated towards the full life of a person. Vocational training will then be no more important an aspect than "training" for leisure. In times of affluence a distinction between these becomes immensely difficult. In the long run this means a functional, useful guiding assessment of the whole person at the end of a "degree course"—not just the proficiency test in set bits of work.

10. The traditional concept of fitting out a person for a set station in life or to get to the top of his field, should change to making a person desirous of learning, of change and of emotional and intellectual development throughout a life span. A development outwards as well as onwards. This then might introduce a

new chapter in world history; innovating will then not be persecuted—and a rational attitude to old ideas and new ones might arise.

11. The integration of all fields of knowledge on a unitary basis should make it possible to learn with far less effort and more meaning over great ranges of subjects. This, together with the revolutions in teaching methods will then make it possible to aim at educating a "whole man" in the Renaissance sense. This ideal we have given up reluctantly only because specialization seemed to make it impossible. The rigid divisions into sciences and arts, and the rigid divisions yet again within these broad fields, will disappear.

12. There should emerge new, useful social groups from educational establishments, i.e. the young married couples with babies and young children will then remain within the fabric of the universities, and within universities will create a fuller context for the other students and establish a new valuable milieu for the raising of young children. The "tight family" in its house or flat has been shown as an inferior environment for upbringing. Students should increasingly create and govern their residential accommodation.

At all levels girls who are expectant or actual mothers will then not be regarded as outcasts. Childbearing and education will come to excellent terms as the age of education increases. The physiological activity comes earlier and with it, earlier reproduction and desire for responsibility. Accordingly, grants for education should become more realistic. Much of today's unnecessary expense will then go.

13. Administration should serve instead of dictate the content, pull and push of learning. This attitude will then be necessary to overcome the many very difficult barriers to the kind of innovations listed and detailed in this book which exist at present. The positive potential of administrators is immense. It should be applied.

14. Far from making educational experiments almost impossible there should be professional and state grants for experiments;

this is proposed in the same sense as urgent need is leading the Federal Government of the U.S.A. to give lavish grants for experiments in public transportation in the face of the problem of private car traffic. The parallel is close: Education faces similar crises of narrow channels ineffectually used.

15. The new approach should consciously educate towards psychosomatic health, co-operation, and the capacity which enjoys and ensures rapid rational change and growth. We should learn how to teach and teach how to learn.

Fig. 8. Catching Staff—an international school of Architecture Sport.—(Cartoon by Paul Ritter after Pete Manton.)

CHAPTER IV

The Techniques of Educreation in Architectural Education

IN THIS book the implementation of educreational theory is illustrated in the field of architectural education. Although it is preferable to have schools of environmental design, and indeed the proposals are equally applicable to such, I want to relate application to what is widely existent and familiar.

Architectural education has traditionally a number of characteristics that make educreational transformations particularly apt and comparatively obvious and easy.

With proposals for improvement it is useful to recognize one particular recurring fallacy. This is to innovate to remedy the specific weaknesses arising out of yesterday education. We can be sure that education as a whole is changing. And though there are likely to be new weaknesses, they will be different ones, not those the remedy for which we can now foresee.

I have heard this invalid argument of basing proposals on the deficiencies of what is not likely to stay with us, so often that I must warn against it. Very much of the report by Mrs. Layton on Practical Experience falls into this trap, most utterances on education in the Council Chamber of the R.I.B.A. in my two years on the council, and, I am afraid, on the Board of Architectural Education.

IV.1. THE ORGANIZATION OF A SCHOOL

At the moment schools of architecture have, by tradition, one professor in charge. Quite rapidly more professors, of building science and environmental studies are being appointed. Whereas the first professor, although it is not stated, is intended to be a professor of architectural education, the additional professors are appointed to "subjects" rather like at medical school or Continental schools. If we now remember that more and more of the first line of professors is made up of very eminent and extremely busy architects and that the function of the second line is obscure and likely to remain confused, the picture of the present chaotic situation emerges.

In architecture, perhaps more than in most situations, there is urgency for the clear division into and appointment of the permanent tutorial professors, on the one hand, and the consultant professors on the other, with various short-term and part-time appointments.

Once we accept that we live in an age of rapid flux, that the development of suitable educational channels out of the present tradition-bound systems will take time, talent and energy, we cannot escape the conclusion that the professor needs these qualities for the educational sphere. His constant inspiration to guide the school as a whole in the many new teaching techniques we must adopt, his help in organizing the growing numbers of consultant teachers into the pattern, and his personal contact with students and staff to achieve that degree of co-operation we must from now on expect—this is the least we can aim for.

The cynicism of the student bodies that read weekly in the papers of further non-educational duties piled on their overloaded and already largely absent professors, is not to be underrated. The fame of the name is in direct proportion to the frustration of not being able to consult it.

It is common for architects to speak of the teams it takes to design and build efficiently. The Guide to Group Practice and Consortia, and much else, has been written on the subject. The staff of a school must be looked upon in a similar way. A team with a goal in view, with strategy in their attack upon it and with co-operation and leadership clearly defined. Staff meetings will then become necessary, purposeful and personal discussions, of educational matters, from the educreational standpoint; an assessment of progress, critical analysis of hindrances in the students' progress, individually or in groups. If the professor is worth his salt he is the key man at such meetings, and they can hardly be less than weekly and take less than half a day. These are work. In a time of deliberate transition, crucially necessary work; a hundred times more so than hum-drum lecturing.

The mistake, common today, that the duty of the professor is fulfilled if he has changed the course structure, introduced a few more subjects early in the course, found the money (if not the inspiration) for research, is a disastrous one. For we should be concerned with evolving live new functions in the schools, not replacing one dead structure by another.

Where eminent men hold positions already and wish to keep their so-called full-time appointments, professors of architectural education could still be appointed. The famous man keeps the fame of being a consultant professor and gains the freedom he needs for his countless activities the world over. It is patently nonsense for a professor with such professional gifts to spend, for example, as the Robbins Report shows, ten hours a week on average on administrative matters. It is not fair on any of the parties that the confusion of ideas makes the proper attention to all the supposed duties quite impossible for any man, while being a famous practising architect is one of these.

IV.1.1. The School Unit of 150 Students

If institutions are to grow large, and the R.I.B.A. has recommended large schools of about 300, then the right way to run such schools is to divide them into units of about 150 each under its own tutorial professor. Observation and experience shows this to be an optimum number.

Their associations and co-operation would vary greatly, although they would, of course, share the facilities and accommodation that can only be provided for a group of three hundred.

It must be stressed that the head of each unit is to be primarily an educator or educreator, and that each unit should be known as a school. In this lie excellent possibilities for diversification, cross-fertilization and many other advantages in a period of rapid change. Administration is simple and experiment practicable.

The same principle of vertical division of the student body should be taken further. Each tutor will then have a group of something like fifteen–eighteen students taken from all years, undergraduate and post graduate. The extent to which such groups are influenced by their tutors will vary, but the personal development, the source of the therapeutic approach and the sense of belonging in a school, is likely to be vested in these groups.

As the matrix of all the school's work is co-operation, many functional sub-groups will be engaged from the very first week in projects, seminars, discussions and many other activities. Contact across tutorial groups and within the "years" will be established in this way.

IV.1.2. Communication in a Co-operative Context

To use to the full the possibilities of spontaneous and planned associations within a school run on co-operative lines, a new approach to communication is necessary. Ordinarily, the student knows what is going on because of a rigid time-table geared to some mythical average student's capacity of work. It includes compulsory lecture courses and handing out dates and handing in dates for projects. This is often rigidly adhered to if schools are run on the normal authoritarian principles now general in education, coupled with competition and fear of failure (both by staff and students!) as the driving force.

In the self-regulative–co-operative–therapeutic approach and atmosphere, the place of the time-tables is taken by very large work-progress charts. These put the individual student "on the

FIG. 9. A communication chart for a school of 150, with ten tutorial groups. Each student has a panel A4 size ($11\frac{3}{4} \times 8\frac{1}{2}$ in.) at his disposal. General school notices take up the highest level. Between each group the tutorial notices take up a vertical column. Postgraduate students communicate within their group space at the base. Such a chart would be about 26 ft long and 4 ft 9 in. deep (for 150 students). It is vital to stress that this is NOT a mark chart, NOT a competitive record, NOT enforced from above by staff, but a means of communication between students and between students and staff, replacing the souless time-table. The chart invites modification, individual interpretation, humour, imagination, creative use. It is flexible, it is a means not an end. Its *raison d'être* is to give greater opportunities for learning and to make co-operation practicable and efficient. It must never be allowed to appear as a piece of administration "required to be completed". It must remain a live, developing means for educreation.

Fig. 10. A possible form that each individual student's chart might take. The function of the first area is to inform all those involved of the current and immediately past activities of "Robert Nero". His design working allegiances are clearly seen. The chart as shown includes the work of a whole year. At any one time only half the working groups shown for the year would be active.

The function of the second area, the weekly diary sheet, is to communicate meetings, whereabouts and activities so that co-operation with others is a workable proposition. Giving a space for every hour of the week allows for realism: many work at night. The proportions of 24 hr spent in various ways is useful to note. As shown, for example, red might denote that a projected date was met. Green might indicate that the work took longer than predicted. Blue might indicate that someone was unreliable and affected the progress of the work.

It must be clearly understood that these records are to make the students, individually and collectively, and the staff aware. They are not to blame or penalize. It soon becomes clear that reliability is vital—a badly needed lesson for the building industry.

Perusal of the chart as a whole can show trends and tendencies which it would be useful to note. The use of colour and many other symbolic devices could be developed I think to allow the chart to fulfil more useful functions than here indicated. It is a collective awareness chart and intelligent study should give anyone interested a great deal of information about the way the school behaves, develops and grows.

Far from putting off, a form-ridden civilization, this creative form should attract, invite, and entice study and participation.*

From the school chart each student can plot his work associations. It is remarkable that in contrast to present schools, where a vague association with the rest of the year is virtually all, the proposals give the following basic work associations (during one year): (red)

(1) Leader in two projects with two helpers each time.
(2) Assistant to four projects working with two others each time.
(3) Studies and subject learning in seminars and with consultant teachers and groups of interested students.
(4) Functional association with those at the same level of progress, i.e. those in the same year in present organization.
(5) Functional relationship with those from all years within the tutorial group.

It is clear that if only a moderate proportion of the possibilities bear fruit the learning process is significantly enriched.

* The example shown assumes that students choose their own project. If the whole year does the same project the only difference is that the kind of help given will have to be stated only. The weekly sheets are mounted on pockets which hold the past sheets. Similarly the four monthly ones.

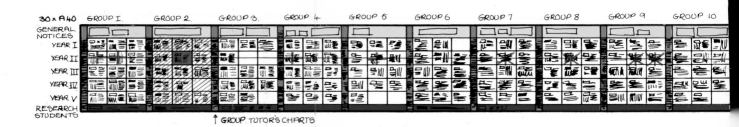

30 x A40   GROUP I   GROUP 2   GROUP 3   GROUP 4   GROUP 5   GROUP 6   GROUP 7   GROUP 8   GROUP 9   GROUP 10

GENERAL NOTICES
YEAR I
YEAR II
YEAR III
YEAR IV
YEAR V
RESEARCH STUDENTS

↑ GROUP TUTOR'S CHARTS

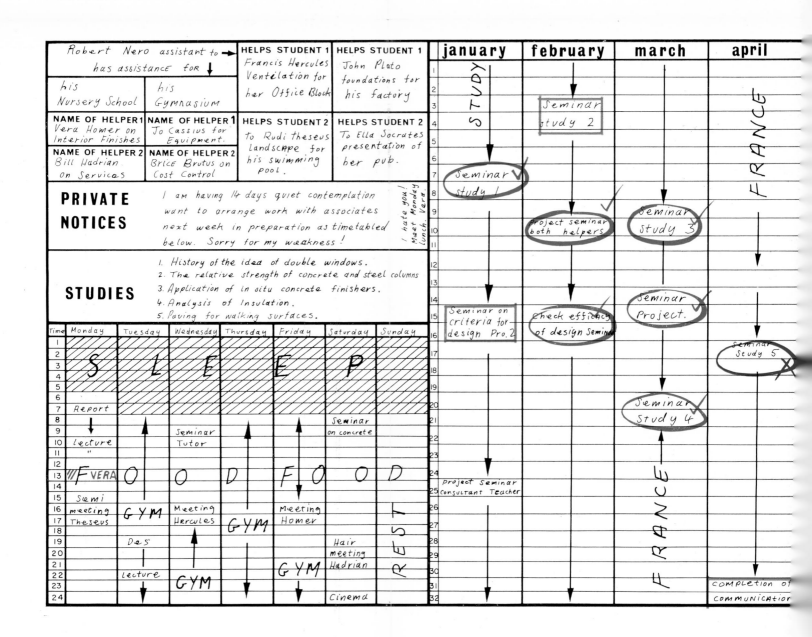

Robert Nero assistant to → has assistance for ↓		HELPS STUDENT 1 Francis Hercules Ventilation for her Office Block	HELPS STUDENT 1 John Plato foundations for his factory	january	february	march	april
his Nursery School	his Gymnasium			STUDY			FRANCE
NAME OF HELPER 1 Vera Homer on Interior Finishes	NAME OF HELPER 1 Jo Cassius for Equipment.	HELPS STUDENT 2 To Rudi theseus landscape for his swimming pool.	HELPS STUDENT 2 To Ella Socrates presentation of her pub.		Seminar study 2		
NAME OF HELPER 2 Bill Hadrian on Services	NAME OF HELPER 2 Brice Brutus on Cost Control			Seminar study 1		Seminar study 3	

PRIVATE NOTICES — I am having 14 days quiet contemplation want to arrange work with associates next week in preparation as timetabled below. Sorry for my weakness!

I hate you! Meet Monday lunch. Vera.

STUDIES
1. History of the idea of double windows.
2. The relative strength of concrete and steel columns.
3. Application of in situ concrete finishers.
4. Analysis of Insulation.
5. Paving for walking surfaces.

Time	Monday	Tuesday	Wednesday	Thursday	Friday	Saturday	Sunday				
1											
2	S	L	E	E	P			17	Seminar Study 5		
3								18			
4								19			
5											
6											
7	Report							20	Seminar Study 4		
8					Seminar on concrete			21			
9			Seminar					22			
10	Lecture		Tutor								
11	"							23			
12											
13	F VERA	O	O	D	F	O	O	D	24	Project Seminar Consultant Teacher	
14								25			
15	Semi										
16	meeting	GYM	Meeting		Meeting			26		FRANCE	
17	Theseus		Hercules	GYM	Homer			27			
18							R				
19		Des'				Hair	E	28			
20						meeting	S	29			
21				GYM		Hadrian	T	30			
22		Lecture	GYM					31			COMPLETION OF
23								32			COMMUNICATION
24					Cinema						

January: Seminar on criteria for design Pro. 2 — Project Seminar Consultant Teacher
February: Project seminar both helpers — Check efficiency of design Seminar
March: Seminar Project.

map", allow co-ordination of activities, knowledge of them, the participation in them, and the initiation of them for everyone in the school. The charts have a multiple function—as a record of work as practice in using charts, and as a means of communication. While the design is a matter for each school, the examples shown satisfy what I consider the basic needs.[i]

The picture conjured up by the long lines of charts might frighten many a freedom-loving heart. But the fear has substance only if an authoritarian atmosphere prevails, with the pressure of competition and the fear of failure.

The charts must not be taken as a regimentation of activities or an opportunity to enforce discipline. They are tools for learning, for co-operating,[ii] for comparison, for humour, for tragedy—a complex diary, inventory, and the total externalized statement of a school's life.

They allow the individual student to see himself, his name, as part of the working pattern of the school. They invite the student to note the promising time ahead of him. They allow anyone to see the life and soul of the place, what is going on in a school, which, for many reasons, is very useful.

The design of such charts is a new challenge, and the example given is just one idea. The scale need not frighten. We are not scared of dictionaries because they include all words. We don't read them but use them as works of reference. The charts would have a similar rôle. The design should spring from the needs. Architects have a habit of letting sophiscated formalism take the place of genuine functional thinking. This should be watched.

Once the charts are used as something which help the freedom to work out one's own pace, and schedules of work, they are seen

(i) Charting activities is developed at the A.A. School where lists of all the lecture activities are put up weekly. In Nottingham we had got as far as arriving at a chart showing the nature and duration of all programmes for all five years at the beginning of the session and a theory and Practice of Building Chart on which students committed themselves to a subject and submission to seminar date and the critic countersigned.

(ii) "Education in architecture should emphasise co-operation rather than competition".—*R.I.B.A. Office Survey*, p. 185, London 1962.)

in an educreative light, as an essential aid to co-operation, and become the expression of the *joie de vivre*, the hilarity and frivolity that are to be found wherever young live animals get together.

The chart in the example shows a school of 150. Vertically the grades or years are first year to post-grad. Horizontally the divisions are into the tutorial groups, the groups which share work accommodation(i) preferably part of a big high room. With each group under the name of the tutor, there is a four-monthly diary(ii) divided into days and hours showing activities and availability of the tutor. On this appointments for individuals or groups may be booked, but this would not normally be expected to take care of all the time, so that there was room for spontaneous actions. There is room for personal announcements to the group and the school by the tutor, the Head, etc. The Head's chart should allow students and staff to see his whereabouts in a functional manner.

At the end of each horizontal line announcements relevant to the year might appear. Below each students' chart are the diaries for appointments with regular consultant teacher. If the subject to be discussed is entered, others interested can then attend.

Each student's space shows his current main studio programme, his associates in this, a list of the people and programmes he is assistant to, and a monthly diary with schedules for his work and diary of meetings. This allows his associates to communicate, arrange meetings noting whether other participants are free. It allows an immediate view of the way a student is working, where he may need help and where he excels and is a good chap to learn from. Above all, it gives orientation to one and all in

---

(i) At one time in Nottingham we even tried to express this physically with superb sophistication: to make the rows in one direction express the group system and, in the other, the years! However, we gave this idea up very quickly; even in our high room it emphasized a regimentation that was the opposite of the basic intention.

(ii) I think it ought to include all days of the week (the full story of work done, staff and student-wise) and all 24 hours of the day. All helps to become aware of who works when.

a hundred matters they would otherwise never have the slightest inkling of and which may be of relevance and interest and lead to fruitful association. Such a chart as I have designed is, not surprisingly, about 4 ft. 10 in. x 33 ft. It should not be displayed in pieces but as a whole, otherwise much of the point is lost. Posters become part of it. (At a level too high to reach for easy writing.)

The chart shows each student's name as he enters the school. This is a fillip at the beginning of the course. Instead of his being an anonymous cog to be coerced to move according to a precise time-table, instead of his year seemingly identical to the others, the chart makes his identity vivid to him, and it is next to a blank space that spells the magic of a year's promise, waiting to be filled by his activities, his plans, his responsibility and initiative. He fills his individual time-table with lectures, visits and aims. He estimates progress, associates, on the chart, making both himself and the school aware of what is happening to him. Many detailed ideas can make the chart vivid from differing angles. Constant development of the idea is desirable.

Take a simple device to this end: say all entries of intentions are black; say that when they have been done according to plan, they are ringed red; if not, green; and if not according to plan, or partially, showing faulty timing, in yellow. This picture is meaningful to the student and to the tutor. Like the temperature chart and pulse rate to the doctor, it allows diagnosis of condition—not assessment of worth!

The chart shows that there are various interlocking groups in which the student functions.

IV.1.3. Working Groups and Associates

(*a*) *Within the group of fifteen or twenty, composed of students from all stages under one tutor:*

This association of the "green" with the mature is particularly useful in the speedy and efficient integration of new students, and in spreading techniques of drawing, model making, printing, production of reports. Not only the sophisticated few but the main stream of new students are standing on their feet in no time. There is immediate contact with experienced people for questions, without involving staff. Labour for tasks, on the other hand (no crazy type of wasteful cross-hatching in educreation!), is immediately available to any particular senior student when a job requires it.

Each "group" will have the specific identity of its tutor. Within the framework of educreation more and more of the work done will be within the framework of therapeutic and working groups rather than "years"; i.e. to anger a student by honest, not sarcastic, poking at his real weakness and anxieties and accept the outburst when it comes as a matter of course, to encourage students to realize that so-called personal problems are not at all personal really; they are shared by many, and talking about them or listening to others cannot but help.

Competition between groups should be regarded as a game, subservient to co-operation between the groups.

The techniques of deciding in which group you belong and for how long can decide the degree of success. Ideally, the student should be able to pick his tutor after, say, the first term—and during the first term his temporary stay in one group or his freedom to change from it should be made clear.

In traditional systems it is clear that the students will have to be divided in fairly equal numbers among the tutors, however popular or unpopular some may be. But the groups need not be rigid. There is no reason why tutors from other groups should not be consulted, of course. In fact, a school running well on these lines can do without its staff quite well for remarkably, even embarrassingly (sometimes for staff) long periods.[i]

To improve the rate of assimilation of new students, to reduce

(i) While, in Nottingham, staff were demoralized to almost non-activity by the extraordinary clumsy and tactless transfer and transformation of the school into the university, the school work continued remarkably smoothly.

the stress on years, to give variety in teaching and, most of all, to bring variety and co-operation where uniformity and competition now reign, the group system of subdivision of a school of creative design is very desirable and effective. The idea was tried for five years at the Nottingham School of Architecture under Donald Notley, and despite all the kinds of limitations of real situations, real people, and the shortage of equipment, the system worked very much better than the year subdivision. (It is desirable in all education.)

(b) Groups of people in the same grade

At the moment, this is, of course, the major "YEAR" grouping in most schools: in fact the only one, orientated very competitively indeed, even when teachers try to arrange group schemes or schemes where jobs are done jointly, in preparing for the design.

It will be with us as the norm for some time. Administratively, it is very convenient and it is efficient for an education which is based on rigid "years" advancing like regiments in step—or that is the aim. There seems little reason for this system to remain. The vertical group arrangement can run side by side. On the Continent, many universities have examinations at various times of the year and candidates sit for these when they feel they are ready. To do a course in the minimum allowed is regarded as unusual and there is latitude even without loss of grants for the slower person to make his way along the course.

The setting of programmes for years will still occur in the traditional situation we are discussing. So will the criticism and jury system. Tutors can still set programmes, taking it in turns, but there is no reason why students should not choose their own programmes. I tried this from the second year onwards and the results were excellent. The advantages are:

(i) Greater interest by students; learns to choose manageable work.

(ii) So, better work.

(iii)   More diverse material: interest in the year and school.
(iv)   Competition alleviated as aims vary.
(v)   Student responsible for brief.
(vi)   Allows diversification.
(vii)   Makes work at individual rate easier.
(viii)   The designs bring a wealth of interest in comparison with thirty or so students all producing variations on the same theme competitively.

The student should be allowed to proceed against tutor's advice with an "unsuitable" subject. The tutor may be wrong but, far more important, the student must be allowed to learn from mistakes.

(c) *The design groups*

Teachers in architecture have faced a dilemma for some time: once it had been recognized that study in depth must take the place of the shallow, showy design programmes, and increased time was required for each project. This meant a drastic reduction in the number of kinds of projects of which a student could have experience. Many regarded this as detrimental as great as the lack of depth that preceded it.

While free choice of subjects enriches the school and the students, and to some extent resolves the difficulty, educreation gives a radical solution to the dilemma.

This not only satisfies the need for depth and breadth of experience but countless other requirements also. As has been alluded before, each student, having chosen his project (or, indeed, even if a group has had it chosen for it, though this cannot continue much longer, surely) he enters it on the work progress chart. He then enters his name alongside two projects of other students which also interest him, and two other students enter their names alongside his. (This is done twice for each session.) The kind of assistance and/or consultation that arises will vary very greatly. It will be discussed, defined and affected by many factors.

This is breakthrough in technique—open to all schools under present conditions—the following advantages can accrue:

(i) Students gain insight into the design approach of two other persons into two other projects. So the individual gains breadth of experience; and with the help of his two assistants he can gain in depth in the study of his project, as they in theirs.

If a student does two projects a year, which should allow thoroughness and time for other work as well as his assistance to two other students, he will have had in, say, four-and-a-half sessions, direct working experience of twenty-five possible different subjects. Beyond the direct work contacts described there are all the indirect contacts with the projects of those who are the assistants or consultants.

(ii) Co-operation and many aspects of management are learned on the basis of experience as leader and as assistant and consultant.

(iii) Purposeful discussion of problems becomes a day-by-day diet and leads to expertise in communication, abilities to express, to understand, and to critical assessment.

(iv) The multiple contact throughout the year through this technique leads to real abilities to work as groups, not the present farcical "group schemes", foisted on to people quite untrained in that difficult task (immensely efficient when mastered) of working together.

(v) A student can effectively specialize in a field of interest in a very realistic way, as a consultant to those he helps. He can choose schemes that are relevant to his interests for his consultant tasks and so "diversify".[i]

(vi) The assessment of students can become so much more valid on the basis of his command of his team and on the basis of his ability to help. The display of ability, the signs of weakness,

(i) What is spontaneously provided is "the opportunity to study in depth a subject in which the student shows particular interest or ability, and for which the school has special resources".—(*Diversification*, a report to the Board of Architectural Education, December 1964, R.I.B.A. London.)

become obvious from every angle. It is highly likely that in such a cooperatively orientated milieu a student lacking in some skill will soon see and make up deficiencies. Assessing students on their methods of work is realistic. The student does not depend on marks at the end of a scheme. He can tell from his work relationships, discussions and progress whether he is doing well or not—and has a good chance of remedying his lacks as they occur.

(vii) Needless to say, the groups of architectural students would, whenever possible, seek to associate with "outside" disciplines, as indeed is already occurring in a number of schools. But the effective vehicle has been missing. The associations have nearly always been "merely interesting", not productive of better work or insights.

(viii) In the past, some of the best practices have resulted from students who have spontaneously learned to work together at school. This sort of thing should arise much more often when cooperation is the matrix of activities. As the age of consortia and similar associations has come upon us, as working with experts becomes more and more an obvious need which we are not able to meet, to learn to cooperate is vital. But it is important, and we should stress, that even if you believe in a traditional type of private practice and imagine you might be the principal, the training described would still be advantageous. This is a virtue; the nature of co-operation adapts itself to individual attitudes and needs. Some people are superb as leaders, others as consultants.

A reading of *The Guide to Group Practice and Consortia*[i] makes quite obvious some of the needs left unattended by traditional education which the educreational proposals would meet. To quote:

"The ability to *think* in terms of "we" before "I" [and I might add "feel"] needs to and can be cultivated. Individuals saying

(i) R.I.B.A., London 1965.

they would like to be effective group members must, as far as possible, discover their basic personal characteristics, remembering that in any field of effort, achievement depends first on deciding to make the attempt.

". . . the conditions of creative work develop natural forces tending to make designers self-centred. While many would agree that shared experienced is enriched, and that ideas grow in or after joint discussion, the very need to concentrate within oneself to find ideas may, if not understood, develop unconscious barriers to collaboration.

". . . at its best, group working is a rewarding experience, particularly in revealing human motives and methods, as well as in developing the self-understanding essential to understanding group working.

"Group fulfilment must be shared out between members in a manner leaving little scope for doubt about the justice of relative emphases. Undue demands by individuals on any of the components of group fulfilment will sooner or later affect unity. Personal contributions to group success are bound to vary according to individual talent, vitality and experience, and in sharing responsibilities, recognition and reward sympathetic formulae must be found.

"When differences in norms become apparent in the decision making phases of group working, the process of control must be brought into play by the leader or chairman. This will aim at getting members to co-operate when they are not very anxious to do so. Areas of agreement and disagreement should then be defined. Sources of disagreement on these areas should be made explicit. The norms related to the sources should be found and discussed. If there is still difficulty in reaching agreement, at least the group know the real reason for the disagreement."

Many of the aspects of management and human relations particularly are learnt with the help of the tutor. Difficulties in co-operation are expected, anticipated, looked for and treated. In fact, this group then becomes one of the possible therapeutic groups in the constellation of the school.

(*d*) *Seminars of students with common projects and problems outside the design group framework*

Beyond the lecture groups we have the seminar groups; this is the most generally useful assembly commonly used. This method of teaching assumes contribution from all participants. It may be on the basis of a statement or object specifically related to one or several of the group, or it may be on a subject. The essential point is to have seating arrangements and atmosphere utterly unlike the one normal in authoritarian student–teacher relationships. It is a chance for changing the "pecking order", as Dr. Abercrombie puts it.

Fresh groups learn quickly to use the seminar situation and manage even without staff help. But staff help is sought intelligently and can be excellent during seminar. Senior students, too, can be very helpful.

Direction and clarity of function and purpose of any seminar, beginning with a brief and finishing with some conclusions, is worth while. The participation of everyone is more likely if the groups are between six and nine, but seminar situations of a number of kinds can be useful with groups as large as fifteen.

I personally feel that to have a chairman, a person responsible for effectiveness of the contributions and the event, is most useful. Seminar learning and committee working have remarkable similarity. This is likely to give practice in the skills of obtaining group decisions, to outline areas of agreement and disagreement. It should also make the committees of the future more evenly efficient. So often appointing a committee is the death-blow to any idea. (Particularly if it's a sub-committee and you can make sure that those on it represent mutually exclusive views on a subject! Many a skilled administrator uses this to block progress and innovation. An action on the face of it designed to facilitate action, but cunningly contrived to make sure the opposite is the outcome.)

The following are other learning relationships which arise as and when required.

(*e*) *The very large group, lectures or demonstrations to the whole university or members from it*

Instead of the lecture or the debate (just an elaborate game) I would suggest the deliberate and scientifically based expressions of differing viewpoints at this level. This could be done during one session or two successive talks or lectures. The students might learn a great deal more than the mere facts and gain more than the inspiration of the talks themselves. To hear the famous disagree is stimulating to the intellect.

(*f*) *Members of the whole university with whom the student has common ties*

With good communications on who is speaking to whom about what, taken seriously, students, by attending cross-departmental lectures, should gain far more than they do now in areas they seem desirous of delving into.

(*g*) *Inspirational lectures to the school of architecture as a whole*

Such lectures should occur frequently from staff and students within the university as well as within the school. They should be triggered off by current developments as much as by presenting the formulated research questions and the hunches undergoing examination in the research. As students become more articulate, they are likely to wish to express strong opinions to their fellows.

(*h*) *Lectures or lecture courses as asked for by interested groups, by inside or consultant staff, to sections of the school of architecture*

(*i*) *Seminars with consultant staff and interested groups*

The manner in which consultant teachers would contribute would obviously largely depend on the teacher's abilities. However, a student body which has learnt to learn, learnt to

H

formulate questions, which is able to give the consultant teacher what amounts to a brief, can be very helpful in creating a fruitful relationship.

(*j*) *Tutorials, singly or with small group and tutor, with strong therapeutic element and great importance*

(*k*) *Trips and visits, summer camps, etc., by interested groups; all manner of ancillary and pressure groups within the school of architecture*

(*l*) *Live project groups within the school*

These will be discussed further on page 329.

(*m*) *Therapeutic groups pure and simple*

These would bring together students from all years under a tutor giving such therapy to those who want to participate, apart and beyond other therapeutically orientated work and actions.

In determining good sizes for activities, guiding principles could be taken from the pronouncements of two experienced "educreators", Paul Goodman and Dr. Abercrombie.

Dr. Abercrombie[i] found in her experiments that those who wished to talk liked smaller classes, those who liked to remain silent, larger groups. When in her experiment the advantages of listening were appreciated by those who concentrated on talking, their objections became less. Her book ought to be recommended reading for consultant teachers.

Goodman writes thus: "I choose the class size of twelve to fifteen as a mean in my own not untypical experience. It gives a sufficient weight of thoughts, objections and questions to oppose and activate the teacher. When the number falls below this, to seven or eight, I begin to feel that I am leading a group therapy;

(i) ABERCROMBIE J., *The Anatomy of Judgement*, p. 68.

I am overly conscious of the individual personalities coping with the subject, rather than teaching the objective subject. When the number rises to between twenty and thirty, I begin to feel I am lecturing the subject, with question-and-answer period, and, perhaps, leading 'discussion'. But of course the mean number varies with the subject, the character of the persons and how the subject is handled. E.g., in teaching a course in writing, I combine several approaches: structural analyses of classical texts, and these are largely lectures, with questions, that could be given to a group of thirty-five; psychological unblocking exercises, and exercises on points of style and technique, for both of which I like the class of twelve to fifteen; reading and criticism of the student's writing which I prefer in groups of five or six and *not* in a classroom. There are similar variations in anything else I would teach . . ."[i]

One of the remarkable anomalies at universities is the exclusion for the purposes of the university assessment, the achievements of the student in the many clubs and associations, for his fellows, at the union or in the department. This is plain crazy. The talents displayed are inevitably closely related to those required in the application in post-university life. Far from getting credit students are threatened and failed because "their course work has suffered". What they have gained instead is not taken into account.

This sort of thing is extreme in schools of architecture where I have known remarkable feats of initiative and skill and directly of an architectural character, regarded as separately from the course. For this, the students got no marks, no credit. Instead, it is once again regarded as "allowing their course work to suffer". B.A.S.A. should see that such shabby, unimaginative dealings cease.

To list a fairly comprehensive range of associations should not give the impression that students are overloaded. If any person lists the associations running in various directions and times

(i) GOODMAN P., *Community of Scholars*, p. 167.

through his life in his present year, he will see that the list is very long, though the pattern is normally taken for granted, and life does not necessarily seem too full. Neither would every student partake of all possible associations.

To make full use of so many possible associations, the chart-picture of the school's work is invaluable. It must not be seen as a tidy arrangement; it is not a mechanical arrangement of parts. The whole is meant as an organic pattern, allowing for give and take and creative development. It sets an effective and dynamic communication network. In the transition from competition, authority and moral impositions, this is particularly vital. But the student who wants to stay outside must be allowed to do so.

With such stress on co-operation, I want to make clear that the most fundamental work group, a person and his thoughts, is not forgotten. The right to work alone, undisturbed, even by tutors and telephones, should be satisfied. All of co-operation gathers its strength from the association and dissociation of groups to privacy—thought, feelings and meditation—to listen to within.

This must not be forgotten. Whereas competition isolates the individual, whether he likes it not, whether it is efficient or not, education based on co-operation can recognize the real need and functions of privacy. This is particularly important in discussions on the nature of the "place"—the architecture of the school.[i]

IV.2. ENTRANCE

IV.2.1. Virtues of Random Selection from Candidates

An examination of the studies of selection procedure have taught me some remarkable lessons:

(a) Students chosen cannot be shown to do better than those rejected by one but accepted by another university.

(b) Selection cannot even pick out those who will not succeed: 14% wastage as an overall average shows this.

(i) See Chapter III.8.

(c) Selection is prejudiced. The bias is against the extrovert, the highly creative and the poor throughout the whole school life of streaming and examinations.[i]

I then asked myself whether a society that can cope with only 20% of those who reach the standard of entry,[ii] should concern, and it seems, fool and preoccupy itself, with the task of selection when the far more important task of providing places for all those who should have them, as a birthright, is thereby obscured? Is not research on selection highly irrelevant in an age that demonstrates ever more the importance of environment? Is not selection an arrogant insult when we certainly ought to be able to help those who want to learn, whatever subject?

I came to the conclusion it was a tragic waste of research funds and talent when teaching methods ought to occupy us to the limit of our facilities and manpower. It is not a matter of trying to find out who will make architects, but how to make architects of those who want to be.

As with streaming in primary schools, so with university selection: once society admits to the right for all to have higher education, selection systems among those who all qualify make no sense at all. They can only be understood, to quote Huxley again, as "venerable traditions that have lost their point", reflecting only the pathetic prima donna pride of universities.

Therefore, I came to the conclusion that entrance selection should be a highly democratic process through random choice from those who submit their names, after a therapeutic meeting designed to make sure the student was choosing as wisely as possible.

Shortly afterwards, I came across the following quotation:

"There is considerable evidence that G.C.E. results are a poor, and often downright unfair, criterion for selecting university students.

(i) See Chapter I.2.
(ii) Robbins Report.

"Prof. Hilde Himmelweit and others found that there was some correlation between A level and economics finals, very limited correlation for sociology, none for law students.

"Headmasters' letters were of some use but O level results (on which preliminary acceptance is often based) were virtually useless, and both together were only slightly better than deciding on a random basis."[i]

Random selection from applicants could, of course, still take into account preference for certain universities, decided perhaps more intelligently after the therapeutic meeting. It would, done on a national scale, lead straight on from the task now carried out ever more efficiently by Central Council on Admissions, which is saving so much previously wasted energy.

The advantages of random selection are:

(a) Students not selected do not feel socially rejected, do not suffer from the worst by-product of competition, the sense of failure; unwarranted as the evidence shows.

(b) The social pressure to provide the places needed for all the increasing numbers who fight their way through to the university entry standard, will be stronger. No easy rationalizations—that the best have been taken so we need not worry too much.

(c) Rather than depressing into inaction those indisputably unlucky ones in the "draw", they are keen to look for alternatives to achieve their ambitions still. And parents' pressure on providing more places will be militant, as it ought to be. Parents are too easily convinced that their children were not good enough and therefore are rightly not at universities. If some very rich and some very talented students were left out it would make the situation vivid.

(d) The phoney feeling of superiority of many of those who have got places would not arise, but a proper appreciation of the privilege to be in this position by the grace of God.

(i) DAVY J., *The Observer*, February 14, 1965.

(e) It would cut out the onerous duty of judging, when fair judgement is precluded, the future of young and often keen people.

(f) The temptation to regard aptitude testing a proper question for research would be avoided. Given educreation, the problem does not arise. The awareness of a person of what he wants to do has no proper substitute. And if there are students who don't know, our job is not to find out for them, but to find out how to avoid producing applicants like that.

One very cheering thought appears (last to those who hate the idea of democracy): the really talented student will find the alternative routes most quickly and will be able to cope with his greater talent in adversity, e.g. in architecture, to qualify externally.

I in no way mean to suggest that the external course of the R.I.B.A., which I have always regarded as inhuman, is a good thing that ought to be fostered. I do mean to suggest that when it is flooded by people who do not feel falsely inferior but who are determined to become architects and have the same share of talent and confidence as those in the schools, we will get more action by the Board of Architectural Education, the universities and the public to provide the proper number of places.

The University Central Council on Admissions 1963–4 Report shows that in universities the number of entrants into the architectural and planning schools fell from 440 in 1963 to 370 in 1964. The statistics produced at the same time by the R.I.B.A., however, indicate an increase of entrants to architecture from 287 to 343. One or more new university schools may have affected the figures, as the applications were made while these schools were outside the Central Council's scheme. So there is little one can say in the light of conflicting figures from official bodies, except to note that even in the more favourable case Robbins figures are not likely to be reached at such a rate of growth. The R.I.B.A. does not say whether it agrees with the Central Council statistics that only 34%

of applicants to university schools of architecture in 1964 were admitted.[i]

In all this we have to cope with the outdated thinking in terms of professions protecting the interest of those who would not find a place if the educational system was overproducing. This is a ridiculous argument in a world crying out for expertise. But the statement below shows how it affects the life of the country— and we should be thinking of the world.

"Doctors are in short supply not because of the salaries offered but because not enough of them are being trained. In 1957 the Willink Committee recommended a REDUCTION in the number of medical students: a recommendation which was universally accepted."[ii]

And, in spite of the immense shortage of men skilled in recreating and creating man's environment on earth, the arguments for limiting the recommended number of entrants into the architectural education by guessing at the future building volume in this country is taken seriously at the Board of Architectural Education.

Information for schoolboys and girls on further education, in spite of several recent improvements, is still quite insufficient. While B.A.S.A. is preparing an independent report to tell students the differences of the various schools, and these are honourable intentions, the changes that occur and should occur rapidly at this present time, preclude a semi-permanent type of information of this sort. It should be a student-produced, independently worded document, but brought up to date regularly. It is these people who have the best idea of how a course might strike those just a few years younger, with very similar expectancies to their own.

The students, without vested interest and ability for candour, would act as watchdog on course depreciation and as a fillip to

(i) The Universities Central Council on Admissions, *Second Report* 1963–4, London 1965. R.I.B.A., *Statistics on Architectural Education* 1964–5, London 1965.
(ii) KLEIN R., *The Observer*, February 2, 1965.

inadequate provisions. If B.A.S.A. had their own "visiting" board to fulfil this function, bringing out the individual advantages and disadvantages, opportunities and limitations of each school, this could be achieved.

One cannot rely on a prospectus. They are grossly pretentious and misleading documents, fashioned to sound as if countless regulations are enforced and advantages there to be gained, that have no relation to reality at all. It is the schism of administration and teaching.

Among the regulations at the Nottingham School of Architecture were to be found:

"Students will be expected to be in readiness to commence study in their respective studios or rooms at least five minutes prior to class opening.

"Students wishing to leave the College before the end of any study period must obtain written permission from the Head of the School of Architecture, or his deputy.

"Students must not leave the College premises . . . during 'break', 10.40–11.00 without the consent of the Head of the School of Architecture.

"All full-time students are required to participate in physical training as part of their course of study—application for exemption will be considered only if supported by a medical certificate.

"Smoking in studios, workshops and corridors is prohibited."

From this one would hardly guess that the Nottingham school was in fact a very relaxed and hilarious environment for higher education where the students who wished to have physical training as part of their course had to beg the administration for it!

IV.2.2. The Advisory Meeting

The advisory or therapeutic meeting would allow students applying to universities for entrance to come face to face with a group of well-informed people trained to communicate to the student what he really wants to know, check on, things he has "heard", or tell him what he had not heard of,

In more detail, the functions of the therapeutic interview are:

(a) To advise the student on the widsom of his choice, to allow an objective examination of his motives and help him to overcome any pressures, parental or otherwise, that may unduly influence his choice of profession, university, etc.[i]

(b) To observe the points of strength from which the student's capacity may spring, to pass this on to his tutor.

(c) To allow the student to ask questions of experts about alternatives and actual schools and universities.

(d) Generally, to make productive the present unproductive, often depressing "interview", with its examination atmosphere.

Such a meeting is, in itself, a worthwhile experience from several points of view. The time taken would be less, for one interview would replace hawking from school to school. The advising teams could be brought together at each university, though there might be no connection between the preference of the student and the place of the interview. Visits to see what schools are like should certainly precede applications where possible.

Meeting groups of twenty-five students together and allowing $6\frac{1}{2}$ hours a day, quarter of an hour a student and twenty-five students a day, a team of advisers could deal with 125 students a week. Given, say, a student population of 250,000, twenty-five weeks for advising eighty teams would be required. There is no need to advise applicants for the same department together. To mix students somewhat might be advantageous from the point of view of a non-competitive atmosphere.

Personnel could be changed, of course, but some people may in fact do substantial duty with very valuable expertise at this advisory meeting. It is not half as bad as the figures might suggest, to be with a group of twenty-five young people for a

(i) Peter Marris found that among the ten classifications of influences he lists, on choice of University of those at Cambridge, for example, only 28% were influenced by the reputation of the course—but 40% of those at Leeds.—(*Experience of Further Education*, p. 207.)

whole day. It is much better than twenty-five young people one after the other for quarter of an hour each. Yet the latter is what many professors or selection teams endure at the moment.

As the proposed meeting is different from the normal interview, it should be described in more detail. First of all, it is difficult but important to bear in mind that the atmosphere of such an interview is other than that at a "selection interview". The positions of chairs should be round a table and the fitting nature of the room considering the larger and diverse collection of people there with the number of older and advising people smaller than the number inquiring. This has a relaxing influence. It is possible, of course, to have single conversations after each group.

In such circumstances it may well be discovered, for example, that a student is coerced by the love or hate of his parents to choose a profession he dislikes, and he may be given that backing he needs to do what his own wishes are.

A host of other matters, when classified, might lead to a change for the better in the student's choice—on reconsidering his first ideas in the light of advice received. One could even imagine a student going up and describing how he wants to apply himself, and being advised what school or course would fit his aspirations.

The tone would be set at the beginning by some such statement by the chairman as: "We are here to give you a real chance to make sure your desires are rationally satisfied by the system we have to offer, full of faults as it is. On my right is Prof. Mathews, Agriculture, Cambridge, Prof. Digs, Mathematics, Liverpool, Dr. Jol, Physics, London, Mrs. Burton, Bristol, etc. etc., as you see on the table plan in front of you, and we can all see from the same table plan both candidates and advisors, where you come from and what your plans are, and the questions you've given with advance notice. You must expect us to disagree, though we will try to tell you why. All those who wish to speak can do so through the chairman, and there is no reason why anyone should not speak repeatedly."

The panel could then start to advise, and the meeting would

deal with each case in turn. But many good techniques await discovery.

Naturally, the character and function of these meetings would become generally known in schools and the students would know that silence is not golden and that pretence is worse. But neither are damning, for both are due to sickness of society. So in the advisory therapeutic kind of meeting: silence and pretence are expected and remedied by expertise.

During this group meeting, with highly skilled people giving their attention to young people for a whole day, it would be using the skill positively if the advisors noted their strong and possible weak points; not to decide their future, but to help whoever is the future tutor of the student at whatever university he might be. The following types of characteristics may be spotted and noted and commented on. The conclusions (they are advisory only) can be given openly to the student—there is no threat involved, only diagnosis.

Enthusiasm
Sensitivity
Insight
Clear thought
Organizing ability
Leadership
Understanding of others
Powers of communication
Powers of description
Powers of expression
Originality
Rebellious attitude
Hunger for skills or knowedge
Possession of skills or knowledge
Powers of judgement and discretion
Social conscience
Personal relationship—love
Vocational eagerness
Character behaviour—aggressive, defensive, etc.

Schools of architecture, currently turning away a great many applicants, have various methods of selection. Some ask the students to come to interviews with folios (as if drawing was relevant!), some with folios and anything else creative they may have. Talking about these things can relax the atmosphere.

At the Bartlett School of Architecture the students have welcomed the applicants and shown them round, in itself a wholesome attitude. We must avoid pretentious exhibitions at such times. All this is, however, accentuating the negative, i.e. that selection remains, and that although we know it is arbitrary we pretend it is not.

IV.2.3. Research at the Bartlett School

At the Bartlett School in London, Dr. Abercrombie is leading research into selection procedure. Statistics show the very questionable implications of making rigid examination requirements of a high standard. A much broader approach to selection is desirable and fruitful. The system on test includes the following: academic record, referee's report and candidate's statement, rating by a team of four. The students are graded into five categories. The top three categories in academic record are considered for interview in relation to the quality of the other two criteria. "The rationale for making the academic record the first sieve is that its predictive value for success in university examinations is known to be fairly good. Success in passing essential examinations is taken as a sign that "a job undertaken can be efficiently done". This remark pinpoints that examinations are, very questionably, taken as the best sign for fitness to do a job. It is, in fact, a very important weakness in the argument for education but a good one for selection. At the Bartlett School, there is more "didactic" learning and there are more examinations to test the "worth" of the student in early years than at other schools of architecture. This selection obeys a secondary truth. But that the early examinations in fact occur and are used as criteria for testing their selection system is remarkably odd. After all, this is a piece of expensive research and there is enough in this book to show that examinations are regarded, with good evidence, as an evil by the vast majority of educated men.

To my mind this research demonstrates the "vigorous quantitative testing" without the inspired question, without the inspired hunch, i.e. highly regrettable waste of time and money and talent.

But one can understand interest in selection if one reads the defeatist attitude of the Robbins Report: although "there has been an increasing degree of competition for entry . . ." it is assumed that "it is inevitable that there should be some degree of competition for entry. For these reasons our estimates do not allow for any relaxation of the degree of competition". Of those who in 1962 achieved two A-levels only 20% went to universities.

Though the Robbins statement may prove to be correct prophecy I abhor the idea and insist that an "educreational approach" would allow so much better use of all money and each manpower and corner of accommodation that more rapid provision than is now thought possible could be made. We must not forget that we are not affording the young a basic right: to be educated when the means are available to be used through the educreational attitude.

I don't seriously think that the undisciplined herd of elephantine university bodies will consider, let alone swallow their shallow pride and adopt, such a rational idea in a hurry. My purpose is to show that all the research and argument about selection procedures, etc., is beside the point. The standard is set by the minimum number of A-levels (accepting A levels for the moment) and the right to have higher education. I am bringing home the irrelevance of selection and its irreverence to humanity.

There is, of course, no reason why a school should not decide to choose its candidates in a random manner. Such an experiment could demonstrate the excellence and importance of teaching method and might indicate to other universities the futility of their selection.

But the situation of shortage of places should not be looked upon as inevitable, as does the Robbins Committee, stipulating the continuation of ever stiffer competition for places: " . . . our estimates do not allow for any relaxation of the degree of competition."

IV.2.4. Emergency Universities

I would like to see heroic projects of "emergency universities" taking shape with what would be an equally talented but rejected series of people and, in makeshift buildings, with likewise rejected and consultant staff, but inspired leadership, as creative experiments. The spirit of enthusiasm and adventure and the challenge of adversity almost guarantees that these emergency universities would do as well or better in many ways than the established, often bogged down, establishments. If some State misses out by not trying out educreation, its economy and efficiency, in this way, it will be a great pity.

Goodman, not primarily because of shortage of numbers but because of the qualities of the American universities, makes a similar suggestion:

"A simple proposal: For the near future the prospect of significant reform in the great majority of schools and especially in the most populous ones, is dim. In the nature of the case the very changes that are needed are the ones that administrations must resist, for they curtail administration's reason for being and jeopardize its security. Decentralizing control, splitting up rather than expanding, dispensing with credits, grading, admissions, de-emphasizing buildings and grounds, being selective about contracting research—all these make pale the hectic flush. It would seem to be self-evident that the only purpose of educational administration is to expedite education, but this thought is entirely naïve and out-of-date. Worse, however, the reforms toward freedom, commitment, criticism, and inevitable social conflict, endanger the Image and indeed nullify the historical role of administration which has been not to protect its community but to pacify it. So let us propose to go outside the present collegiate framework. The simplest remedy is the historical one, for bands of scholars to secede and set up where they can teach and learn on their own simple conditions. Such a movement is difficult but not impractical. In my opinion, if it could succeed in a dozen cases—proving that there is a viable social alternative to what we have—the entire system would experience a profound and salutary jolt."[i]

And Goodman goes on to describe in some detail the plans for such a "community of scholars".

IV.3. THERAPEUTIC TECHNIQUES

IV.3.1. The Variety of Possibilities

In an educational system which is orientated towards awareness, towards coming alive, and the creative processes, the individual student is likely to experience his problems and frustrations vividly. This in turn will lead to the desire to do something about it, particularly in an atmosphere where this is the norm, the accepted and expected behaviour.

The therapeutic, as indeed the co-operative and self-regulatory attitudes, would be explained to new students in intellectual terms. The group master would normally do this.

The symptoms of sickness were diagnosed in the psychological, and physiological and the social aspects of human beings in Chapter II.2. Correspondingly, a three-pronged therapeutic attack can be made on the underlying energy malady. From the physiological standpoint, the famous work of Matthias Alexander[ii] and the lesser known but more impressive principles of Feldenkrais,[iii] show attack via posture and bodily symptoms on the ills of the total personality. Any avenue can be effective, and Wolfson has developed a well-known voice therapy.

The psychological avenue is, of course, the most frequently used. Psycho-analysis as developed by Ferenczi,[iv]

(i) GOODMAN P., *Community of Scholars*, p. 159.
(ii) ALEXANDER M., *The Universal Constant in Living*, London 1941.
(iii) FELDENKRAIS M., *Body and Mature Behaviour*, London 1954.
(iv) FERENCZI S., *The Further Development of an Active Therapy in Psycho-Analysis*, New York 1953.

Halmos,[i] Braatoy[ii] and many others, has used the approach through the mind but seen it as part of a wider unified field in each person.

Sociologically, Moreno,[iii] with his socio-drama, Lewin,[iv] Klein,[v] Foulkes,[vi] etc., and, most deliberately for our purposes, Infield,[vii] have shown how the social context of life can have therapeutic application. Group therapy as such combines some of the above ideas.[viii]

It is the great advantage of Wilhelm Reich's[ix] unitary approach that all the above can be seen as expressions of the same therapeutic endeavour, namely to get the basic energy pattern functioning freely and rhythmically. Reich's own work, not surprisingly, includes perhaps the most effective techniques for therapy for they combine work on the body, on the mind, the emotions and the social context. All aspects can be most effectively seen and so exploited as relief to the blocked energy economy of the person. Lowen and Perls[x] have developed some of Reich's concepts in special ways.

From the immense pool of possibilities hinted at above, each situation with its particular organization, its tutorial and consultant staff talents, will allow more or less direct application of a therapeutic approach. From the attitude of a single tutor to the change of the whole system there are in the educational context many crucial points for effective application.

(i) HALMOS P., *Solitude and Privacy*, London 1952.
(ii) BRAATOY T., *Fundamentals of Psycho-analytic Technique*, London 1954.
(iii) MORENO J. L., *Who Shall Survive?* New York 1953.
(iv) LEWIN K., *Field Theory in Social Science*, New York 1951.
(v) KLEIN J., *The Study of Groups*, London 1956.
(vi) FOULKES and ANTHONY, *Group Psychotherapy*, London 1957.
(vii) INFIELD H., *Co-operative College Papers; The Sociological Study of Co-operation*, Loughborough 1956.
(viii) "The attempt to pierce to common humanity by self-awareness in groups is more realistic . . . than . . . teaching the common great books and philosophy".—(GOODMAN P., *The Community of Scholars*, p. 144.)
(ix) REICH W., *Character Analysis*, London 1959.
(x) LOWEN A., *Physical Dynamics of Character Structure*, London 1958; also PERLS, GOODMAN and HEFERLINE, *Gestalt Therapy*, New York 1951.

Various kinds of therapeutic approach are emerging in ever growing numbers of social contexts: education, industrial relations, marriage guidance, institutional groups of many kinds. We must expect a manifold development of techniques in the next few years. The examples quoted give an insight into the kind of possibilities which may be developed under several headings.

The therapeutic approach takes several routes, and I will isolate and give examples of the following:

(a) Individual: aided personal efforts.
(b) Co-operative learning in free group discussions.
(c) Group tackling work obstruction, solve difficulties in co-operation.
(d) Group getting together to tackle personal problems.
(e) Group psychotherapy proper.
(f) Co-operation as a security-creating phenomenon.

IV.3.2. Individual Therapy—Aided Personal Effort

It is feasible that talented tutors may give individual therapy to certain students. This may be the most effective application, but it is also time taking and has the important disadvantage that positive and negative transference, hate and love for the tutor in question, can be a disturbing element emotionally, even if the rest of the students understand the situation intellectually.

The tutor, while involved as tutor, must remain independent in the sense that love relationships with his students would seriously impair his position, his effectiveness as a tutor *vis-à-vis* the students. (Exclusive love relationships, that is.)

The individual therapist's therapy must always be rare. Other therapies will be the rule.

Gestalt Therapy,[i] as vividly described in the first section of the book of this name, allows the student to help himself beyond the awareness which is intellectually introduced during his studies. This approach has been used by undergraduates with good results.

The first 225 pages of the book deal with eighteen "experiments",

(i) pp. 84 and 85.

all to be repeated by the student during his day-to-day life rather than in any specific therapeutic situation or place.

The book allows a student or a tutor to understand the technique sufficiently to use it if circumstances are at all favourable. To bring together Gestalt psychology and the "armour" theory of Wilhelm Reich makes a powerful combination. The general attitude is shown by the following quotation on "Contacting the Environment":

"It does no good for people to insist that you 'pull yourself together'. It does not make it any more feasible even if it is a psychoanalyst who says, 'Just relax, don't censor, and remember the details of your childhood'. Except very superficially, these things cannot be done by deliberate decision!

"What can be done is what you have started to do in these experiments—that is, to become aware of your efforts and reactions and to acquire toward them an attitude of 'creative pre-commitment'.

"First, let us distinguish between what is habitually called concentration and what is genuinely healthy, organic concentration. In our society concentration is regarded as a deliberate, strenuous, compulsive effort—something you make yourself do. This is to be expected where people are forever neurotically commanding, conquering and compelling themselves. On the other hand, healthy, organic concentration usually is not called concentration at all, but, on those comparatively rare occasions when it does occur, is named attraction, interest, fascination or absorption.

"Watch children at their games and you will see that they are concentrating on what they are doing to such a degree that it is difficult to draw their attention away. You will notice also that they are excited about what they are doing. These two factors— attention to the object or activity and the excitement of satisfying need, interest or desire through what one is attentive to—are the substance of healthy concentration."[i]

(i) Ibid., pp. 84 and 85.

What these eighteen experiments in the book are like is well explained by the following excerpt from Experiment 3, Attending and Concentrating:

"The more complete the felt-contact between you and your environment, and the more honestly you feel and express to yourself your feelings of desire, loathing, coldness, boredom, disgust, with the persons and things you come in touch with, the more you will have a relevant context in which the 'inner conflict' will emerge during the experiments.

"The following will facilitate your felt-contact with the environment:

"Let your attention shift from one object to another, noticing figure and background in the object—and in your emotions. Verbalize the emotions each time, as, 'I like this' or 'I dislike this'. Also, differentiate the object into its parts: 'It is this in it I like, but that I dislike.' And, finally, when this much comes naturally to you, differentiate your emotions, thus: 'For this I feel disgust' or 'For this I feel hatred,' etc.

"The resistances you are likely to encounter in yourself during this experiment are embarrassment, self-consciousness, the feeling of being too harsh, presumptuous, nasty, or perhaps the wish to be paid attention rather than give attention. If, with respect to the persons you are in contact with, these resistances should become too strong to tolerate and tempt you to abandon the experiment, restrict yourself for a time to animals and inanimate objects."[i]

How they combine mental and bodily awareness can be exemplified by this quotation from Experiment 6, Sharpening the Body-Sense:

" 'Now I am aware . . .' applied to all your experiences will, unless yours is a very conscientious, obsessional character (in which case you will nullify the experiment by some other means), lead invariably to your wandering off into daydreaming, 'thinking,' reminiscing, or anticipating. As you deviate thus from the

(i) Ibid., p. 20.

experiment you will lose awareness that you are now doing so, and you will wake in chagrin that such a simple task should be so hard to perform. Don't expect at the start to be able to carry on for more than a few minutes without slipping. But come back again and again to verbalizing, 'Now I am aware . . .' until you get the feeling that 'I,' 'now,' and the object of awareness constitute a unified experience.

"The aim is to extend the boundary of what you accept as yourself to include all organic activities. By slowly but persistently doing this, you will gradually become able to do without effort much that was previously impossible no matter how great the effort.

"So we proceed in such a simple fashion as this: 'Now I am aware that I am lying on the couch. Now I am aware of the wish to do the awareness-experiment. Now I am aware of hesitating, of asking myself what to do first. Now I am aware that the radio is playing in the next room. That reminds me . . . No, I am aware that I meant to listen to that program. I am aware that I have stopped myself from wandering. Now I feel lost again, I am remembering the advice to stick to the surface. Now I am aware that I am lying with my legs crossed. I am aware that I have a pain in the back. I am aware of wishing to change my position. Now I am doing that,' etc.

"Notice that processes are going on and that you are involved in and concerned with these processes. To realize such continuous involvement is extremely difficult, and most persons escape by accepting as their own—by identifying themselves with—only those processes which are deliberate. But bit by bit you are to take increasing responsibility for all your experience (we do not mean blame for it!)—including your blocks and symptoms—and gradually to acquire both free acceptance and control of yourself. The notion that 'thoughts' on their own initiative and without any help from you 'enter your mind,' must give place to the insight that you are thinking the thoughts. At present it is sufficient to notice that thoughts are not like objects floating in space, but that they are processes which have some temporal span.

"Now, still accepting and identifying yourself with all your awareness, begin to differentiate as follows:

"Try first to attend mainly to external events—sights, sounds, smells—but without suppressing other experiences. Then, in sharp contrast, concentrate on internal processes—images, physical sensations, muscular tensions, emotions, thinking. Then, one by one, differentiate these various internal processes, by concentrating, as exclusively as you can, on images, then on muscular tensions etc. Follow these through, as previously, by detailed recognition of the different objects or activities and, if possible, of whatever moving dramatic scene they may be components.

"The rest of this experiment and the following two are devoted to helping you to differentiate 'body,' 'emotions' and 'thinking'."[i]

Giving emotional development a rightful place in education is a long-sought-after aim. *Gestalt Therapy* shows techniques whereby this, obviously remedial aim for our society, can be realized. In this way emotion can be developed after children have been brought up with an "emotional limp". But our attitude must be therapeutic, not merely a matter of developing the limp:

"From this it follows that emotions in themselves are not something to be rid of on such trumped-up charges as being impediments to clear thought and action. On the contrary, they are not only essential as energy-regulators in the organism/environment field, but they are also unique deliveries of experience which have no substitute—they are the way we become aware of our concerns, and, therefore, of what we are and what the world is.

"This function of emotion is grossly maligned in our society. As stated previously, it is regarded as arising only in crises, and even then only if the person 'loses control of himself' and 'gets emotional'. Calmness is prized as the very antithesis of emotion, and people strive to appear 'cool, calm, and collected'. Yet

(i) Ibid., pp. 84 and 85.

calmness is not without emotional tone, for it is born of the directly evaluative experiencing of this particular situation as one which can be effectively handled, or, at the other extreme, as one about which nothing can be done. It is the fluid, open-ended situation, where one feels that he has much at stake and where his own actions may swing the balance, that is truly exciting. To affect calmness in such a situation is a 'front,' achieved by suppressing manifestations of concern. To fool others in this way may be worthwhile if they are enemies, but to fool yourself is to mistake yourself for a foe and to deny yourself awareness of 'What's up'."[i]

"What the 'adults' do not guess and bitterly resist having revealed to them is that their impatience in getting the child to 'control his emotions' is rooted squarely in the fact that in their own childhood, too, 'the authorities' had this same warped, apprehensive attitude toward emotion.

"This whole crusade for 'control of the emotions' is, of course, itself emotionally grounded, and it is prosecuted in a most emotional fashion. It does not fail to get results, but the results achieved are not those which were offered in justification of the program. It does not eliminate 'undesirable' emotions from the person, for it cannot repeal the way nature designed organisms to function. What it does succeed in doing is to complicate further the already intricate organism/environment field by setting up a great number of situations which, unless avoided, are immensely emotion-arousing!"[ii]

To get the most out of "verbalizing" a Gestalt therapeutic attitude is useful:

"Healthy verbalizing usually takes off from what is non-verbal —objects, conditions, the state of affairs—and terminates in the production of non-verbal effects. This is not to say that verbalization may not on occasion be useful when it is about what is already verbal—books, plays, what someone said—but this

(i) *Gestalt Therapy*, p. 96.
(ii) Ibid., p. 97.

tendency to talk about talk is in our times a disease! When one fears contact with actuality—with flesh-and-blood people and with one's own sensations and feelings—words are interposed as a screen both between the verbalizer and his environment and between the verbalizer and his own organism. The person attempts to live on words—and then wonders vaguely why something is amiss!(i)

Students certainly suffer frequently from this malaise— talking until two and three o'clock in the morning so often, with what results? I suspect very often words are then used as a screen "between verbalizer and his own organism". A genuine relationship is blocked by an ulterior one.

Gestalt Therapy, dealing with what Dr. Abercrombie would group under schemata, has this to say and to recommend in "Experiment 10, Converting Confluence into Contact":

". . . many of our habits were not freely developed and are not maintained because of their efficiency, but are confluences with someone who taught them to us, with a model of some sort, or with some abstract conception of duty, propriety, or utility. We take for granted that they were spontaneously acquired, but any attempt to change them brings us up against resistances so strong as to be unmistakable evidence of unhealthy confluence.

"Notice some of your habits—the way you dress, the way you brush your teeth, the way you open or close a door, the way you bake a cake. If they do not seem as efficient as they could be, or if some alternative seems just as good and has the advantage of offering variety, try to change. What happens? Do you take pleasure in learning the new way? Or do you encounter strong resistances? Does changing some item in your usual schedule throw off the rest of your routine? What happens if you watch someone perform a task similar to one of your own? Do you get annoyed, irritated, indignant at small variations from your own procedure?"(ii)

(i) *Gestalt Therapy*, p. 105.
(ii) Ibid., p. 120.

The contents of volume 1 of *Gestalt Therapy* list the experiments and are therefore of relevance:

PART 1. ORIENTING THE SELF

    I The Starting Situation
   II Contacting the Environment
         Experiment 1: Feeling the Actual
         Experiment 2: Sensing Opposed Forces
         Experiment 3: Attending and Concentrating
         Experiment 4: Differentiating and Unifying
  III Techniques of Awareness
         Experiment 5: Remembering
         Experiment 6: Sharpening the Body-Sense
         Experiment 7: Experiencing the Continuity of Emotion
         Experiment 8: Verbalizing
         Experiment 9: Integrating Awareness
  IV Directed Awareness
         Experiment 10: Converting Confluence into Contact
         Experiment 11: Changing Anxiety into Excitement

PART 2. MANIPULATING THE SELF

    V The Modified Situation
   VI Retroflection
         Experiment 12: Investigating Misdirected Behaviour
         Experiment 13: Mobilizing the Muscles
         Experiment 14: Executing the Re-reversed Act
  VII Introjection
         Experiment 15: Introjecting and Eating
         Experiment 16: Dislodging and Digesting Introjects
 VIII Projections
         Experiment 17: Discovering Projections
         Experiment 18: Assimilating Projections

In the development of new and better methods of learning, design skills, and process sequences, it is obviously of great advantage to become aware of the hindrances. Many aspects of the awareness studies detailed later are closely related to Gestalt therapeutic concepts.

IV.3.3. Free Group Discussion

The "free discussion group" as used by Dr. Abercrombie in her experiments with medical students are a well-documented example of a therapeutic approach to group teaching. Here we have an "awareness study", in my language, because the whole exercise is devised to make the student aware of the "anatomy" of his judgement. (It is not the group therapeutic situation which arises when a group are facing stumbling blocks in their work.) To quote Dr. Abercrombie:

"Formal education is concerned largely with reality-adjusted thinking, psychotherapy largely with autistic thinking as it interferes with reality-adjusted thinking. The teaching method presently to be described had characteristics of both traditional teaching and psychotherapy.[i]

"The essential difference between teaching in free group discussion and by ordinary didactic methods as in a lecture, is that the students talk to each other . . . in free group discussion . . . the students are presented with the same information (for example an account of an experiment), but it soon becomes clear that they do not extract the same information from it, and learning depends on the fact that each extracts something different.

"Discussion . . . [emphasizes] the importance of individual differences in the store of information. . . . The organization of the discussions is directed towards encouraging the students to talk freely and to listen to each other, and many environmental factors such as size of groups and seating arrangements have complex effects on this . . . . For administrative reasons it was convenient to have groups of twelve, and although groups of eight or nine persons is generally considered the optimum . . . .[ii]

(i) ABERCROMBIE M. L. J., *The Anatomy of Judgement*, p. 61.
(ii) Ibid., p. 68,

"Much of the work ordinarily done by the teacher in tutorials, questioning, criticizing, asking for evidence, controlling the too vocal or encouraging speech in the silent—is taken over sooner or later in various ways by members of the group. This acceptance of responsibility is itself a maturing process which must be encouraged, and perhaps the teacher can best assist by having faith that it will occur . . . .[i]

". . . it may legitimately be stressed that in free group discussion techniques there lies a promising tool for investigating those hidden processes of our own and other people's thinking which so powerfully govern our behaviour, and about which we know so little."[ii]

Given that co-operation takes the place of competition and that not only the isolated experiment taking up a few hours a week, but the whole of the course, is more or less orientated towards this kind of teaching, Dr. Abercrombie's approach blossoms into something far greater than she describes. On the other hand, her experiment shows how talent can, in the adverse conditions of the normal educational set-up, achieve considerable gains, in readiness to advance when the opportunity arises.

Dr. Abercrombie demonstrates how the seating arrangement around a table varies, with the "tutor" taking up a different position each time, quite casually, to stress the informality and random seating. The point of this is that people communicate with anyone to whom comment is relevant in free discussion, not in any preferred direction as in lecturing, or "question-and-answer situation".

"Another important difference between this method of teaching and the didactic lecture method is the extent to which emotion of various kinds is aroused and expressed. One gets the impression that many personal affinities and antipathies already established between students are brought into the discussion. . . . Serious disagreements may arise . . . . It is inevitable that some aspects of

(i) ABERCROMBIE M. L. J., *The Anatomy of Judgement*, p. 80. Dr. Abercrombie was for five years associated with Foulkes's group psychotherapy.
(ii) Ibid., p. 81.

the course should be painful to some people, since it continually exposes the inadequacy of their customary approach to problems."[i]

Dr. Abercrombie describes well that the tutor in the teaching situation must learn to listen, and reminds us how hard that is for those used to standing and talking in front of classes only.[ii] She stresses how praising or criticizing individuals has an adverse effect on the free discussion and how the teacher must skilfully take the inadequacies back to the students to sort out, if he intervenes at all.

"It is the teacher's job to make clear the relation of . . . significant red herrings to the main topic.[iii]

"Learning in free group discussion is a process of identifying, through verbalization, the associations between schemata, so that the new information can be dissociated from those schemata with which it is automatically associated, and can be seen to be potentially relevant to many schemata, instead of to a few only.

"By studying the reactions of many groups of students to the same scientific topic it was possible to identify and describe recurring patterns of behaviour or modes of employing schemata. Reference to these was made at appropriate points during the subsequent discussions to help to clarify and broaden the students' understanding of their own ways of behaving."

Subsequently ". . . alternative judgements of the same patterns are discussed . . . and judgement is improved after this experience."[iv]

My own experience and experiments bear out all Dr. Abercrombie's conclusions. It must be recognized that free group discussion represents an approach generally valid for educreation and replaces, if we accept the evidence of its effectiveness, very

(i) ABERCROMBIE M. L. J., *The Anatomy of Judgement*, p. 73.
(ii) In my own experiments on these lines I felt I had achieved something when the students told me to "shut up", explaining that they wanted to get on with the discussion.
(iii) ABERCROMBIE M. L. J., *The Anatomy of Judgement*, p. 77.
(iv) Ibid., pp. 79–80.

largely didactic class teaching and lecturing. The immensity of this inevitable conclusion has obviously not struck even those who admire Dr. Abercrombie's work.

It combines, as she herself says, teaching and therapy in an effective way. It throws the student back on to his own devices, encouraging self-regulation. The size and function of the group encourage many aspects of co-operation, being devoid of competitive intent or moralistic judgement of any kind.

IV.3.4. Group Tackling Work Obstructions

Co-operation as such is a therapeutic catalyst. The emotional contact with others, the energies roused by the desire to solve problems, and the vivid experience of frustration, can make the individual aware of the nuisance of shortcomings while it gives him security and capacity to help himself and so the group.

Infield, studying and experimenting with co-operative groups like those in the Kibutzim in Israel, or those preparing for such life, has contributed most in this field. It is directly relevant to any situation where co-operation and the therapeutic attitude go together.

Infield has devised fairly simple sociometric tests which diagnose the groups' integration and brings to the fore what characteristics of what relationships may be the disturbing factor. Dealt with in this way by the outsider, the tutor, the therapist, members of the group do not see diagnosis in terms of blame but in terms of the first step in therapy. This intellectual understanding will go hand in hand with emotional resistance, and this is where the security and help found in the group and through the therapist becomes vital. The starting point is the insight of the rightness of co-operation as such and the wish to be able to contribute well.

Infield stipulates that not only is co-operation a therapeutic circumstance, but, when incorporated, as in educreation, a prophylactic one. He feels it vital in an age when the wealthiest nations show the greatest degree of mental disintegration. I interpret this in the following way: poverty ties energies and poses continual real problems which attract, fuse and liberate for more real problems. Affluence liberates great energies but poses, or allows recognition of, in our sick, disintegrated society, fewer and fewer real problems, so that attraction–fusion–liberation do not have a strong enough field for application in the energy economy of the person (or community). The disintegrated personality has lost its "tone" through lack of problem-solving work. (Like the 'spoiled child'). And the mental disintegration is strongly related to the rotting, stale, unchannelled extra energies. The solution is not to ask for poverty; or the privilege of being able to afford neuroses to an ever-increasing extent; or suffer results of freedom without love, as in delinquency. The solution lies in a highly realistic therapeutic approach which allows particularly the young to get to grips with the many, many real problems and responsibilities that beset the world.

To give the flavour of Infield's approach we quote from a case: Of the capacity for co-operation and the actual performance of the group, Infield writes:

". . . the apparent lack of group coherence could not be due to lack of co-operativeness. . . . there was an obvious discrepancy between the capacity of the members for doing things together and their actual performance. This was confirmed by a comparison between co-operative potential and sociometric position."[i]

Probing of individual scores showed that the most responsible and influential position in the group was held by a girl he calls Irene. Irene actually resented the group and the group suffered from her leadership. It was the therapist's task to let Irene know that she was in a wrong position, to show her that this was in conflict with her real wish for the community or group, to work

(i) INFIELD I., *Co-operative College Papers, The Sociological Study of Co-operation*, Loughborough 1956, p. 46. To read the chapter on the human factor in R.I.B.A. 1965 report on Colloquia and Group Practices brings out the pertinence of Infield's approach well beyond education to professional groups.

well and to resign as a rational act subsequent to the scientific diagnosis of the situation. The group regarded this action highly and Irene immediately had more respect, love, etc., from the group. What is more, her action set a new standard of co-operativeness in the group.

In educreation, the involvement and the remedial actions may not be as complex or deep as those in a totally knit community such as a Kibutz. The practicability of examining working groups, together for a year's project, perhaps in this way, is very real, and the application for good results essential in most instances. In an atmosphere created by an educreational approach students would have therapeutic application to groups outside their own orbits of action quite frequently and not every bit of remedy would fall on the shoulders of the tutors.

IV.3.5. Group Psychotherapy

Group psychotherapy as described by Foulkes and Anthony[i] involves groups of varying kinds who meet together for the express purpose of therapy. Such groups should not include students who have to work together, and their relevance is to inter-departmental groups. This, indeed, should be a standard form of hygiene at any university. A number of such groups should be there for those who wish to participate, perhaps with tutor's, advice, under the guidance of qualified therapists.

"The most significant features which group-analytic psycho-therapy originally introduced are the following:

"1. That seven or eight members meet for one and a half hours, sitting in a circle together with the analyst.

"2. That no programme or directions are given, so that all contributions arise spontaneously from the patients.

"3. That all communications are treated as the equivalent on the part of the group of the free association of the individual

(i) FOULKES and ANTHONY, *Group Psychotherapy.*

under psycho-analytic conditions ('group association'). There is also a corresponding relaxation of censorship.

"4. That the therapist maintains throughout an attitude which corresponds to that of the psycho-analyst in the individual treatment situation. (Transference figure: helps to clarify and interpret content, process, behaviour, relationship).

"5. That all communications and relationships—which are of central importance for the therapeutic process and the analyst's therapeutic activities—are seen as part of a total field of inter-action: the group matrix.

"6. That all group members take an active part in the total therapeutic process."[i]

IV.3.6. Co-operation as the Therapeutic Factor

Yet another variation on the therapeutic theme is the groups which are formed to perform tasks and, by the very co-operation, needs are met and therapeutic tendencies activated.[ii]

The premise that social relations are a necessary aspect of life leads straight to the deduction that in a sick society the incapacity to associate with others leads to loneliness. And the job to be jointly undertaken gives the impetus for getting together. This aspect of therapy has its clearest demonstration in emergencies which give people the strong motive to co-operate and to come to life through it. The 1939–45 War brought this sort of thing in many ways, and it is this which makes folk nostalgically look back at times of stress. A co-operatively orientated course would fulfil this therapeutic function by its very nature (note the initiation ceremony, p. 242).

Enough has been quoted and described to show to the edu-creative tutor just how many possible therapeutic applications arise out of the new kind of teaching situation. Development of such techniques will be very widespread in the next few years, and

(i) FOULKES and ANTHONY, *Group Psychotherapy*, p. 28.
(ii) THELAN A. H., *Dynamics of Groups at Work*.

the training of tutors will, of course, include the therapeutic elements.

IV.3.7. Staff Involvement

A therapeutic course will make the tutor experience the truths involved and he learns to know himself and his weaknesses. From this the individual and proper application of each person according to his talents and capacities can more easily follow. Without this there is the obvious danger in messing around irresponsibly in a field that feeds many common neurotic traits— wish for power, control of other people—without a realization of this.

But one aspect is very reassuring: when a group is therapeutically involved the element of risk, the insurance against harmful personal influence of a misguided tutor, is far greater than in individual therapy.

At staff level, the therapeutic approach continues. One of the functions of staff meetings of tutors will be an exchange of therapeutic observation on the work of the school. The Head should be capable of resolving the problems that might beset a staff, such as those described by Infield with regard to the Kibutz. In the main, the help to one another in the process of educreation would be more the purpose of staff meetings than the organizational matters now discussed.

Many will be horror-struck by this very idea of bringing emotion and therapy into a staff room. But this merely points to the unsuitability as tutors (not necessarily as consultant teachers also) of those who react that way.

IV.4. INITIATION
IV.4.1. Functions of Initiation

Change of group loyalty is a crisis accompanied by energy mobilization.

Initiation is an ostentatious, deliberate attraction–fusion–liberation rhythm contrived to take advantage of the mobilized

I

energy. This experience then creates and ingrains a strong feeling of belonging. This applies even if it is a cruel procedure; but there is no need to rely on cruelty to make the deep impression. In many primitive cultures mutilation of the genitals was (and is) an expression of the emotional plague: a direct insurance that the young would not experience too much pleasure when they joined the adult class.

The stress on the gravity of joining, on the importance of realizing that joining means something, is general. It has got to be a considerable experience to fulfil its basic energetic purpose. As has been shown, the students' initiation rites had degenerated into almost pure sadism with rare exceptions. The function was to make all the little proud head prefects who had been kings of their schools into humble freshers. Now it is dying out, and with it the primary purpose—to give the feeling of belonging. Students now just ooze into school, as if it was nothing special.

With educreative concepts we can approach the subjects with a little more deliberate finesse. I will list some main functions which an initiation ceremony should fulfil:

(a) To give the individual a feeling of belonging, both to the group of freshers with whom he starts and to the school as a whole.
(b) To give the group of freshers identity.
(c) To make co-operative endeavour obviously the right thing.
(d) To include the hilarious, and have feast, fun and games.

To satisfy these requirements considerable tension must be built up, endurance expected and a far wider range of talent, and volume of work, demanded than any individual could manage. In fact, the tasks asked of the group should be related to the talents there might be known to exist in the group.

IV.4.2. Proposals

The idea suggested here does fulfil the functions listed. It is conceived to engage the capacities of as many students' talents as possible. (Note, for example, how the foreign student comes into his own with a translation.) It is designed to bring about that state of emergency which makes it easy for people to co-operate.

The freshers are asked to appear at an appointed place, in an extremely official and vital-sounding notice, at the said time, say 5 a.m. or 6 a.m. Landladies should be told they will be away that night. When the time comes each person is searched for food, cigarettes, books, etc. Male students are asked to remove their ties and female students all their make-up. This can be requested beforehand. Pretence has no part in this experience. Ties and make-up make puppets out of people. This they are told.

Late-comers are kept outside, are asked to write down, copiously, in note form, why they are late. They are told that the group, i.e. someone else, will have to produce a 5000-word statement on why they were late, going into biographical, psychological and characterological as well as technical details so that the notes must be extensive. Before he can enter, the group must ask for him, i.e. at least two hours after the commencement. Depending on what sort of a person the late-comer is, the waiting time can be filled in a judicious way. Whether he is the arrogant public school boy, the timid one, or a foreign girlie will make the difference. But the mystery of what is happening inside, the urgent need the group has of the individual, and the gravity of the disastrous unreliability, are the main points stressed.

The students, having been searched one by one, get inside the room where they are to spend at least the day together (it should not be an over-large room—the requirement for tolerance of working "on top of each other" is useful). Here they read the following official-sounding notice:

"See-co-th-Edu-Group Identity Project. (University Accept-ance Dept.).

"Before you, as a group, are accepted in the school of archi-tecture you must achieve identity as a group. You will therefore be kept in this room until you have dealt adequately with the problems posed, in the opinion of the 'select committee', which will receive work and is meeting at two-hourly intervals. They will give their judgement half an hour later. Work can be submitted in any sequence when deemed completed.

"All the resources in the room can be used.

"You are in contact with the outside world through a telephone. Only the wearer of the dress, specially designed and made by you for the purpose (to adequate standard), may address the select committee, having struck the gong five times. No person may address the select committee twice.

"Sooner or later you will realize that if you can co-operate you will be out sooner and in contact with food. The longest period so far taken to complete the tasks and endured by a fresher group, was four days two hours. Those with stamina carry on when those exhausted have to be removed.

"All the following tasks have to be completed to the satisfaction of the select committee before anyone from the group is allowed out:

"1. A name for the group must be coined bearing in mind the relevance of the year in world history.

"2. An original motto must be created, bearing in mind the need to humour the select committee, and the group, for the next seven years, and to eternity.

"3. Permanent, physical, symbolic embodiment of the occasion is demanded, including name and motto.

"4. A hymn to the glory of the group and the institution is to be composed. Both words and music must be original. Words must be translated into three other languages and the music written for at least the piano. The whole must be properly produced and bound.

"5. A drama depicting the fate of a student who was not accepted in the school is to be written and produced for the select committee, with scenery. Performance to begin and end with the singing of the hymn to a rich musical accompaniment.

"6. Each person has the following tasks to fulfil before anyone is allowed out:

"(a) To know the full name of everyone else in the group; on exit this will be required from everyone before anyone is allowed out.

"(b) To answer the questions deposited in the labelled, individual envelopes. This is a strictly private affair and no knowledge of questions or answers must be allowed to leak to any person. This is why you are supplied with invisible ink. Eat your question papers after you have completed your tasks. (You will be hungry enough ere long). Your names must be on the answer papers. Hand them via your spokesman to the committee when you have finished. The ink will be made visible by the select committee.[(i)]

"Questions:

"1. EXAMPLE: The flamboyant, orectic pilgrimage, of Richardson into the pityless architectural past, contributed more to the rigmarole of the monition of functionalism than the orgonomic if mithridatized theories of the crapulent therapists ever granted to the cumulative index of the behaviourists, resident in the fictional Walden II.

Question: Do you agree with this statement?

"2. EXAMPLE: Industrialized modulation of current epistemological concepts in the foundational sciences has demands to make from the increasing manpower of the economic constructional surplus (TEDDY) which surpass the Royal Institute of British Architects' and its President's and Council's fanfaronades on this theme or its panegyrized variations.

Question: Do you feel it is just that a Royal Institute ought to produce less surplus?

(i) In fact all the questions are exactly the same, highly pretentious but nonsensical. The invisible ink encourages a student to commit himself. Part of the festivities after is to read out the answers once it's known the questions were nonsense!

"3. EXAMPLE: Interplanetory interpenetration in cosmic spaceology has brought the archi-scientist face to face, metaphorically speaking, with his own front-door hinges. The question is, how much does now depend on the screws fixing the hinges (to speak literally)?

Question: Taking this figure of speech at its most ostentatious, comment on the space-time aspect of the critical path studies ushered into the repertoire of the constructivist philosophy, and indeed technology, in the last five-and-a-half years. Do you feel panification and osculation are here relevant? How?

"4. EXAMPLE: Purely from the practical point of view would you evaluate in order of preference, and from the point of view of the opposite sex, giving reasons, the following: prophylactic sheath (washable and not washable), total abstinence, Kraus-Ogino safe period, dutch cap (rubber large), greifenberg ring, dutch cap (gold small), contraceptive pill, withdrawal, self-control, as many conceptions as come.

"7. Write briefly, and, by God, honestly, your attitude to:

(a) You and air.
(b) You and food.
(c) You and sex.
(d) You and love.
(e) You and clothes.
(f) You and shelter.
(g) You and one other nation.
(h) You and education.
(i) You and the world as one.
(j) You and your parents.

"8. A minute-by-minute illustrated diary of events of the group from the moment you enter the room is essential; each person can add what he wishes beyond the central chronicle to be kept.

"9. All written work to be done on the sheets supplied or materials cut to the same size. (A4.)

"10. For those who have arrived late the group, not the person, has to provide a 5,000-word report on the person and his or her lateness."

The room should be furnished so that the students have much chance for improvization. A chemical lavatory or two ought to be provided behind screens or partitions so that no one leaves the room. To heighten the fun and tension the rooms could be without daylight and the light might be made to fail occasionally. A telephone should be provided but there is no reason why the exchange should not be bedevilled at times! There should be no clock (via telephone only). A typewriter and a piano should also be provided. It would, of course, be wonderful fun to have one-way vision of the group through windows or mirrors.

Tools, instruments, raw materials like rolls of brown paper and corrugated cardboard, paints, wood, etc. etc., should be provided *ad lib*. Food ought to be stored in secret places, and dictionaries or other useful books which would be shown only afterwards, unless the students looked very thoroughly and found them.

Only water should be provided—no food, which is an incentive! A first-aid kit should be there (it heightens tension if ostentatious).

How long the whole performance lasts, what extra difficulties are introduced and how often work is rejected as sub-standard, depend on individual circumstances and the art of governing the whole thing.

Ideally, the rag should be followed by a celebration feast of the whole school, and by an exposition on how the thing could have been done very much more efficiently by skilled co-operation and planning. Further, reading out the answers given to questions should make a fitting ending to the procedure.

The creations of the project are, of course, ceremoniously installed, blessed, or whatever architectural students might devise.

This outline of what a deliberately designed framework for a rag might be, will, I hope, attract student bodies to have fun to good purpose and use their imagination and their art to enrich and develop this kind of idea.

There is a real need and function for initiation. As shown, it can be done without relying on fear, the cowing of frightened freshers and the indulgence of power complexes and sadistic outlets. If the criteria and the real functions of the occasion are borne in mind, it can be, educreationally speaking, a very valuable, considerably enriching, gorgeously frivolous occasion—something that really fuses new students with the school, and liberating their energies as part of it.

IV.5. PRIMARY AWARENESS STUDIES

General points:

The initiation of students and placing them into common, friendly, group-spaces, with others at various advanced levels, loosens up servile school attitudes. The awareness studies continue this process, but do much else. They should be designed to shock the student awake, infect and involve him with the enthusiasm of the school, make him brilliantly conscious of the responsibilities, possibilities and scope of his education.

A first term spent in this educreational way will have a powerful therapeutic effect and trigger off emotional reactions and outbursts. The tutor has a key position. Energies are liberated to tackle the fundamental emotional problems that arise when areas of life and aspiration, long dormant, are reactivated. Anxieties can effectively be shared and wonder heightened by joint action and experience.

During this time the student makes enormous advances, but these are in the development of his personality. Where work is produced this must be independent of any kind of marking or other comparative assessment that may make him associate his activities with the authoritarian educational pattern from which he is only just emerging. He must be allowed freedom to idle, a reaction essential for many a schoolchild before work is desired for its own sake, motivated by the desire to find out, to master a skill through sheer curiosity.

It may be said that presumed participation in awareness studies implies the very compulsion that educreation tries to eliminate. The secondary truth that applies here is this: in spite of telling students they don't have to take part, the fresher is likely to; still under the spell of school, used to being told what to do next, he is curious and has genuine interest in learning.

During the awareness studies relevant lectures by consultants might well be taking place—for the voluntary attendance of anyone in the school who is interested. Further, all students should be free to attend any lecture they choose.

Once he begins to have the strength and independence to opt out, this has to be used therapeutically by the tutor. It can either be a rational action (if, indeed, he has better things to do), or as an irrational defence (not "lazy" or "bad"), as missing something that he might enjoy and use to very good effect in his development. An explanation of his likely hate for learning and school work should be added. The response to this might well be an emotional outburst; a sign that the curative, enlivening process is at work.

Awareness is the keyword. Every sensory path is involved. Not just intellect nor just emotion, but both—as aspects of a unitary energy economy of the whole personality.

Many of the studies, particularly at first, are aimed to expose shallowness or artificiality of the student's normal reaction. They have a game-like nature which encourages participation, and a surprise element involving humour or insight. They must not degenerate into a parlour game—even if therapeutic—because some of those participating will not require any therapy. So they must have intrinsic value in practising a skill, acquiring knowledge or know-how. But at this stage awareness comes first—success in the pursuit, which is the vehicle, is of secondary relevance, and the tutor shows this to the student.

"Thought is born of failure."[i] This spells a basic right in the

(i) WHYTE L. L., *The Next Development in Man*, London 1944.

development of students. They must be allowed to make mistakes and encouraged to commit themselves, without fear of judgement, without the noose of "fear of failure" tightening round their necks with each discovered error. Fear of failure is a terrible and common deterrent to creative work. It is worth trying hard to tackle it in the first term.

During the first term, ideally, a student should be engaged very intently for some periods. He should also have lots of time to find his way about, engage himself therapeutically and explore the many new avenues open to him. Lecture courses and didactic work should not occur in any form beyond the strictly inspirational and such as might deal with aspects of methodology. Seminars, free group discussions are, of course, an indigenous part of the awareness studies.

The examples which follow are some of an innumerable variety of awareness exercises that can be thought up by the teachers of the future. I don't claim they are the best, but they have been designed to fulfil specific functions. These are stated at the outset and must be borne in mind. One can easily lose the point, when one's imagination is active, and confuse one's own needs as a student with those of today. Again, the "awareness" aspect can get lost. This has, in fact happened severally to my structural awareness studies. The idea was first published[i] in 1953, and having been adapted here and there by many schools in the English-speaking world, I have had the idea explained to me (!) in some schools and noted the complete absence of the original "awareness" context, though the origin of the idea was clear.

Some of the awareness studies are best run by tutors, some with help from fellow students, always easy in the group system. Small groups are good, but tutors may combine, or the year work as a whole with tutors variously engaged. The awareness studies are advertised on the work-progress charts, and participants take their choice.

(i) RITTER P., Testing of Model Beams, *A. & B. N.*, April 9, 1953.

The examples are given partly in the form in which they might be handed out to students, as "programmes" have been handed out in schools of architecture for a long time. Much more of the function is explained than is customary. From the beginning the student realizes that the programme is to be examined critically, not just accepted as "authoritative" pronouncement.

The tone of communication should place the ball into the student's court again and again. The help in co-operation takes the place of continual teacher orientation. Questions such as "What do you want us to do now?," "How shall I do it, Sir?," should be used to make the student aware of

(a) Missing an opportunity in not thinking for himself or with his fellow students.

(b) That his question is useful only if either he says what he wants, or seeks advice on his criteria for wanting to do something or inspiration on how it can best be achieved.

The importance of formulating the question (the brief, the definition, the problem, the frame of reference) before tackling any solution should be brought home to the student whenever possible. After all, a brilliant question or formulation of a problem is as exciting as any other aspect of problem solving. It's just that education has been concerned with answers only, for centuries.

IV.5.1. Critical Faculties—Do I still think?

(a) *Critical faculties awareness lecture*

Aim: to indicate to the student that, unlike at school, he is responsible for himself, that his elders and teachers must not be blindly regarded as authorities.

A supposedly, or actually, famous lecturer is invited and carefully announced as a particularly wise and important if slightly abstruse kind of chap. This carefully chosen and briefed person addresses the students for at least two hours with long meaningless sentences of unmitigated but highly intellectual sounding rubbish.

To the senior students present it should be amusing. Their presence reinforces the freshers' tendency to regard it not as nonsense but "above him".

Questions should be put to students immediately afterwards so that they commit themselves on paper to being intelligent about nonsense. (Seniors can pretend to fill in the answers to egg on the gullibility of the freshers.) Before much longer they are told that they have been listening to sheer twaddle and left to stew in their own realizations as the older students walk out.

This will encourage students to use their critical faculties and to ask when they lose the trend of an argument in a lecture or seminar: a vital lesson.

(If you are wicked and know a lecturer who needs to have his wits sharpened, and who is abstruse, you invite him a little later making it seem as if this was a similar exercise, letting it "leak" to the students. This can have salutary effects on both sides!)

I had experience of this kind of thing when it was done as a students' rag at Liverpool. In 1943 there was a large first year at the School of Architecture and very few seniors. This would have made the usual violent goings on a little dangerous for the seniors (Liverpool always had a large Irish influx). So, ingenious as ever, and with splendid actors about, it was a fine way of ragging freshers.

An alternative to the above is to give out a nonsensical programme such as shown below. This will be effective only if the fellow students co-operate and help the freshers on to commit all sorts of daft things to paper, stupidly believing advice merely because it comes from those who are older.

EXAMPLE: "Design a new city today, giving particular attention to water supply, drainage, pedestrian and motor traffic, public transport, elevational treatment, height restrictions, the colour problem, site treatment, the position of offices, cemeteries, undertakers, sports fields, hospitals, school systems, museums and the architectural continuity of the past styles of Bulgaria, where the city is sited."

It is also a good exercise to turn the tables on the new student; hitherto, everyone will have asked him why he wants to be an architect, will have told him all about the possibilities of being an architect, and so on.

To exercise his mind in the opposite direction will enliven his critical faculties. The programme would read thus:

"You are to assume that you have been fooling one and all that you want to be an architect because a legacy of £100,000 was conditional on this. You now find that it is in fact exactly the opposite and you have to find good reasons for not becoming an architect, and convince the university authorities and the trustees."

IV.5.2. Staff Introduction—"Who are the staff?"

Who are the staff?

Aims:

> to allow each teacher to introduce himself to the students;
> to show what expertise is to be found where, so the staff may be used in an efficient way;
> to show the student with whose philosophy or attitude to education he has affinity, and where he might expect empathy;
> to show that there are a variety of points of view on most matters, including the subjects of study;
> to indicate that the relationship between staff and student is not a school-type. The introduction suggests consideration of the student, and the deliberate effort to form a good working relationship;
> to allow the student to express preference intelligently in whose group he would like to be.

Possible methods:

(a) Formal lecture with questions and discussion.
(b) Informal talk.

(c) Providing published works by tutor, or references, for the students to peruse, with subsequent questions and discussion.

(d) Visit to tutor's work on site, and exposition of working method and views, with discussion.[i]

There is, of course, no reason why students of other years should not attend the introductions. It is a matter of recognizing that serious discussion of members of staff and their work is useful.[ii]

The time taken for the introduction and discussion is not likely to be less than half a day, and where the time is available, a day may suit some staff better.

It may be argued that it is not right to expect staff to make really personal contact. The answer is that given a therapeutic attitude to education, the core of tutorial staff, as previously described, must be capable of such contact with their students to do their job. If this is impossible for them it means they should teach only as "subject consultants" or not at all.

An example: There was no such introduction at Nottingham, and I made it my business to give the first year some idea of the particular usefulness they might find in the various members of staff. With that highly English vice of mock-modesty, which is really a matter of keeping others in ignorance about things they ought to know, a student might miss much that is good.

Again, because no one else talked to the students about orientation in broader than architectural aspects, I spoke to them in a series of ten lectures on Values. This was nominally the introduction to "Theory and Practice of Building", and there was pressure on the head by the staff to stop me giving "lectures on free love". Always the same old smear!

(i) In each case a discussion within the student group (of all years) should follow.
(ii) It is a suitable time to indicate change in ideas and the development of one's work year by year.

Titles of books and references were given to the students.[i] I don't think many followed the references. Those who did, did it avidly. And many more discussed and spoke on the subjects raised. None forgot that to think in terms of values—quality rather than quantity or virtues—was a possibility. The information below was given to the students beforehand:

"Freedom from hunger, from fear, of speech, for education, of worship and freedom to work. These are basic aims not fulfilled by far. But in the bio-technic era (Lewis Mumford) we go beyond these to more positive values and qualitative aims.

"1. The world we live in.
Ref.: (*The Culture of Cities*, London 1939, *The Condition of Man*, London 1937, both Mumford).

"2. Healthy food (in contrast to many processes which spoil it).
Ref.: (*The Living Soil*, E. B. Balfour, London 1943).[ii]

"3. Healthy air (not foul city fumes).
Ref.: (World Health, *W.H.O. Journal*, Geneva, May 1961).

"4. Healthy love (in contrast to our masochist-sadist ambivalance).
Ref.: (*The Origins of Love and Hate*, I. D. Suttie, 1935, Penguin 1960; *The Function of the Orgasm*, W. Reich, New York 1948).

"5. Healthy community (instead of the tight family).
Ref.: *Sociological Study of Co-operation*, H. Infield, Loughborough 1956; *Mutual Aid*, Kropotkin, P. London 1910).

"6. Healthy development (instead of Victorian "knowledge" and virtue education).
Ref.: (*Summerhill*, A. S. Neill, London 1962; *The Free Family*, Paul and Jean Ritter 1959).

(i) It should be added that the books were at least brought into the lecture room so the students saw them, but they could not borrow them. (Guess why?)
(ii) The lecture on healthy food resulted in bread-baking classes on demand in my house (the students having tasted samples of the bread and told of the simplicity of the recipe).

"7. Healthy work (instead of hated work—longed for "free time").

Ref.: (*Fear of Freedom*, E. Fromm, 1954).

"8. Healthy spiritual development (not moralized, organized doctrine).

Ref.: (*Ether, God and Devil*, New York 1949, *The Murder of Christ*, New York 1953, both W. Reich; *The Man Who Died*, D. H. Lawrence; *The Next Development in Man*, L. L. Whyte, 1944).

"9. Healthy environment, architecture, homes, communities, towns to enhance all above (not narrow "scientific" functionalism on the present mechanistic basis).

Ref.: (*The Expanding Environment*, E. A. Gutkind, Freedom Press 1953; for excellent discussion of ideas of many people on architecture, *A.J.*, June 2, 1949).

"10. How organised education may lead to the above.

Ref.: (*Aims in Education*, A. N. Whitehead, New York 1949)."

Today, I would add these items:

Refs.: World Design Decade Phase I (1963), Document 1, Inventory of World Resources, Human Trends and Needs; World Design Decade Phase I (1964) Document 2. *The Design Initiative*. Both Southern Illinois University, Carbondale, Illinois, U.S.A.

If a number of lecturers introduced themselves and gave leads in terms of bibliographies and what they believed, such a ten-lecture course would not be necessary unless it had virtue as an inspirational course.

IV.5.3. Architecture—What have I begun?

Awareness study 3. Duration, perhaps one week.

Aims: To bring the student face to face with the multiple enormity of the phenomena now relevant to him; to indicate how orientation through purpose and classification of knowledge is valuable in defining fields of interest and areas of relevant ignorance; to show usefulness in sharing his gains (co-operation) with other new students; to give introduction to techniques of work and communication.

Method: A number of themes are displayed and it is indicated that each student can choose that which attracts him most. Those who have chosen the same programme represent groups. They are born of a common interest or purpose. A real reason for working together. Examples of four themes:

PROGRAMME 1. Assess the various kinds and quantities of buildings to be erected in England in the coming year. Relate this to the number of registered architects in the country and discover what proportion is likely to be designed by architects. Write a brief report of method of work and findings.

PROGRAMME 2. Attempt to design a classification which will allow the cataloging of all literature on architectural and allied subjects. Compare this critically with the S.F.B. classification in the Building Manual of the R.I.B.A. Sort out one journal with S.F.B. classification marked on its items and one without. Report in writing on the possibilities and difficulties of filing.

PROGRAMME 3. List all the features in the environment of the room you live in; from the position of your top shirt collar button to the effects of sunshine. List and note which aspects are under your control and which are not. Report and recommend on ways of improving your environment.

PROGRAMME 4. Report on the organization of the architectural profession, its policies and means of expression.

There is no reason why other themes and other groups of individuals should not emerge spontaneously. Each group should record their results for permanent record and easy reproduction.

To give students some idea of a possible work pattern a time-table is suggested. Time-tabling is introduced as administration to maximize possible participation.

Like the initiation, this would appear on the work-progress chart in the area concerning all first-year students. Students would enter their choice (or abstention) into their own diary spaces. (This pattern would follow in all the studies.) Announcements to the year or the school about each group would go by the chairman's diary.

Suggested time-table

Monday: Decide by 11 a.m. your interest and sign your name in the relevant column.

11 a.m.—meeting of group—election of chairman—decide on procedure—staff advise only after students' decisions have been made.

Say, Monday noon until Wednesday noon: Development of work.

Say, Wednesday 2 p.m.: Groups meet to collate material, organize report production and produce it.

Say, Thursday 2 p.m.: The four reports are presented in manner deemed suitable by group to the rest of the "year". Discussions and report should include reference to work methods as well as content; sharing experience as well as knowledge with others. Chairman for meeting from students. Tutors present for their own study at least. If possible for whole period as this is the crucial beginning.

Say, Friday 2 p.m.: Tutors comment on work method and content in seminar. Remarks will be constructive only; comment on comparative worth of finished result will be out of order—tutor to be chairman.

6 p.m.—celebration of achievement. Formal handing over of reports to library (those who wish to have copies should be able to reproduce them themselves at a later date).

Improvements of time-table should be made or suggested at a useful early date—and carefully communicated.

The arrangements of similar short-range work schedules becomes a matter of course for each study. Student initiative should bring them about. (Students may have to experience chaos first!)

IV.5.4. Design Skill—"As easy as falling off a bicycle"

Awareness study.

Duration one day. Best carried out by tutors (one hour per student). Free discussion seminar follows this.

This is the most profoundly important study of all. Design is here defined as "the skill to arrange to advantage preliminary to execution".

". . . there is less difference between their outlines of thinking and bicycle-riding than our self-esteem would make us believe. Both are governed by implicit codes of which we are only dimly aware, and which we are unable to specify."[i]

"Skill"—capacity for complex behaviour which does not lend itself to intellectual analysis (like riding a bicycle);

"To arrange"—compose in a preferred manner;

"To advantage"—to satisfy specific functions;

"Execution"—realization in concrete form.

Aims: To allow a student to become aware of the meaning of "arrange" and "arrange to advantage", and to gain vivid insight by direct experience into aspects of the design skill, where intellectual analysis is precluded; to allow the student to become clearly aware of the nature and the usefulness of aids in design.

This exercise depends on surprise for its impact, so beyond the title and the time the students should not be given any information. (The environment should be plain—no paper, pencils, models, etc., should lie about.)

STAGE 1. Ask the student to compose in his mind's eye six short hexagonal tubes with one end closed (better shapes will no doubt emerge). When after a minute or two he says he has done this, ask him to draw it giving pencil and paper.

(i) KOESTLER A., *The Act of Creation*, p. 44.

Lesson 1. Limitations of one's imagination. When the student tries to draw what he has imagined, it is usually either impossible or different from that which he thought he had in his mind.

STAGE 2. Ask the student to draw what he now considers to be his preferred arrangement.

Lesson 2. Immediately point out how pencil and paper prove a design aid. They talk back and allow you to develop ideas by replying with further lines. No need to finish or comment on drawing.

STAGE 3. Hand the students models of the six hexagonal tubes closed one end. (These, like the pencils and papers, have, of course, been out of sight!) Ask the students to arrange models to their now preferred arrangements.

Lesson 3. Relief at seeing something concrete. Point out models are a more vivid and a simpler design aid than pencil and paper. Design aids really aid design.

STAGE 4. Ask students now to arrange six models i.e. to their liking *and* so they would catch the maximum of water.

Lesson 4. As decisive as lightning and obvious as thunder, the integrated functional element in architectural design (coming after the first four stages) strikes the student once and for always.

STAGE 5. Ask the students how to arrange the hexagonal pipes to catch the maximum of water and so that the outlet pipes leading to one common pipe are as short as possible.

Lesson 5. Services in buildings! (A student may be offered or ask for pencil and paper again, showing advantages of that aid in abstracting.)

STAGE 6. Ask the students to arrange the six models as if they were timber, to be lined with lead, to create as much water holding volume as is possible.

Lesson 6. By composing six volumes, without further material, a seventh can be created. Economy. Structure and finish.

STAGE 7. Imagine the hexagon models are concrete tanks closed on all sides. They now need only to store, not catch, water. Outlet not to be considered, but minimum of ground surface should be covered.

Lesson 7. The vertical element in building—the site—density—ground use.

The students are shown that the skill of design includes the simultaneous application of the economic, functional, aesthetic, and constructional aspects, just as riding a bicycle entails balancing, steering, pedalling, braking, at the same time. This, better than anything else, shows the need for practice.

It is absolutely essential not to comment at any stage on the quality of the student's solutions but to stick to the awareness lessons. He expects again and again that you will "judge" his solution; the force of your comments, the strength of the awareness lies in part in the unexpected observation of the tutor and his disinterest in any marking or judging.

This awareness study has been tried. The "eureka" look, on the student, convinced the several onlookers, educational and design experts, that this was a powerful experience. Even merely to relate this study to older students or architects, as I have now done in many small and large groups, makes some realize vividly what had been left hidden in their own training.

IV.5.5. Motives—"Why are we here?"

Duration one week (two days for statements, three for discussion).

Aims: To bring out into the open students' motives for studying architecture, to bring an honest attitude and better understanding between students, and between staff and students.

In schools of architecture in the past, fresh students were asked to write an essay on "Why I want to be an architect". A collection of more or less polished hypocrisy was the result. The sincere soul was not encouraged.

As a newcomer you can hardly be expected to trust your teachers enough to write "because my mother bullied me", even if you realize it, and expect not to suffer for it one way or another.

So you are asked to report sincerely, anonymously, if you wish, and concisely, to the best of your ability why you think you find yourself at the beginning of this course. All submissions will be typed so that they are identical in form.

No essays, please, unless you especially wish. They are a complicated and sophisticated art form quite unsuitable for many purposes where, for purely traditional reasons, they are now deemed right, without the matter being given a rational thought.

Groups of students in free seminars will discuss the various reasons, backgrounds and possibilities. Those who feel sufficiently secure can associate themselves with their descriptions.[i]

IV.5.6. Anatomy of Judgement—"Are you sure? Pity we are so sure!"

The name of this study is taken from Dr. Abercrombie's book which is so valuable, short and clear that every tutor and later student will have read and re-read it. Whereas the book implies how teaching techniques in general can be influenced by her findings, the awareness study is designed to jolt the student out of the comfortable, smug highly subjective and limited little world that limits his work and clear perception.[ii]

(i) Notes for tutor: A surprisingly large number will do so as trust is gained and the obvious help of having others understand and share their plight is noted. Unconsciously or consciously, dishonest accounts can be the basis for a group therapeutic approach. Those with similar problems might get together and ask a tutor's help. Those who strut about pretending they want to build a better world, though nothing could be further from their minds, and those who cynically say they are only in it for the money or the cushy job, or because they could not get into anything else, can all be "nursed" to a fuller and more opportune attitude to their life.

(ii) See also CRAWSHAY-WILLIAMS R., *Comforts of Unreason.*

Abercrombie's "argument", given at the end of her book is worth quoting as a suitable introduction to the seminars following on the awareness exercises:

"The argument of this book runs as follows. In receiving information from a given stimulus pattern we select from the total amount of information available (that is, from the complex of the stimulus pattern in its context) and from our own store of information. The receipt of information therefore involves making a judgement, but in many cases (as for instance in seeing familiar things) this is done so rapidly and automatically that we are unaware of the extent of our personal involvement in the act, tending to regard the information as given. In such cases we might obtain more valid information if we could consider alternative selections from the information available.

"Many factors of which we are unconscious influence our judgements, both in cases where we are not aware of making any (as in seeing) and in those where we are (as in evaluating evidence from an experiment). It is postulated that we might make more valid judgements if we could become conscious of some of these factors. A situation (free group discussion) is described in which alternative judgements of the same stimulus pattern are discussed, and some of the factors influencing the judgements become apparent. The validity of the contribution of the various factors can then be assessed. The results of a test support the hypothesis that judgement is improved after this experience."[i]

EXAMPLE 1. (Day session): Awareness of the influence of "what they say".

Let the student body look at a prepared and mounted series of photographs showing on the one side buildings by celebrated architects and on the other work by unknown people.

Ask the student body to make comparative comments on these two parallel series. Having collected the comments you announce that, unfortunately, the names were reversed!

And then the awareness seminar begins by reading the com-

(i) ABERCROMBIE M. L. J., *The Anatomy of Judgement*, London 1960, p. 142.

ments and noting their validity in the light of the new information. "They say—What they say?—let them say!" (Bernard Shaw.)

Famous architects are, of course, only one example. Other fields where this technique is obviously applicable are literature, stained glass, music, painting, landscape, design, and, of course, one can also combine various fields. (It is a sobering experience to walk romantically in the country, admire a gorgeous white flower from afar—and then find it's a bit of rubbish someone has thrown away!)

A variation on the above theme is to find genuinely inferior products of famous artists and superior works of nonentities. The tutor then backs the judgements of the students on the basis of "everybody silly sometimes".[i]

Another worthwhile variation makes the student see the emotional involvement and shows him that his tutor is aware of it also. The recipe runs as follows: select a little known "indecent" painting by a famous painter (Picasso, Courbet, etc.) and a Victorian nude but very arty "decent" counterpart. After comparative comments by the students the free discussion seminar will elicit worthwhile clarification in many students' minds relating to art and sex.[ii]

Sir Kenneth Clark's *The Nude*[iii] is highly relevant reading. He maintains that there is an erotic element in genuine appreciation of any nude.

EXAMPLE 2. (Half-day session or day session.) This can involve any of the simple or complex devises evolved by Gestalt and perception psychologists, and reproduced in such books as E. H. Gombrich's *Art and Illusion*,[iv] Jane Abercrombie's *The Anatomy of Judgement*, or textbooks of perception psychology.[v]

(i) Author's family motto.
(ii) It seems astonishing that the fifteen-year-old student gets plonked in front of a nude live model expected to get on with it without any sort of emotional preparation.
(iii) Pelican Book.
(iv) New York 1960.
(v) Illustrated in *The Anatomy of Judgement*, opp. p. 43.

Two lines which seem to be of different lengths merely because the arrows at the ends face opposite ways are the simplest example. Direct experience in terms of two similar bananas laid parallel, where the inside one always looks the bigger, is useful, for this activates the childhood memories of most of us: the fear of having the smaller one.

The most ambitious experiments are in terms of the scale model or full-size mock-up of a room, where the perspective is so falsified that the most astonishingly grotesque illusions occur.[i]

The variations on this theme are endless and an imaginative tutor can improvize in many ways.

Given the basic principles of Gestalt and Ground relationship in a lecture, the students might even devise original applications for their entertainment and enlightenment.

EXAMPLE 3: Comforts of unreason and emotional deadness.

From Crawshay-William's book specifically and the work of psycho-analysis generally, there arise clear views of blocked senses and perception, and, of course, the analyst and Crawshay-Williams show these weaknesses also. For architectural students the following exercises might be particularly stimulating:

(a) Ask students to try to remember what any of the buildings on the street outside look like. This illustrates how select-ively we see.

(b) A student could be asked to write a hundred words on a subject he feels strongly about. A free discussion group could note how his prejudices are reflected in his statement. To quote from John Locke might be a good introduction to the seminar.[ii]

EXAMPLE 4: Phoning or writing letters. Discussing the nature of aversion to become aware. If you don't like phoning or writing, do you find a reason why phoning is not a good idea? It is as well to be clearly aware of such weaknesses; they have remarkably far-reaching effects.

(i) See also NOBLE J., Social Psychology, *A.J.*, March 6, 1965.
(ii) *Essay concerning Humane Understanding*, originally published 1690.

EXAMPLE 5: Some questions can throw light on the variety of culture patterns represented in the years. Answer the following questions briefly. Then hold a free discussion seminar.

(a) A mother hits her child of nine; a child of nine hits his mother. Which action would you condone more easily?

(b) "Love your neighbour as yourself." Is this a uniquely Christian aim or virtue? (It is, in fact, also in the Old Testament.)

IV.5.7. Communication—To each his own

Aim: To make students aware of the wealth of choice and need for choice in communication.

From the awareness that drawings talk back to you, it's an easy step to realize the drawings talk to other people. The whole field of communication should be conceived as one where basic thinking pays at all stages. In other words, if you are feeding information to a computer the nature of the computer has to be borne in mind. And if you are sending a form into a planning authority, the function and nature of that, too, and so on, a very long list of different lines of communication demanding "design" process and skill for their proper execution. The relationship determines the nature of the effective relation, not unnaturally!

So an awareness study might be:

Design the passing of the following information to:

1. The builder, and a fellow architect concerned with the design.
2. An old workman.
3. A harassed housewife of twenty-five with seven children (an actual example).
4. An old, old maid.
5. Yourself, for clearer thinking of the solution to the problem.
6. The planning authority and the health department.
7. The education officer.
8. The local newspaper.
9. Record on a punch card with many similar items.

Each student picks one and presents his result in seminar. The critic acts the part of the person who has to be persuaded, or the computer to be fed.

"Information:

"Something will have to be done about the architectural fashion of providing 'crinkly' at ground-floor level in the Square because the result of using these recesses for urinating are found there every morning, and offend the public.

"You, in the interest of a client who is also building there, have been asked to influence people coming under the preceding headings and are to devise effective communication so that they are sure to vote or influence against more 'crinkly' along the same street. It is obvious that truth is merely a rare form of expression in public life and your design would seem to adopt judiciously to the various secondary truths but maximize the effect by the manner of your communication, which will in each case be private."

The various safeguards against behaving in the normal manner, i.e. scientific method, learning to look and to feel, not minding being wrong and against public opinion, finding out why one is all these things, should be explained by tutors if they don't crop up. To admit ignorance or inability, to decide with insufficient knowledge, evidence or feeling, must become normal and expected. If decisions made on weak bases are challenged it is worthwhile to retract and examine one's motives instead of arguing to defend the judgement.

IV.5.8. Structural Awareness Studies—Forces fight form and materials

The idea of using structural models for teaching purposes in the awareness sense was pioneered eight weeks after I started teaching at Nottingham in 1952. I was utterly frustrated at having myself learnt so little about structure and thought hard to find a solution for the students I was to teach. The early, dramatically successful experimental runs (even the lecturers and the Head were laying bets on which beam would be best) were dampened down by staff fear of enthusiasm and the inability to see the relevance beyond the sheer fun which, it was thought, was all right maybe once every few years. However, the results were published[i] and my experiments went on[ii] year by year, hounded from room to room by senior staff, and I was feeling guilty because students were keen and enjoyed what they were doing!

However, some years later the A.A. put on a whole course based on the idea independently developed by Lisborg.[iii]

In Nottingham, the first-year students of the Engineering Department, at the wish of the professor, have joined in some of these exercises since 1962, and I believe we made history in producing the first joint project for the first years of these two professions. Those who said that this was impossible (before it happened) were partly so sure because the School of Architecture was, of course, still part of the City College of Art and Crafts at the time. However, where there is a will (and co-operation) there is a way.

Today, many schools in the English-speaking world and beyond are using the idea. But herein lies a lesson. The awareness which is crucial to the whole idea, has frequently disappeared as an aim, and only so much rather meaningless sophisticated high jinks remain. And, of course, the results get marked.

Aims: To give direct experience of the nature of materials, and form in structure, prior to mathematical appreciation and teaching of formulae.

Method: By loading to breaking, with primitive methods, structures most of which he has himself designed and built, the student learns to feel for structure. The fact that it is his own work makes all its shortcomings and its behaviour far more vivid than the testing of standard structural members by sophisticated machines. Materials not normally deemed as structural, like chocolate or an eggshell, are effective just because their use in unfamiliar context increases awareness. The series of studies

(i) *Architect and Building News*, London April 8, 1953.
(ii) *Architecture and Building, London*, May 1960; *Architects' Journal, London*, October 18, 1961.
(iii) *A.A. Journal, London*, January 1960.

given in this book were worked out to cover the essential aspect of structures.

In writing short reports for seminar discussions, students are specifically reminded not to bother with a straight report as if describing a physics experiment at school. They should instead provide some individual comment, however naïve, on their awareness, and regard this as the first page or two of a loose-leaf book on the subject for adding to throughout their studies—or, indeed, their professional lives.

Taking a view of structures which is in sympathy with this approach are two books which should be freely available to the student. Preferably, he should possess both.[i]

In the studies described relevant references to in the Lisborg book are given in each case. The American book is beautifully produced and has exceptionally fine, clear diagrams. In fact, it has so much empty space in it that it could be adapted as a "cobo" (contribution book) for the student's notes, comments and references.

STRUCTURE STUDY 1. Natural forms.

Aim: Awareness of strength of forms and economy of nature.

Procedure: Without introduction a strong student with a large hand and courage is given an egg to crush, applying even, all-round pressure. For several reasons he ought to take off his jacket and roll up his shirt sleeves. If lucky, the man's muscles will swell. The egg will virtually explode in all directions. The drama of the occasion is of educational value.[ii]

(i) LISBORG N., *Principles of Structural Design*, London 1961; SALVADORI and KELLER, *Structure in Architecture*, London 1963.

(ii) When I visited Prof. Cowan's famous laboratories in Sydney he pointed out a machine designed to break egg-shells. "We empty the eggs first, of course", he said laughingly. I know his enlightened attitude to education so I described how we did it in Nottingham and asked him whether he thought that was the better way of teaching the lesson. "Of course", he said, "but how could I mess up the lab. walls?" Administration, or the cleaners, once again dictating the educational process! Even so, to break an egg one can always go outside. Plenty of room at Sydney University! The direct experience is vital.

The seminars dealing with this subsequently would deal with the affinity of architectural forms, and materials, of the relative force of the fist and the weight of the shell, the weakness of the shell to other forces. Fuller's work and many other interests can take this as a starting point for individual study.[i]

STRUCTURE STUDY 2. Materials.

Demonstration: Heat simultaneously three similar bars of chocolate carrying a similar load with a similar source of heat (birthday-cake candle I found useful), one bar fully wrapped, one bar fully wrapped in foil the other not (see illustrations).

Seminar points: Ways of breaking, visiostatic and non-visiostatic tension, compression (bending), shear (torsion) fire and fire resistance by use of second material. References: Lisborg, pp. 164–7, 262, 299, 324, 354.

Report: Personal comment.

STRUCTURE STUDY 3. Combination of materials.

Design for test: Two plaster beams cross-section $\frac{1}{2}$ x 1 x 14 in., one of them with thin brass wire reinforcement to be specified, one without. Plaster mix to be the same for both. The above cross-section is a maximum. Plaster may be reduced to a lesser dimension or holes or dents carved, or cast, to achieve the maximum self weight–load carried-ratio. Fourteen-inch length is fixed. Load to be hung, as point load from 1 in. wide webbing strip at the centre of the beam.

Seminar points: Structural combination of materials against tension and compression; chemical combination; resistance to forces; fire or water; nature of failure of beams; reinforced concrete. References: Lisborg, pp. 178, 181.

Report: Personal comment.[ii]

(i) McHALE J., *Buckminster Fuller*, New York 1962; also World Design Decade 1965–1975, Phase I (1964), Document 2, *The Design Initiative*, Illinois 1964. PETTIGREW J. B., *Design in Nature*, London 1908.
(ii) If the wire is gauged rightly some beams fail in tension and some in compression, very useful object lesson. Casting of the beams should be done a day prior to testing if heat for drying is available. Otherwise—and this is better—more time should be allowed for "curing".

STRUCTURE STUDY 4. Forces.

Design to test: Build a model beam or truss to span 2 ft 6 in., clear span 2 ft 4 in., maximum depth of beam 2 in., maximum width 1 in. The criterion of worth of the beam is the ratio of self-weight to load carried. The model is to be built of timber as specified and Balsa cement. The load will be applied by a 1 in. wide loop of webbing, girding the truss or beam, to suspend from it a concentrated load in the centre (see illustration).

Seminar points: Tension, compression (bending) shear (torsion) kinds of shear, determining what forces shall be encountered; forms in structure. References: Lisborg, pp. 4–16, 32–35.

Report: Personal comment.

STRUCTURE STUDY 5. Forms.

Design for test: With one sheet of typing paper and glue, to be specified, make the tallest possible free standing structure capable of supporting a 6 lb. brick. The brick will be put on a thin piece of plywood to allow careful placing. Wind will be excluded.

Seminar points: Forms for compression (hyperboli), forms for tension, for bending, stressed skins, pinned arches, direction of forces, stability. References: Lisborg, pp. 20–27, 45–52, 27–28; *Architects' Journal*, March 3, 1949; Samuely, Force and Form— *R.I.B.A. Journal*, March 1952; Samuely, *Space Frames and Stressed Skins.*

Report: Personal comment.

STRUCTURE STUDY 6. Stability.

Design for test: Repeat materials and test as before with the following variation: wind will be simulated by strongest possible blowing from student body from a distance of not less than 2 ft.

Seminar points: Wind force, bracing, triangulation, three supports or four, connections and continuity. Reference: Lisborg, pp. 20–21.

Report: Personal comment.

STRUCTURE STUDY 7.   Continuity.   Three dimensions.

Design for test: Prepare direction for a design which will be built by another student for the test, without your aid; given a piece of timber 2 ft long and 3 in. wide and 1 in. thick it is to be supported one brick height from the ground ($4\frac{1}{2}$ in. approx.) over the maximum, completely unobstructed area you can devise. (Similar to the problem of a diving board.) Six bricks may be used in your design.

Seminar points: Communication of ideas (continuity!), comparison of each individual's approach; fixed ends, rigid and non-rigid structures, continuous slabs, the ground, foundations, buttresses to thrust; timber connectors, welding; problems in prefabrication; roots of trees. References: Lisborg, pp. 217–26, 40–42, 45.

Report: Criticism of the way the design was communicated and proposals to illustrate the point of continuity in future years, and any ideas evolved on other structural awareness studies.

IV.5.9. History—"You are, whether you like it or not"

Aims: To show
(a) The concept of time vividly.
(b) The frail substance of records.
(c) The techniques of finding and using sources.

1. Lecture and seminar to make vivid that:

Everything is or will be history.

Ten persons of the age of 100 connect verbatim to the year A.D. 965. (Twenty to what the world was like before Christ!)

History records records. But how are records made? What determines them?

The facts behind history; i.e. biography of Charles Reilly *Scaffolding in the Sky*, London, 1938.

2. The frail substance of records. Trace the ultimate source of one single well-known historical detail, i.e. how do we know what Egyptian paint-brushes were made of? How do we know

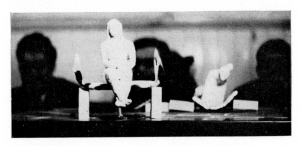

FIGS. 11, 12, 13. Structure awareness study. The pictures demonstrate a pioneer project. Three bars of chocolate were used as structural elements, one unwrapped, one with silver paper and one fully wrapped. Loaded by plaster figures a birthday candle was simultaneously lit under each bar. The relevance to the structural behaviour of steel in fires, of wood, the question of insulation, etc., made the starting points for the seminar.

This exercise with its direct unusual experience should be carried out during the first few weeks of the students course. It is a structure *awareness* study.

FIG. 14. A little boy of $1\frac{3}{4}$ years can manage every aspect of a three-speed radiogram: traditional education artificially restricts the use of aids until such time as adjustment to their use becomes difficult. The knowledge of the exact tunes on each of twenty-five records, recognizing the pattern of the writing, the colour, etc., the gestalt of the record, precedes the ability to read by years. Similarly, the use of the typewriter, the knowledge of the look and position of letters of the alphabet at the age of just three, precedes the ability to write by a considerable time, in the same little boy without any special tuition whatever.

Fig. 16. I attended Fuller's first Design Decade talk to B.A.S.A. in London and brought back the idea of the globe to carry data on world resources trends and needs to make vivid the world is one "space ship". This was just in time for the Nottingham students to develop John Morton's idea (see Fig. 20) for the centenary exhibition of the local architectural society. A grant of £300 and virtually all their own time and initiative, independent of staff, resulted in this, the first globe of this kind, in the world (1962) carried by Morton's tensegrity. The prototype had of course weaknesses, but it was a great triumph for Nottingham School of Architecture, College of Art and Crafts. (The school was moved to Nottingham University to be entirely restructured under new leadership, in remarkable sets of circumstances, two years later.) The dome is to be rebuilt in improved manner by B.A.S.A. for the 1965 Paris International Architects' Universal Conference, the subject of which is Architectural Education in 1965. *P.S.* It was a spectacular success at Paris and will be re-erected for the R.A.I.A., conference in Perth, W.A., in 1966.

Fig. 15. Even in adverse surroundings, with ramshackle tables, broken-down chairs and curtains hanging torn from windows, seminars of about half a dozen students, four simultaneously, in one room can do good concentrated work. This is the dungeon-like lecture room at Nottingham School of Architecture, College of Art and Crafts.—(Photograph by Mr. Butcher.)

FIG. 17. Structural Awareness Study with primitive equipment ideal for vivid experience for students.

Fig. 18. The structural awareness studies as carried out with first-year architectural and engineering students (see p. 267). The danger of sophisticated testing apparatus taking the place of the student directly loading and so experiencing the load his structure is taking must be resisted when schools or departments of engineering are involved.

Fig. 19. This extension of a small village school at Halam, Notts., designed by the students of the Nottingham School of Architecture, was carried out as a development of the life-project idea pioneered by the Birmingham School of Architecture. The responsibility for design and supervision was far greater at Nottingham than with previous examples. Further detailed description and assessment see *A.J.*, 20 June, 1962.

Fig. 20. This tensegrity structure arose out of an independent search by a student for a solution to a design problem. It was an original question and an original hunch which led to an answer which was found later to be like the work of Buckminster Fuller— but not before the student (John Morton in his fourth year) had lectured to junior years on the emergence of his idea from the problem.

about Egyptian geometry? etc. Pictures, observers—degrees of reliability—newspapers, compare a dozen of one day.

3. Finding and using sources. Make a study of the history of some small object or idea that has interested you for some time. Write a report on your detective work and comment, e.g.:

History of gowns for academicians

Knife, spoon, fork

Door and hinge

Writing from left to right

Meal times

Age of consent

"Time is money"

Shortage of land

Professional monopolies of doctors and lawyers and not architects and engineers

Classroom education

Going "out" to work

Separation of babies from mothers' bodies into prams

Idea of cutting and building columns in bits

Medieval use of "lighting up" at night

Medieval lifting of very heavy members of timber

Drains

Egyptian paint-brushes were made of?

Why is central heating called that and what is the origin of the name?

Why is Ruberoid called by its name?

How far back can you name a relative? What sort of socks did he wear? How and where did he have his hair cut?

Did Napoleon have a favourite colour?

Does Le Corbusier know about Parkhill and what does he think of it?

Can the Lord Mayor pronounce "architect"?

What is the earliest use of metal windows in your town?

The idea of the exercise is twofold. On the one hand, the sheer excitement of finding out is to be aroused; there must be something a person wants to know which is specific. Secondly, the

K

awareness of sources. A list of sources[i] should be given to the students and the meaning of the classifications becomes vivid in their search. A librarian is often a valuable consultant teacher.

As the subjects are not trivial the written reports on (a) the search, (b) the results, will be of use to the student body and the library. If there is a clever co-ordination a sizable amount of useful knowledge can be unearthed and fitted together. But this is of secondary importance.

IV.5.10. Economics—"Price me a pound of cathedral, please"

Duration: one week.

Economics of building.

Aims: To show:
(a) The basic nature and power of economic factors.
(b) The relative cost of items.
(c) The current prices of land and buildings.

Methods: Introductory lecture with horror stories about architects' neglect of cost factors, and other introductory matter: ministry grant restrictions, university grant policies, loans, interest rates and repayments; all these in outline so that the student learns to take them for granted and look for them, rather than forget about them until he faces them as "nuisances" in practice.

> Groups study together on basis of common interest, to investigate:
>
> Cost of various kinds of local land.
>
> Cost of building per pound(!), per square foot and per cubic foot.
>
> Elemental cost analyses—what are specifications? Quantities?
>
> Capital cost and maintenance cost awareness.

(i) CHANDLER G., *How to Find Out, A Guide to Sources of Information*, Pergamon, Oxford 1963.

Free discussion seminars at which discoveries are presented, individual corrections brought together; group and year reports reproduction. Consultant teachers may help.

IV.5.11. Environment: The sins of our fathers—our opportunity.

The interest of students in the environment is used to collect over the years a record of many of its physical characteristics, to be deposited in the library.

This idea leaves enormous scope for personal interest. Individuals should do this task alone as it has special relevance to work methods. The following fields might be examined:

> What tree species flourish in the locality. Why?
> What scales do architects and planners use? Why?
> What libraries exist in the locality? Why?
> What building materials are produced locally? Why?
> In what regard does the layman hold the architects of the town? Why?
> What Victorian buildings in the town would you preserve? Why?
> Trace the history of local newspapers.
> What is the relation between architects and planners in your town? Why?
> How many and what kinds of light fittings are to be found in the town? Why?
> How many kinds of bollards? Why?
> How many floor surfaces externally? Why?
> Pedestrians—only ways in the central areas? Why?
> What areas of the town are slums? Why?
> What is the purity of the local river and who controls it? Why?
> What is the purity of the local air and is this changing? Why?
> Find and list the various means of transport to London, Liverpool, Manchester, etc. etc., for use of the school.

What are the outstanding qualities of the local museums and art galleries? Why?

What is the local position with regard to concerts, opera, ballet, choral music? Why?

What are the outstanding merits of the academic constellation of your university (college)? Why?

IV.5.12. Responsibility—The world is one

Aim: To show the student the world is a spaceship (Buckminster Fuller), and each person's responsibility is world wide. Application is feasible for the first time on this world scale.

Method: Buckminster Fuller's Design Decade idea. The globe with the plottings of resources, development, disease and population information, etc., etc., can be continually developed by first-year students to make the information fuller and fuller (no pun intended). The possibilities, if the initial outlay is generous, are immense and involve the use of computers. To be able to learn their nature early, or have some people about who have done this, would diminish the worship of these mysterious intimidating beasts.

IV.5.13. Work Method Progress—"Where am I now? or Christmas is coming (in the Northern Hemisphere)"

All the work done so far can serve the purpose of studying work method by free discussion groups not only on the findings of each person, but more deliberately on their approach, on the way they got the task done. This will take some considerable time and might be best achieved by making the seminar groups small, perhaps six or seven persons.

This could develop into an end-of-term discussion of the development of each person during the term—not a marking kind of competitive assessment. The following questions could be a lead:

Work method:

How do you learn best? Remember?

How do you store knowledge?

How do you record sources of knowledge?

What disturbs your concentration?

What compulsive habits sap your energy, absorb your energy?

What effects do you rely on?

What are the motives for your work? Mother? Self? Teacher?

Summary of awareness studies.

The time-table below shows how these projects can be accommodated in one term of ten weeks allowing plenty of time for other work.

In a school where regimented time-tabling is important, the work could indeed be indicated in the way shown. Otherwise this is an indication of when and how the work might be timed.

It can be assumed that students will do all the work, out of choice, or they will choose from the programmes what they wish to do (some things perhaps more thoroughly), or that one or other of the awareness studies is carefully grafted on a more traditional type of first term. This is what had to be done in Nottingham for some time, and is likely to be the most frequently acceptable solution, at least in the near future.

It should be borne in mind that, though students may do some projects only, they can learn a very great deal by attending free discussion seminars and lectures on some of the others.

It must also be assumed that students will, on their own initiative, have desires to study, read, work, encouraged and helped by staff and older ones from the group. This will allow them to develop to their limits.

It is my firm belief that a term spent in this sort of way, with the accent on awareness of many kinds, with co-operation and a strong sense of belonging, with a clear indication of possibilities and responsibilities, would produce student bodies significantly more capable of learning than those we have today.

FIRST-TERM THEORETICAL TIME-TABLE

Week 1	Week 2	Week 3	Week 4	Week 5
Initiation and critical faculties awareness; lecturer's introductions		What have I begun? And seminar method	Design awareness, study and motive awareness	Anatomy of judgement

Week 6	Week 7	Week 8	Week 9	Week 10
Structural awareness, history awareness, economics awareness, environment awareness, running concurrently				Work method awareness

IV.6. DESIGN PROCESS: METHOD, ANALYSIS AND AWARENESS

IV.6.1. Common Functioning Principles in Design Process Method

"The meeting decided to pass a blanket resolution: 'B.A.S.A. affirms the need for a systematic approach to design, and should foster experiments in this field to encourage the use of conscious design methods in schools. The emphasis on design programmes in schools should be shifted from the results achieved to the methods by which they were achieved.' "[i]

Now students are quite confused about what design entails. This chapter's explanations and awareness studies can make the process clear. It will also show the marginal relevance of computers. The newsy status value of these high-powered technological design aids gives them a prominence out of all proportion

(i) Report of Annual Meeting of B.A.S.A., *A.J.*, October 14, 1964.

to their value or relevance. The danger that they are confused with design method itself, that they dictate design methods and so architecture—not for better architecture but so that their use can be defended—is very real.[i]

Earlier, the students have been made aware of the design skill[ii] and how aids are employed. We will now see how this skill, like a vizor, slides along the design process with a specific rhythm.

Related methods have been evolved and published. But there seem to me decisive advantages, especially for architectural design, in my own formulations. They will be the context for the exercises themselves. Once again we find a three-beat rhythm. Reviewing all the seventeen papers given at a conference on design methods, Professor Page said:

"In scale the design problems have ranged from the geographical region down to the scientific instrument and there only seems to be one common point of agreement, and that is that systematic design is a three-stage process . . . analysis, synthesis and evaluation."[iii]

Attraction–fusion–liberation (building and realization are processes of "evaluation"). We even recognize the description of a common functioning principle of analysis–synthesis–evaluation recurring and appertaining to each part of the three-beat rhythm.

". . . how we might design . . . this is itself a design problem." And ". . . the selection of what to analyze is a design problem."[iv]

". . . we have explored most closely . . . the processes whereby we can improve our techniques of analysis rather than synthesis or evaluation—I think the first thing we can recognize is the cyclical process involved. It is very nice to believe that you can

(i) WHITEHEAD B., and ELDARS, An Approach to the Optimum Layout of Single Storey Buildings, *A.J.*, 17 June, 1964.
(ii) See page 259.
(iii) Conference on Design Methods, Oxford 1963, edited Jones and Thornley, papers by 17 authors.
(iv) ESHERICK J., Problems of the Design of a Design System, in Conference on Design Methods,

go straight through from analysis to synthesis to evaluation . . .
but . . . in practice you go round several times."[i]

If we draw a chart (or "model" is now the fashionable term)
of this phenomenon of recurring cycles and cycles within cycles
to the same three-beat rhythm we have an extremely useful picture
of the temporal design process, and we can see from it that the
multiplicity of the skill is found at all stages of work. We have
a design method check-list. A check-list not of items or subjects
but of aspects and thought processes. A check-list for proper
employment and deployment of the design method itself.[ii]
Where as for the student this is of special use, it retains its value,
of course, in practice.

———→

D E S I G N I N G S K I L L	I Analysis and Data			II Creation, Synthesis and Judgement			III Realization and Evaluation		
	Anal- ysis I.1	Crea- tion I.2	Reali- zation I.3	Anal- ysis II.1	Crea- tion II.2	Reali- zation II.3	Anal- ysis III.1	Crea- tion III.2	Reali- zation III.3
	A C R	A C R	A C R	A C R	A C R	A C R	A C R	A C R	A C R

———→

Design process chart: the breakdown, the degree of detailed study will be
greater in some areas so that the regular picture given here is purely
diagrammatic. The DESIGN SKILL moves along the DESIGN PROCESS.

To summarize:
The scheme for the design process has several uses:
(a) To make the student aware of the common functioning
    principle in design, whether in detail or as a whole.
(b) To orientate the student as to the time programme of
    any job.

(i) A review of papers presented at the above conference, p. 209.

(c) To show where and when aids and assistants come into the scheme of things.

(d) To allow logical investigation for the sources of weakness which has arisen in any particular stage of a design.

(e) To act as a check-list for the operations involved in any particular design job.

(f) To show how the actual work done follows a pattern, and the relation of this pattern to the ideal diagram which will rarely be followed in an exact manner.

IV.6.2. Other Methods

D. G. Thornley[i] has published a design method in architectural education as introduced gradually at the Manchester University School. Together with Buttle's version this allows the student to see that the design process is not merely a vague progress from doodles to buildings. But the many specifically named stages actually given to the student to work through seem to me to have weaknesses: it looks as if this was a complete list yet it cannot be of all the items he should study and all the work he ought to do; the lists are given under four headings.:

1. Accumulation of data.
2. Isolation of a general concept of "form".
3. The development of the form into the final scheme.
4. Presentation of the final scheme.

The worst of being spoon-fed with titles and directions is that all these headings are really already answers to questions which the student needs to learn to ask. In Nottingham we merely demanded an "analysis", and, arising out of that, the "criteria" which were to guide the design and assessment. The sort of list of considerations which Thornley or Buttle provide then followed from the individual's application. The vital difference was the students arrived at that list. They did not start with it.

(i) In Conference on Design Methods.

To have to formulate the questions, to think through "what is relevant?" gives a thorough understanding of a problem. It allows original departures for original thinkers. It encourages development and a positive critical capacity. The student can design his own design method over the years.

The Manchester list is so detailed, so aligned with strict timing and sequence that obviously it cannot allow for individual variations in work method or work speed.

The design-process chart shown in this chapter is methodology pure and simple. It describes no more than the natural rhythm of learning, of scientific discovery,[i] as severally diagnosed, and applies this to design. There are no subjects headings such as "4. The position and nature of special planning elements (e.g. kitchens, lavatories etc.)", as found in Thornley's system. But there is a clear indication that in some instances the cycles within cycles will advance much further than in others: that is, the need to discover, and find out, and create, and judge, will arise, according to the building under design, more in some areas than in others. The student is not told; but he thinks and finds for himself what sort of information is required before one can start realistically imagining a building. He envisages how complete and what kind of communication and information is required before a building might be realized.

In seminar discussion, the various attempts made by students, to formulate "Manchester type" lists of subjects to be covered and the critical-path for this design stage, will supplement each

[i] We have a parallel in the stages of scientific method:

I. Attraction
{
1. Problem noticed,
2. Observations,
3. Hypothesis.

II. Fusion
{
1. Hunch,
2. Experiment,
3. Results and deductions.

III. Liberation
{
1. Theory,
2. Application,
3. Evaluation and development.

Each of the above nine is open to further useful analysis into its three beats, other. They can be added to by further comments from the experiences of the tutor.

Jones's method of systematic design comes far closer to this kind of thing. Jones is concerned with the combination of imagination with "rigorous mathematical or logical treatment". (Why do they always couple "rigorous" with mathematical?—as if all else was slovenly).

Jones's system is developed to deal mainly with smaller, simpler items of design and invention: cutlery, transformers, etc.

Important differences arise between design for production of the sort which requires setting up of expensive machinery, for example, and that which changes with each use or application: the prototype for preliminary trial or evaluation is sometimes, in the former case, not possible and, in the latter, of very limited value. Jones's stages of systematic design are:

"1. Analysis	1.1.	Random list of factors
	1.2.	Classification of factors
	1.3.	Sources of information
	1.4.	Interactions between factors
	1.5.	Performance specifications
	1.6.	Obtaining agreement
"2. Synthesis	2.1.	Creative thinking
	2.2.	Partial solutions
	2.3.	Limits
	2.4.	Combined solutions
	2.5.	Solution plotting
"3. Evaluation	3.1.	Methods of evaluation
	3.2.	Evaluation for operation
		for manufacture
		for sales"[i]

(i) JONES J. C., A Method of Systematic Design, in Conference on Design Methods, p. 55,

Jones brings in the imagination by free association sessions:

"Any idea . . . that comes into their heads, however mad or eccentric . . . This is deemed a useful technique, under the name of 'brainstorming' in the beginning of the creative stage."[i]

(Synectics[ii] has developed and worked with this concept most effectively for many years.)

The "three-beat" can be spotted also within each of Jones's three stages from the substance of the sub-headings.

I maintain that to become aware of this rhythm clarifies thought and leads to more effective action. And this is the basis of the many kinds of design method now advanced on many sides.

IV.6.3. Computers as Design Aids

One can see that in the analyses, the computer might have application. Though its clumsiness in use is usually more trouble than its worth, and only special design problems would be fed to it, in exceptional circumstances.

On the basis of the "three-beat" we can distinguish between design which lends itself to mechanical solution, in terms of computers and operational research data pure and simple, and other different design which requires value judgements and creative, original, thinking at every one of the myriad of "synthesis" (fusion) stages, in all the cycles, and cycles within cycles etc. In the latter, the use of computers is of marginal importance:

"Digital computer techniques are important but the computer never excites me very much as a design tool. I look upon them as instruments which can take some of the slog out of life, but I think that there are certain dangers in using computers for systematic design, for people are very unwilling to discard programmes when the boundary conditions change. We have not had very much of a discussion about analogue computers,

(i) JONES C., *A Method of Systematic Design*, p. 55.
(ii) GORDON W. J. J., *Synectics;* to be described in greater detail later.

and I think that this is a pity because there are a number of different types of analogue computers like electrolytic tanks and so on, and many of these provide design information directly in a visual form (often in two dimensions). This may be more useful for design purposes than a set of numbers on paper produced by a digital computer print out system. Analogue computers are much less flexible than digital computers because they cannot solve a large number of different types of problem, but the programming is often much simpler. There are difficulties with hardware, but we should still realize that analogue computers have a much bigger field of application than has been considered in this Conference. With digital computers the basic problem is clearly the programming of the input and there are great dangers here, I think, from the point of view of systematic design. Once you have programmed the computer there is a great temptation not to do any more systematic design. It is easier to let the machine churn out the answers for the wrong design. I think that this is a very big and fundamental problem with all present digital computing methods. The digital computer obviously has its place, particularly for solving well established type problems, for example structural design, but I think that computers contribute practically nil to creative design.[i]

It is the nature of an organism to be roused by difficulties to creative thought: "Thought is born of failure." To a computer a difficulty can only be fed as a "constraint". At best, it could set into action another programme, or a few, to see if new combinations can meet the difficulty. This is nothing compared with the wealth of a lifetime of experience of a human being on which he draws for original combinations in the creative act.[ii]

Having made plain that he distinguishes between design where processes are known, and design for unknown future growth process, Esherick echoes Page:

"It is a matter of the greatest importance to understand what

(i) PAGE J. K., Review of Papers at Design Conference, p. 213.

great damage could be done by trying to solve the second type of problem as though it were a problem of the first type.[i]

And whereas this is generally acknowledged the tendency of saddling the architect with the duty to think in terms of the computer arises repeatedly. To demonstrate this I quote from a report on the computer course at the Architectural Association School of Architecture in the autumn of 1964:

". . . before the advantages of computer aids in decision making can be realized, problems and methods must be precisely formulated in logical terms. Most single faceted architecture problems can be stated in this way, but little advance has been made in procedural theories for the 'whole process' of designing.

". . . It is the architect's immediate responsibility to formulate his method so that, with machine aids, he may provide a more thorough and rapid service to client and user."

However, there is no evidence that this will make the service better.

". . . Any attempt to group optimum sub-problem solutions in order to achieve the best overall solution is mathematically and architecturally invalid."

". . . computer help is unobtainable till architects rationalize the design methods they use to reconcile sub-problem solutions and thus move towards an overall optimum solution. The existing procedures for optimizing single design functions in isolation (for example, circulation cost, heating, lighting, etc.), may hinder rather than help the designer to achieve a balanced overall solution."[ii]

Maybe it's not a bad thing, as computers are *a priori* accepted as a decision making aid, that:

". . . in architectural practice, education and research, little consideration is given to methods necessary in design to meet the user's needs with the means available. The development of

(i) ESHERICK J., *Problems of the Design of a Design Method*, p. 78.
(ii) NUTT and PEARSON, A.A. Computer Conference, London, *A.J.*, September 30, 1964.

computer aids for planning and design will be retarded until this problem of 'design method' has been tackled."[i]

We have here not only an example of unwarranted assumption that it is the computer aids we need (rather than better development of human skills) but also the expressed aim to change architectural design methods to suit the computer's quantitative language. We have the fashionable linking of the work "design method" with computers. We have the assumption, quite unwarranted, that "tackling" the problem of design method will give a computer orientated solution. The two are in no sense synonymous. Computers are a mighty heavy tail and, as Page suggests, once we start it wagging, the dog of architecture is likely to wag with it, willy-nilly. In our present state, of the rapid development of a sick society, we cannot afford to jettison the degree of vigilance and flexibility that goes with human decision making.

I see still a different specific danger in the use of scientific paraphernalia in design. I know how susceptible architects and students are to fashions, gimmicky words, clever sounding phrases without ever grasping their meanings. I also know what a mystery mathematics is to most of them, and that they stand in great awe of a thing like a computer. Further, we know that many of those who work with computers believe in them passionately—like the teaching machine addicts—and, of course, the two things have strong links.

So what with the religious fervour, the mathematical incantations and the mounting pressure of salesmanship and the desire to "be with it" there is a likelihood of the profession succumbing to the computer. Perhaps another contributory factor is the fashionable stress on the architect's inefficiency. However, it is the architect's inefficiency that is our specific worry. The incredible waste of abilities and capacities that result, for one and all, as a result of our traditional education should be our chief

(i) NUTT and PEARSON, A.A. Computer Conference, London, *A.J.*, September 30th, 1964.

concern. A radical improvement through educreation, of the deductive, inventive and emotional aspects of life is of primary importance.

"I see no dangers in our use of science or mathematics—so long as we act as men, using all our powers of thought and feeling", says Esherick. But this is a vain hope in an academically hidebound, emotionally limping collection of individuals and groups.

Like the teaching machine, the computer is, for designers, most active as a red herring—the cleverest red herring ever. It can talk back you know!

IV.6.4. Design Process Awareness Study

The following awareness study should be given to students as a very important exercise (pressure to participate on functional grounds). It would occur before the first architectural design programme, in the first week or two of the second term, in the first year.

The programme reads thus:

"The 'design skill' of which you were made aware in the first term is at work throughout the design process of planning a building. The design skill is complex and so is the design process. But just as, for the purpose of insight, we separated the 'arrange' from the 'arrange to advantage' and showed how formal, structural, economic and service aspects combined in the total complex skill of design, so the complex temporal process of design can also be analysed.

"A three-beat or stage rhythm has been detected and used by very many system designers. This can be related to nature's general movement in cycles of three-beat rhythms.

"The following words will associate familiar processes with the three-beat:

"I. (Attraction)
    "Data, Analysis, Involvement, leading to

"II. (Fusion)

"Synthesis, Judgement, Invention, Creation, Evolving, leading to

"III. (Liberation)

"Realization, Production, Testing, Evaluation, leading to data for further design processes, of the same rhythm."

The diagram showing the three-beat rhythms within such rhythms looks very simple:

⟶

Design skill:	Data	Creative Stage	Realization
Economic			
	I	II	III
Aesthetic			
Structural	I.1 I.2 I.3	II.1 II.2 II.3	III.1 III.2 III.3

⟶

The awareness studies now suggested are designed to give a clear indication in concrete terms what the abstract formulations might stand for. Each exercise relates to one of the nine groups one might have if one analysed the design process not only into its main three rhythms, but each one of these into three sub-rhythms. I think such a ninefold division is the least to have clarity and scope for designing an effective approach to an architectural problem.

It must not be taken that these awareness studies are in fact what a student might evolve in doing a design. They are indications of the kind of thing that would go into the categories. They merely show within the diagrammatic framework given real items occurring in the architectural design process.

EXERCISE 1, STAGE 1 (Data analysis, involvement, etc.)

Exercise: Each student writes a letter posing as a client, giving information about a building he wishes to have designed, with invitation to act for him. Letters are "posted" in a box and students then take out letters—other than their own— from the other side of the box.

EXERCISE I.1 (Data analysis). Each student then writes an answer asking all the things he needs to get the best possible understanding of the problem.

EXERCISE I.2 (Creative thought and judgement on data). Evolve what are the areas of ignorance which you will have to study and look up in respect to the building in question.

EXERCISE I.3 (Realization of data). Set out a framework for the information as it is gathered so that it is directly useful for the next creative stage.

EXERCISE II.1 (Data for creation). Working backwards from a well-known building try to deduce what the criteria were in guiding the architect's design and give careful evidence for your detective-like deductions.

EXERCISE II.2 (The creative act). Find an example of the actual creative moment of an experienced designer, and establish what had brought about the "idea", "insight"; what notions came together to form the original concept?

EXERCISE II.3 (Checking, evaluating the creative act). Note and study some examples where realization changed and developed considerably from original design. Try to analyse and report on this and the reasons, e.g. What happened at Sydney? What happened with Clasp? Relate the three stages.

EXERCISE III.1 (Data for realization). What legal permissions are necessary for the building in question? Or: Make a survey of the availability and time lag in delivery of building materials in the town.

EXERCISE III.2 (Creative judgements in realization). Pre-planning, critical path planning,[i] time schedules, progress charts, are all means to minimize waiting, of any sort, in construction (and before). Each student should collect an actual example of waiting at a building site, discover its reasons and discuss the point in seminar. The total collection should give a reasonably comprehensive picture in a report.

(i) JEANES R. E., Critical Path Method applied to overall process of building, current papers, D.S.I.R., Watford 1964.

EXERCISE III.3 (Realization and evaluation). The use of buildings is hardly ever studied—buildings are not regarded as experiments testing hypotheses. But they can be, even if the mathematical aspect of the tests is only a minor one; either formulate the hypothesis, for which a building can be the experiment: can you deduce or discover age, flexibility and looks of buildings in your town? A close look at some of the main streets' buildings would give valuable information with regard to (a) alterations done; (b) frequency of facelifts (shop fronts); (c) flexibility missing, in terms of owners' needs. The reports and conclusions of discussions will make you aware of one of today's most fundamental architectural problems: is permanence still the normal requirement in architecture?[i]

The entire set of design process awareness studies can be done in a fortnight. Through seminars and discussions and inspirational lectures, the various aspects of the design process rhythm should have real meaning for the students.

IV.6.5. Design Process Chart Use

The next stage is to show the detailed use and application of the design process chart.

If we imagine a student having received a letter from the fellow student posing as a client, which does not give enough information, he must decide on some further action. What? How? It will come to him fairly soon that it might be another letter. Now this is where we begin the demonstration of the effect of the application of the three-beat common functioning principle to every stage and sub-stage of the process: cycles within cycles.

What are the three stages in sending a letter?
1. Compose it; 2. Write it; 3. Post it.

So how do I "compose" it? Three stages again:
1. Note points; 2. Order points; 3. Make a rough copy.

(ii) HAVARD T., John Week on Indeterminacy, *A.J.*, October 28, 1964.

But this is a nervous student; he asks, "How do I 'note points'?"

1. Concentrate; 2. Ideas will come; 3. Put them down in words.

He is too tense to follow; "How do I 'concentrate'?" he says.

1. Are you aware you need to do it? 2. Relax; 3. Energy will become available.

Or, let us take the architectural problem of heating in a building. How shall I heat it?

1. Get the data; 2. Decide after weighing up; 3. Check your decision.

But how do I collect the "data"?

1. Find out; 2. Write, phone or go there; 3. Collect or receive. But how do I "find out"?

1. Analyse your sources; 2. Judge which might be best; 3. Check.

But how do I "analyse" the sources?

1. Collect all you can; 2. Organize information; 3. Put into clear form.

But how do I "collect" it? etc., etc., back to being "aware", "relaxing", and finding "energy" once again.

We can translate the letter example with some additional breakdown into diagrammatic form. This is the normal way of working with the design process formula. It is necessary to show clearly how a plan of action follows if the diagram (evolved from left to right) is now read from right to left. All the rhythms in the design of a building could not possibly go on to a two-dimensional diagram. But we get an inkling of the number of rhythms involved, we realize why many decisions are ill-founded because the rhythmic beats are not habitually gone through, even mentally, as an experienced designer in fact would. It is important to remember that to each rhythmic beat the design skill is applied, the combination of economic, aesthetic, constructional and realization considerations.

Writing letter

Design skill →
1. Composing.
2. Writing.
3. Posting.

Design skill →
1. Note points.
2. Order points.
3. Rough copy.

Design skill →
1. Concentrate.
2. Ideas.
3. Verbalization.

Design skill →
Design skill →
1. Awareness of task.
2. Relax.
3. Energy becomes available.

Design skill →
1. Consider resources.
2. Choose.
3. Check working order.

→
1. Sit down.
2. Decide use of page.
3. Put pen to paper.

Design skill →
1. Get implements.
2. Write.
3. Read through.

→
1. Recap function of letter.
2. Check on effectiveness.
3. Amend as necessary.

Design skill →
1. Envelope, stamps.
2. Take to post.
3. Collection.

Perhaps I should stress again that it is not a matter of distributing sheets which have any work process diagram on. The crux of the matter is for students to become aware of the meaning of the three-beat rhythm in the process, its cyclical nature (spiral), its usefulness, and to have practice in applying them again and again until, like maths or language, this becomes another basic symbol system to help comprehension, as language furthers communication and mathematics calculation. I know this is a large claim. Like maths and language it becomes a habit.

If the student records his work in this kind of way (and language and mathematics also have their constraints!) then faulty logic, change of values and criteria, additional factual information and contradiction of previous "factual" information can be traced in their effect and their origins. This is an immense gain not only in university education but the continued process of educreation through life.

Let us take an example:

The answer to the letter in our exercise contains something that does not seem to make sense. We trace this on the chart to the questions in the original letter. Having found the source of the trouble there we can then note how it arose. Were the points not presented in proper order? Was the writing illegible? etc., right through each stage and related beats. And the findings show what needs to be watched more carefully next time: a systematic way of learning by experience!

We are here dealing with methods that the students would probably be able to learn much more quickly than their present teachers. A closely co-operative school would develop the expertise among its student body and would in fact teach the staff who are slower by demonstrating the idea again and again. This is what in fact happened at Nottingham with regard to the introduction of the three-stage analysis–design–communication. Many of the staff learned slowly, but they learned.

One or two people at staff level should feel the advantages of this way of doing things strongly, so that they grapple positively with the problems that crop up. Even this can come from senior students, however, where the co-operative atmosphere is mature.

IV.7. DESIGN PROCESS PRACTICE:
STUDIO WORK: PROGRESS AND ASSESSMENT

IV.7.1. Analysis of Present Studio Work

The deserted studios of many a famous seat of architectural learning are not to be taken as failure of the project approach. They are signs of the inferior educational atmosphere of the place. Places where professors are busy managing all manner of other things but are a rare treat for the mere student; places where the staff is concerned with practice and things running smoothly and without hitches on pre-planned, albeit inefficient lines. Places where there is absolutely no point in turning up, for the good students hide their good ideas, to keep ahead in the competitive scheme of things, and the poor ones merely propagate the fear they have of failing.

In the past, coolly considered "studio work" has suffered from the following weaknesses which should be remedied by new proposals:

(a) Programmes handed out have been uninteresting, irrelevant, sometimes nonsensical, showing an artificial origin and lack of care and imagination in preparation.

(b) The student has not known where to start or how to progress.

(c) He has not known how to judge what he has done.

(d) He lacks the ability to ask meaningful questions or to get useful advice from studio instructors.

(e) Subsequently, it is easy to get fed up with any programme and long for some "real life".

(f) There is little point in coming into the studios—when you do, few people are there anyway.

(g) Competitive attitudes depress all but a few.

(h) Marks are based on arbitrary judgements made by juries more often than not ignorant of the student's criteria and approach.

(i) Criticisms are either too long, boring and repetitive, or too short and mention only a few schemes and a few points; they are usually flavoured by the bitterness born of competition (these things are beyond a game) and the unfairness of judging on the very incomplete story the finished presentation drawings tell, with all their hidden faults and misleading gloss.

(j) "Design drawings" are regarded as an entity before commencing "working drawings".

(k) Interest is limited and competition heightened by bundling into one studio, a year at a time, all engaged on one and the same programme and helped by perhaps one or two studio instructors—trying to help dozens of students solve the same problem! An extraordinarily barren set-up when one comes to consider it. And, sure enough, little grows from it. The best work is done alone at home, in spite of studio instructor's advice.

IV.7.2. Alternative Views on Remedies

The highly inefficient picture described is widely agreed. It has led to two points of view:

(a) The narrow rationale that students waste time trying to design because they have not mastered the background SUBJECTS. The remedy suggested is a curtailing of studio time, particularly in the first three years, and the filling of this time with didactic lecture teaching of many more subjects. This attitude is gaining ground with alarming rapidity. Its simple sound seduces.

(b) The second attitude springs from a fundamentally different approach: it suggests that the interest and so study of the subjects is born and achieved through their relevance to the design process. The whole of the course becomes interdependent, relevant and related, from the outset.

Before imaginary comparisons are made, between (a) and (b), and between these and the *status quo*, it must be stressed that the educreational attitude of (b) is made effective by the kind of new teaching techniques described in this book. These could begin at once; they do not await better conditions or better staff. The beginning can rest on more effective use of present resources.

A study of a cross-section of thought on educational techniques shows a tendency in many fields to move towards the kind of project teaching that architecture has long fostered. Architects repeatedly model their arguments of "didactics first" proposals ironically on courses about to undergo fundamental changes towards the very thing architects wish to abandon!

If agreement on the ineffectiveness of studio work is the starting point then, given the above tendency towards project work, the obvious thing is to look for ways of making studio time effective. Not, as the architect is so prone to do, throw the baby out because the bath-water is dirty.

Enough has been suggested for the organization of a school of architecture to make clear that the drifting, purposeless studio atmosphere—enlivened only by the prima-donna competitive spasms at marking time, and the occasional accident of interest coinciding with work set—can be replaced by more positive and defined attitudes.

A key to this is the comprehension of what is entailed in design. The student has been made aware of the design skill and design process. Now he needs repeated practice, as much practice as is possible to try his skill, make mistakes and learn from them.

The student's desire to work, find out, create, must from the outset have efficient outlets. The awareness studies prepared the way for this and the first programmes involving planning of a building must be orientated as much to the methodology used as to its result in terms of design. Pains are taken in all schools to teach subjects, from Theory of Architecture to Drainage. But the deliberate attempt to teach design process methods is only slowly coming to one or two schools.[i]

(i) SUTCLIFFE S., letter in *R.I.B.A. Journal*, September 1964: "Any studio instructor will tell . . . that the problem [of providing technical and social science teaching] is administrative child's play compared with the

The design skill now practised for the first time in a realistic framework, should give a deliberately good start so that the habits which grow from it will affect favourably the work of the person, not only for the rest of his school days but for his whole professional life.

IV.7.3. Seminar Methods to Further Team Work

Seminar discussions are often referred to in this book, and the meaning should be defined. Reading about Dr. Abercrombie's free discussion groups[i] gives a good idea of many of the aspects a seminar should show. But to get the most out of seminar discussions I repeat that to have a chairman, (not the tutor) is a good thing, and also a subject, report or aim for discussion. If a report is to be discussed then a critic should have had access to it to prepare his response. The chairman's duties, to keep the orientation of the seminar, and to judge on such matters as chairmen have to, is excellent practice for life, as is practice in the art of criticism. We, as groups, are hopeless at getting somewhere collectively. The irony is that committee work, so important in democracy, has normally no deliberate training in school.

For an architect to have the experience in running professional kinds of meetings for some five years is of immense educational importance, and would lift the efficiency of professional training significantly in terms of purposeful communication.

The tutor's job is to help. Not so much in the factual errors that may occur in the discussions, though these are usually worth a comment, but on the way the seminar is or is not achieving optimum or maximum efficiency in the purpose it has set itself. And just as it is a really worthwhile technique to read examination questions very carefully, so it is worthwhile also for the chairman,

(i) ABERCROMBIE M. L. J., *The Anatomy of Judgement*, London 1960.

problem of teaching the synthesizing process of design. All the social studies and technological skills will become no more than sterile brick upon sterile brick unless the architect is capable of this process".

as a matter of methodology, to open with a short statement of what he thinks is the function of the meeting. The summary of the achievements, maybe conclusions at the end, is the complement of this.

For students who, in the present run of things, hardly open their mouths before the third year, to be put in a position of chairman or critic repeatedly as a matter of functional routine, has fine effects, as students testify.

It is this training in purposeful discussion which makes the groups of three engaged on a project, or possibly groups of six, (two groups meeting together because of joint interests and the possibilities of co-operation in some way) such a powerful learning technique.

It is within this framework that the help students can give each other is maximized and staff used to the full, to comment on developed problems, carefully refined questions, to carry on when the seminar has got stuck, and teaching students how to help one another. Staff, instead of moving from board to board, individual to individual, would attend to designers and their teams, at crucial times marked on the work-progress chart. Staff would thus address at least three people and all those others who wish to listen in. A better use of their time. This would also teach students how to help one another.

IV.7.4. The First Project

It is within this framework also that the first project for the design of a building can get an orderly step-by-step progression: the student's individual endeavour (always heightened by co-operation unless it's gone awry), meeting together in seminar with his group or two groups, and discussing problems or proposals, findings, deductions or ideas. It is at these meetings the decisions on how the "assistants" or "consultants" might help the "leader" to achieve his end. It is such activities and their results as well as the student's drawings which will show clearly his maturity, his development, progress, weaknesses and strong points—above all, it will give him the chance to strengthen his weak spots as soon as they become obvious in dealing with his group.

The student has during his first term already worked up to this sort of activity. He has seen and taken part, thanks to the vertical division of the school into groups, in the endeavours of senior students, giving a great deal of insight and information.

Certain general recommendations can be made for the nature of the first programme, whether student chosen or set by tutors:

(a) The size must be limited to allow a thorough treatment of the whole design process.

(b) There should be a functional and spatial relationship of a number of rooms, i.e. one main cell with a few subsidiary spaces.

(c) The users of the building should require specific consideration so that nothing can be taken for granted, i.e. used by an animal. (This means thinking about doors, handles, strength of finishes, too often applied blindly to design.)

(d) The construction and structure must be capable of a variety of interpretations.

(e) The students must be really enthusiastic about the idea.

The choice of an animal as occupant of the building to be designed, with a secondary human use, has been very successful in satisfying all the above requirements. (Donkey stable at seaside and bison house for a park.)

Although awareness and methodology remain a major function of his education at this point the main driving force becomes the student's desire to create a good solution to his problem.

For some time students will have been discussing the design problem they might tackle during the spring and summer term. As they have seen with other years, so first year is recommended to proceed as follows:

1. Register your project (say "elephant house") on your space in the work-progress chart. (Individuals may all have their own subjects, or there may be choice from, say, three, or all may do the same programme.)

2. Register your name as assistant or consultant against two other problems of other people, noting briefly what your contribution might be (i.e. "as needed", or "services" or "materials", etc., etc.), bearing in mind that this is the beginning of a two-term work association. It is worthwhile discussing this association on the basis of preliminary ideas before finally getting on with it.

3. Arrange, with the help of the work-progress chart, which indicates availability of each person, a meeting of your own team. Note your required attendance at other meetings that might be relevant to your interests.

4. The meeting should establish a work pattern, areas of responsibility, and sufficiently defined prediction in terms of rate of progress and co-ordination to check actual events against this prediction.

5. Subsequently with meetings of the group, and through seminars, incorporating others beyond it, with or without tutor's presence, the design should develop according to the common functioning principle rhythms of the design process chart as a backcloth and to guide.

6. The effectiveness of your work should be judged taking the answers to the following questions as criteria:

(a) Is the data adequately processed so that design decisions can be undertaken on the basis of clear criteria, and defined constraints and areas of freedom?

(b) Do the design decisions follow the criteria set and exploit opportunely and imaginatively the resources and possibilities available?

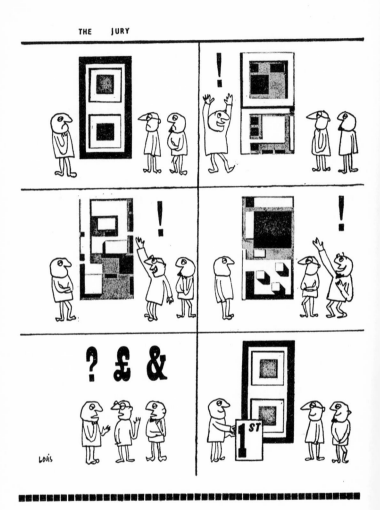

Fig. 21.   Reprinted by permission of the *Architects' Journal*.

(c) Is the creative stage process of the emerging design carried out in such a way as to optimize every compromise that has to be considered and with techniques that allow a smooth development of the valid, previous ideas?

(d) Is the communication of your ideas to those involved with your work, clear so that misunderstandings do not arise?

(e) Are you able to use to the full the talents of your helpers?

(f) Are you able to contribute to the two (or three) projects in which you are assisting, to the greatest gain of the chief designer?

(g) Are you employing design aids to the full when it really merits it?

(h) Are you contacting authorities, inside and outside the school, effectively? i.e. are your questions meaningful and specific, are the answers of value, are you becoming clear where areas of ignorance exist, not only in your mind but the knowledge of mankind?

(i) Is the work rewarding and joyful and full of new insights?

(j) Have you a solution that satisfies the criteria and gives you pleasure (and at least some others, perhaps?) or do you have a thorough understanding of the weaknesses and lacks of your design and how to act to avoid these?

V.7.5. Assessment Aids

Beyond these questions the tutors, particularly those who need to provide marks for the administrative appetite, could use the critical thinking scale quoted below from Burton, Kimball and Wing. How vastly superior this would be than the analysis, even on several counts, for marking, as is done, for example, at the Bartlett School and as we did for many years at Nottingham.

"A Critical-Thinking Scale[i]

Name of student...

"DIRECTIONS:

"The following items describe certain kinds of behaviour associated with the skill we often call 'critical thinking'. A careful rating of a student on each item will give an index of his or her critical-thinking skill.

"The ratings should represent your best estimate of the student's typical, day-in-and-day-out behaviour. Do not rate a person according to his or her performance in one unique or spectacular situation. To help obtain ratings which represent typical behaviour, it is requested that no ratings be prepared until at least one week after you receive this rating blank.

"For each of the items you are to place a check ($\sqrt{}$) at the point on the scale which seems best to describe the person being rated.

"1.   Ability to recognize a problem.

Rarely notices any sort of problem.	Identifies only superficial problems.	Notices obvious problems; overlooks subtle ones.	Maintains questioning attitude; is intelligently curious.	Has penetrating mind; consistently identifies problems.

"2.   Tendency to stick to a problem.

No capacity for a sustained attack on most problems.	Many problems not held clearly in mind; wanders, introduces irrelevant ideas.	Solves average problem efficiently.	Is persevering; is reluctant to leave a problem without completing it.	Is unusually persistent in all problem-solving efforts.

(i) BURTON, KIMBALL, WING, *Education for Effective Thinking*, New York 1960. This book is full of excellent material for any teacher.

"3. Tendency to be rational.

Is gullible; easily swayed by own beliefs, values, prejudices.	Makes clear effort to be rational; is hampered by limited intellectual ability.	Attacks most problems in rational, objective manner; troubled by highly controversial issues.	Regularly attacks all problems in a logical manner.	Is unusually adept at logical analysis; attacks all types of problems in a logical manner.

"4. Ability to clarify a problem.

Does not attempt to make a problem specific, precise, definite.	Usually unable to select and clarify key ideas.	Usually grasps central idea in ordinary problems.	Detects and clarifies central ideas even in complicated problems.	Consistently locates and clarifies very obscure points.

"5. Ability to attack a problem in a flexible and original manner.

Abandons problem after one attempt to solve.	Relies on steady plodding, shows little ingenuity.	Shows average resourcefulness.	Has only occasional trouble, suggesting new, effective ways to attack problems.	Is highly imaginative; displays unusual ingenuity.

"6. Awareness of need for evidence, for facts.

Feels "one opinion is as good as another".	Rarely presents or demands any sort of supporting evidence.	Generally seeks the facts of the situation.	Regularly seeks evidence; is a good judge of reliable and pertinent data.	Consistently bases conclusions on all facts, properly evaluated.

"7. Ability to draw accurate conclusions.

Often reaches conclusions contrary to the known facts.	Does not interpret data carefully; draws unjustified conclusions.	Usually forms acceptable conclusions.	Regularly forms acceptable conclusions after sound analysis of all facts.	Competently organizes and interprets even complicated data, notices obscure inferences.

K

"8.   Willingness to suspend judgement.

Jumps to conclusions.	Considers alternate solutions only very super-ficially.	Usually makes reasonable choice among obvious alternatives.	Critically examines most possibilities.	Reaches decisions only after a careful analysis of all available data.

To allow the student, his assistants and his tutor and others involved, a proper perspective of his development, particularly useful in the educational process, the student should keep all in the way of drawings, notes and models that he would tradi-tionally throw in the wastepaper basket. As soon as this attitude takes roots, and without any self-consciousness once it is estab-lished, in the whole school, the format and the clarity and the interconnection of the various bits of pieces of thought and paper will be better co-ordinated.

Then the documentation exists by which, at any given point, the effectiveness of previous work and the points of ineffective-ness can be shown.

I think it is, generally speaking, true to say that the stuff thrown in the wastepaper basket at the moment, is educationally speaking, more valuable than the prissy thing hung up to fool juries and, worse, often fooling the student. We are assessing a complex skill, not the personal likes or dislikes of the result.

Assessment of the folio of work produced at the end of a session where necessary, becomes more a matter of noting grave lacks and making good of possibly recommending reconsidera-tion of career than pass or fail. Each student has within his volume of work not only the scheme for which he was responsible with its background and the help of others clearly shown. It also has the projects of the two or three students to whom the one under examination acted as assistant, with his contribution clearly marked. And all that has been said can apply to all five years of the course.

IV.8. GAINING SPECIFIC KNOWLEDGE

IV.8.1. Existing State and Robbins's Recommendations

In schools of architecture, as elsewhere, by and large lecture courses on a number of subjects, arbitrarily separated out from what is a unitary field of knowledge, follow a set syllabus and aim at satisfactory examination results. These lecture courses are supposed to cover the "essential groundwork" or "the field" or similar. The dilemma of the past ten years and more, of pressure to teach more and more specialist subjects which the student "really could not do without", has become entirely accepted: we just don't bother to find a solution and we feel it's just inevitable that some things are included in the sacred syllabus and others are not.

Voices in the wilderness are hoarse with crying, "Teach the student how to learn, so that he can help himself from that overflowing bowl of knowledge as he needs it, with maximum efficiency". To date, it's all to little avail. The external examinations of the R.I.B.A., for example, are relentlessly geared to what is bound to be out of date by the time it has passed all the stages required of a reform. The only way this problem can be solved is to write the need to keep up to date into the requirements, to demand change, not forbid it.

Professional education is particularly restricted in development by the requirements of the statutory bodies the professions set up and with which they control education. Used positively, this can be an inspiration and a help. But in times of rapid development the conservatism that attaches itself to professional bodies is anything but the stimulus education requires.[i]

Of this we have multiple examples today. All they tend to think of is making courses longer and longer. Why? To purge their bad consciousness, at having begun practice themselves utterly unprepared. They forget education can become more efficient. To depend on didactic teaching, because fresh students are used to it, is short sighted.

(i) It is interesting to read of the origin of the Board of Architectural Education: REILLY Sir C., *Scaffolding in the Sky*, London 1938, p. 115.

K*

It is quite wrong to say that if, for example, lectures in physics were given to architectural students design would improve. It is right to say that if students are made aware of the design process then they will be interested and will want to learn about the relevance and the application of certain elements of physics. This is better done by delving into a search of what they first define as relevant, with guidance, than having another man's lecture notes rammed down their tight, unthirsty gullets to vomit up in examinations, and sit for hours, dutifully filled by the drowning voices of irrelevant instantly evaporating words.

The Robbins Report criticism of what I might term "subject teaching" is very enlightened. It takes note of progressive views long held and sets the scene for an "educreational change".

"We have received from both university teacher and student organizations extensive complaints concerning methods of instruction. The substance of these complaints has been nearly always the same: undue reliance on lectures, often delivered with too little consideration of the needs and capacities of the audience, and insufficient personal contact. The remedy generally demanded is the adoption of what is called 'the tutorial system', though what exactly is meant by this is not always clearly defined by those who desire it. . . .

"But we do not believe that this desirable state of affairs can only be achieved by individual tuition, every pupil enjoying one hour a week by himself with a tutor, or that it can always be best achieved by this method of teaching. The tutorial properly conducted is an arduous affair on both sides: the pupil has to take a very active part. For the great majority of students we believe it to be too exacting. They would gain more from being members of a small class of three or four in which they did not have the responsibility of making all the running. Even in the older universities of England the single-pupil tutorial has to a considerable extent given way to the double tutorial and to small classes. Less than half the tutorials given in Oxford and Cambridge are given to a single pupil. We think that for those capable of taking part in it the single-pupil tutorial gives better results than any other method of teaching. But it is costly and extremely wasteful of the teacher's time if it involves a great deal of repetition of material which all students of a subject have to learn to handle. It was invented as a means of educating a small élite reading for honours schools. As a method of educating large numbers of students it is impracticable and we believe undesirable."[i]

"Conversely, we are not in sympathy with the view that the lecture is an archaic survival from the days before printing was invented. We think that a well-planned and well-delivered series of lectures can give a sense of proportion and emphasis lacking in tutorial discussions and seminars where teaching, in following where the argument leads, may often stray into byways. It should bring to students modifications of what they find in their textbooks, suggest wider reading, and, when given by lecturers in touch with recent developments, be a source of stimulus and inspiration."

". . . we are particularly thinking here of lectures to large audiences in which a genuinely synoptic view of a subject is given. Lectures of this kind which lay down principles and survey a subject widely are particularly valuable for first-year students. Attendance at lectures gives them a necessary frame to a week's work, makes them feel a part of a community of learning, and leads to wider intellectual contact with their fellows than membership of small classes alone can give.

"We are in favour of diversity and believe that in a well organized course of instruction different types of teaching should be combined. We are struck by the evidence . . . that a high proportion of instruction is received through lectures. On the whole we think that there is little virtue in formal lectures delivered to very small audiences. A lecture should be something of an occasion and, except in large universities where in a big lecture list there is a room for the highly specialized lecture which only a few genuine enthusiasts will attend, time spent in preparing

(i) Robbins, *Higher Education Report*, H.M.S.O., London 1963, pp. 186–7.

courses of lectures for small audiences would be better spent in giving more classes and in regular and systematic correction of pupils' own work. We are impressed by the evidence that students do little written work during the term and get too little detailed criticism of what they do submit."[i]

Although the concepts are still couched in traditional terms, the evidence presented emphasizes the need for other effective methods of learning, beyond the lecture and not as time-taking as the single person tutorial. This is, of course, where co-operative free discussion group work comes in. And the other point that Robbins omits is, of course, the possibility of developing and helping a student along his chosen interest, and not along a "set" course. Then the "regular oral and written work presented" is not what has been set by another but what, according to the work-progress chart, he has set himself.

We will differentiate between different kinds of learning, but first we must remember that the relevance of a subject and the desire to study it, can arise from a student interest or from staff inspiration. And this is, of course, the talent of a good teacher, to inspire interest. The present curriculum and syllabus-bound, examination-orientated kind of teaching does not give the teacher a chance. Let us further bear in mind that unless learning springs from interest it will be inferior.

IV.8.2. Methods of Learning

Let us assume then that interest in a subject has been aroused and list the different kinds of learning relationships that might evolve:

Learning from print.

(a) Books, journals and other obvious sources are at present insufficiently used. The student is orientated towards lectures and, particularly in architecture, reads and looks up far too little. As the amount of information available to the world is

(i) Robbins Report, pp. 187–8.

doubling every ten years this emphasizes the problem of making sources available, and of making the student aware of the best methods which develop. Not the least important is the technique of finding out quickly whether a book, however falsely promising or misleading the title may be (and they certainly tend to be) is giving the information he requires and whether it is doing it in a way and with a method that fits his own pattern of development, learning methods and manner of assimilating knowledge. Einstein wrote of the growing importance to learn to recognize which books not to read. This is profoundly true and we must arm students with a shrewd critical faculty assessing the basic worth and attitudes of books to them by a minute's glance at the strategic points.[i]

Worthwhile books can be studied alone. But there are books which offer individual reading and lend themselves to weekly free discussions (i.e. Lewis Mumford, Norberg-Schulz). Books with a point of view and an argument. Studying textbooks in this way can often cope collectively with difficulties that might have stopped or slowed down each of the individuals.

The deliberate and careful acquisition of worthwhile books and bibliographies, kept for one's future ease of reference, follows naturally.

Where books are developed of the kind suggested earlier, the cobo, or contribution textbook, it is obvious how work with the book becomes a more positive activity than mere reading.

However, while the normal kind of book is with us exclusively, it is a matter of showing students that it is to be regarded as something which should evoke their response. Notes taken from books or interleaved with books should have a critical quality.

(i) I suggest: (a) the contents list, giving scope; (b) the footnotes, giving orientation; (c) the conclusions and (d) expression of personal opinion wherever in the book; (e) check on the one point in the book you know most about; (f) note when the book was written. Never go by a review unless you have long checked whether the reviewer's views tally with yours.

(b) The step beyond that is to formulate a criticism or develop subjects in books and present a paper at a seminar so that others can share the thoughts and in their turn criticize and contribute.

An advantage is that the student presenting a report or paper, having been interested in the subject, will tend to sound interesting to others.

(c) To observe or experience and record and comment for seminar discussion is a technique we have used a great deal in Nottingham and found exceptionally useful in taking the place of whole ranges of lecture courses. "Theory and Practice of Building" lends itself to this arrangement particularly well, and it will be dealt with in another context also. The relevant point for this section is the satisfaction expressed by the Visiting Board. They saw the demonstrations of the knowledge in the work examined by students who had learnt in this unorthodox, free way, from using textbooks and consultant lectures independently, functionally, where applicable.

(d) To learn from the "discoveries" of other people in the school, during the course of studies, encourages students to recognize the value of their own thoughts, use them to the full where they are valid, and dispose of them where they turn and take unrealistic pipe dreams, etc., in seminars. However, what occurs to students as a discovery is often shown to repeat or to be closely related to previous work. This brings the student into touch with the world of knowledge on their own terms and indicates the need for experience for "veterans", as Goodman calls them, among the staff, who have a wide background.

(e) There is a method of learning which may have an ever-increasing use as we understand it better and use it more efficiently and selectively. This is sleep learning. Basically, it involves a short course in relaxing as you go to sleep to make you receptive. And then it is a matter of playing the very quiet time-set instructional tapes into the tiny loudspeaker under your pillow. The previous relaxation exercises have made sure that, on the one hand, your sleep is deep, and on the other, that the loudspeaker does not disturb your sleep. It seems quite feasible that the claims made that better sleep results is true. For the dream-filled sleep of most people, tensed up for the night (without even being aware of it) can readily be improved by the relaxation. If then it is realized that only a short time of the night is taken up in the learning process, of sleep learning, so little understood as yet (as sleep itself is not understood either)[i] then better sleep and use of time normally spent in not particularly refreshing sleep makes good sense on the face of it. Such learning has been used by famous actors to learn their roles and foreign languages, and also by the Forces in the U.S.A. and Russia. But the use has not spread to date, and better techniques may be forthcoming. Here is a field which seems to me more full of promise than the teaching machine.

That scientific discoveries are made while asleep and moments of insight occur, is well known.[ii] So why doubt the possibility and advantages from sleep-learning, if we learn how to do it properly? Most people have a strong immediate reaction against the idea: "Not in my sleep as well, leave me alone, please!" is the background of this. But once it is brought home that their dreams or nightmares do not leave them to sleep in peace anyway, a more rational attitude is often forthcoming.

"History", "theory", "services", "acoustics", "mechanics", "cybernetics", "ergonomics", "sociology", "ecology", "mathematics", "strength of materials", "specification", "professional practice", and so on—all the specialized subjects lend themselves to the approach described in terms of other subjects.

A school enriched by the developing individual talents of each student, by the co-operative attitude and the work-progress chart communication, making each student fully aware of the talent that is available, (and so often with the traditionally English vice of modesty, hidden from others) has a stimulating and generating power unknown in higher education to date.

(i) CRILE G., *The Phenomena of Life, a radio-electric interpretation*, London 1936, p. 160, has an interesting theory of sleep.
(ii) See, for example, LOEWI O., in KOESTLER A., *The Act of Creation*.

There is no insurmountable difficulty in "subject" teaching even for exams. At worst the student specifically swots for an exam. A necessary if anachronistic chore that is a nuisance, but should be seen as such and then one can get it done. And students do learn things that seem at one time impossibly unattractive.

The frustration of lacking maths or physics to meet mystery after mystery finally gets the student who has a dislike of these subjects from school to gather the energy and initiative to get the hang of the fundamentals of the language (maths) or the discipline of the subject (physics). The help of his fellows is significant. One finds a small group of students tackling ignorance that has annoyed them.

With the five-year course as it now stands, this sort of educreational potential is particularly feasible in a school orientated towards satisfying desire for knowledge spontaneously, allowing students and staff to strike while the interest is hot.

This view of five years suggests how short-sighted it was for the Layton Report to look at existing schools, see boredom, and thence suggest for the future (when courses will be entirely different) that a student needs a break in the middle of his course for a spot of "real world" and professional practice.

IV.9. REALITY IN THEORY OF ARCHITECTURE

The Principles of Architectural Composition, "An attempt to Order and Phrase Ideas which have hitherto been only felt by the Instinctive Taste of Designers", written by John Beverly Robinson, was published in New York in 1899.

It is particularly interesting that Howard Robertson's book, also called *The Principles of Architectural Composition*, published in London in 1924, attempted "to formulate some of the guiding principles of architectural design . . . as the judgement of design has been so largely a matter of individual taste . . . ". Robertson does not mention the American book, although the foreword describes him as "a student of theory both in America and in Paris". The books are quite similar in a number of ways, and to me it is particularly interesting that their disagreement is categorical on the matter of quality.

Theory of architecture and architectural composition are subjects still taught at most schools. They are by and large based on Howard Robertson's book[i] and deal with "unity", "contrast", "duality", "rhythm", "scale" and so on. It has long provided the basis for criticism of the aesthetic aspects of architecture in schools.

This sort of teaching is becoming less popular. The problems it raises because of its shallow *a priori* assumptions on what is right and wrong. I had an almost traumatic shock when, in my first term at Liverpool, I thought I had, for once, done really well. I had placed as the centre-piece of five anxonometric and highly rendered, simplified, geometric abstractions of buildings (for a "composition programme") a symbolic continental gothic cathedral. But I was told in the "crit" that this form, to me sacred and wonderful beyond criticism—so I had been imbued in my childhood—was not a good choice because "it suffered from duality"! If only I had known of Robinson's book to defend myself! To this day, I wonder about duality and the west fronts of cathedrals, where symmetry and two towers dominate. On the other hand, it took me years to get used to English spireless cathedral towers. They all looked to me unfinished, unsatisfactory! Later on I learnt the Freudian interpretation of spires and domes, and this clicked. (Most students are still afraid to take this seriously and *feel* its rightness.) The energetic approach of Reich allowed me to understand why the "Aedicule",[ii] why enclosures large and small, built or painted, should have a special significance.

The work of Rensch[iii] and others has shown that some animals prefer regular patterned cardboard pieces (birds, monkeys), but

(i) Robertson H., *Architectural Composition*, London 1938.
(ii) Summerson J., *Heavenly Mansions*, London 1947; Ritter P., *Enclosure*, Nottingham 1954; Sharp T., *Anatomy of the Village*, London 1946; Sitte C., *The Art of Building Cities*, Vienna 1889, London 1949.
(iii) Rensch B., Malversuche mit Affen, *Zeitschrift für Tierpsychologie*, Berlin, Sonderdruck, Vol. 10, No. 3; Die Wirksamkeit asthetischer Faktoren bei Wirbeltieren Sonderdruck, *Zeitschrift für Tierpsychologie*, Vol. 15, No. 4, Berlin.

fishes prefer irregularity; that man prefers the Golden section,[i] monkeys prefer to paint in certain patterns (fan shapes,[ii] red ants prefer vertical stripes to horizontal.[iii] These things must have more meaning than we can give them at the moment.

I remembered two characteristics in myself which echo, I think, students' experiences:

(a) Symmetry, the way candlesticks and clock are arranged on our mantelpiece and sideboards, has cultural roots which are considerable and influential.

(b) The copying of ideas from contents of the "glossies" made up, on a vast scale, the basis of "design". Here lay a guarantee that others might approve. Without this the student is lost.

These two aspects, on contemplation, have basic meaning. On the one hand the student cannot trust his "spontaneous" (it is a cultured spontaneity, of course) formulations and, on the other, he does not trust or depend on direct experience of physical environment to inspire him to arrange forms accordingly.

In spite of Norberg-Schulz's[iv] bold and learned effort to give us an integrated theory of architecture which goes further than anything before, in marrying Gestalt psychology to architecture, it leaves out of consideration the influence of the individual's personal blockages in seeing, sensing and building in a sick society. (This affects the comprehension of the theory also.) I feel one should start off with man, but not in the intellectual way that Piaget studied children, but with the motives in mind and the emotions which, for millennia, have been those of individuals with emotional limps, neurotic desires and religious plagues, making up societies suffering similarly. Only this will allow an understanding of most actual phenomena. In other words, a complete theory of architecture needs to include the secondary truths as well as primary truths.

(i) BRISALIEVITCH M., *The Golden Number*, London 1958.
(ii) MORRIS D., *The Biology of Art*, London 1962.
(iii) JANDER and VOSS, Die Bedeutung von Streifenmustern für das Formsehen der Roten Waldameise (*Formica rufa* L.), *Zeitschrift für Tierpsychologie*, Berlin, June 1963.
(iv) NORBERG-SCHULZ C., *Intentions in Architecture*, London 1963.

Liking or disliking a building (as differentiated from those functional or technical qualities which are measurable) is a matter of personal communication and relationship. The student might be made aware how one can get to like a person after starting off with dislike. That, in fact, quite a few film scripts are based on the phenomenon of disliking vehemently at first sight, later changing to love. So with buildings.

A slide lecture might be given illustrating:

> "Fire-stations looking like churches (Victorian) and
> Churches looking like fire-stations (modern);
> "Factories looking like schools,
> Schools looking like factories;
> "Flats looking like rabbit hutches,
> Rabbit hutches looking like flats;
> "Flying saucers looking like lamp shades,
> Lamp shades looking like flying saucers," etc.

Students should become aware of what they associate with architectural names and why they like building or not—but real buildings!

Students ought to be made sharply conscious when they comment on buildings which they have not experienced. If they have experienced them, did they see what the journals said was there, or did they see other things also? Was it their experience? Or did they repeat someone else's?

I think once the students agree that to criticize buildings one has not experienced is a highly dangerous and appallingly fashionable vice, a fine might be agreed for each such judgement or critical conclusion or deduction, etc. I think if all architects had been conditioned in this mild but precise way their outlook might have been different.

The punishment should fit the crime. The older the student, and, even worse, with a tutor or consultant who has come into the building, the larger the fine ought to be; and the fund that accrued would naturally be used to allow the students to go and visit buildings and environment they really want to experience.

M

"Do you know what you are talking about?" should invariably lend itself to the answer, "Yes. I have touched it, smelt it, seen it, experienced it", to this and that extent. This leaves the door open for further knowledge from the questioner. A famous building may look very different two years after it was built. Full or empty, the four seasons, time of day, weather, the nature and the current temper of the observer and his company at the time, all have to be borne in mind. And the influences can be understood with Gestalt psychology[i] and developed psychoanalysis.

Only in some such way will we stop the rot of running to the journals in schools of architecture and practises the second a design is set. And the even worse habit of marking designs according to what the tutor has seen only in photographs.

It would lead to direct experience of architecture on an unprecedented scale! To go round Cambridge first without the guide book and ignorant is much more fun and better mental exercise. Having been immersed in other matters I knew little of what was going on in Cambridge and to give myself a treat I took an American student round. I stopped him from buying the Pevsner Guide first. Things look fresher to me when I am not told what to look for, in the first instance anyway.

So we came across lots of new buildings, some vaguely familiar from pictures, some not. Under construction we found a monstrous white mausoleum type building. I assured the student I was merely looking round it because I enjoyed jokes and unfinished buildings. He shared the joke and I said that of course he will not find this college in the Pevsner Guide; but it was there, with some very famous names attached. Would we have dared laugh if we had seen the names first? Still in Cambridge, I remember my fury because when as a second-year student I liked the arch in Caius College from the Senate House side, I said so. I was reprimanded and told it was "Victorian". I was looked at askance, as a damned ignorant heretic who averted his eyes from

(i) GOMBRICH, *Art and Illusion, A Study in the Psychology of Pictorial Representation*, London 1960; ARNHEIM, *Art and Visual Perception*, London 1956 (particularly p. 64).

the only true glories to be seen, the Senate House and King's Chapel. Well, the Senate House was not cleaned and looked a grey mess to me and the yellow warm stone of Caius appealed to me more. And the arch still does.

Stroke sculpture; caress architecture with your eyes; feel the spaces and the floors, the temperature and the quality of the air; note the faces of the people moving about; hear the noises, touch the materials; sense the movement; sit on seats; and become aware of the delight and the frustrations.

Sterling and Gowan's engineering building in Leicester University has been almost deified. I, too, like it very much, particularly the drama of its sculpture from across the playing fields through the trees, and the play of surfaces and spaces inside. And just because I like it, a little part of my "everybody silly sometimes" lecture deals with it. (It is a lecture based on my family motto which shows students how even the greatest and famous architects can make mistakes.)

The Swedish architect who had joined me to look at this building also liked it very much. We breathed in volumes of delight. And, appreciative, we sat down in the lecture theatre seats—only to rise astonished. We tried again. Either we were both odd or had someone made a mistake? The seats seemed to have excruciatingly shaped back rests. The kink came in the wrong place. (I am average, the Swede was tall.) O.K., we all make mistakes. But, and this is why I am telling the tale, a few weeks later the *Architects' Journal* issued as one of its working detail sheets no other than the details of the very seats we had sat on, as an example of specially careful anthropometric design . . . and I can just see all the students who see it, using the detail again and again without having sat on these seats to evaluate. That's my point.[i]

Much of the writing in architectural theory is sophisticated

(i) James Stirling has explained to me that the seats are designed for leaning forward for writing only—according to the brief of the professor who has strong views on teaching techniques—what happens when the next professor has different views?

one upmanship and allows the student to shroud his awkward position in a fog of arbitrary generalizations to get lost in the darkness or side-tracked by limited views. No wonder Norberg-Schulz calls his "an integrated theory"—it's the right "Intention in Architecture" anyway!

IV.10. THE REAL WORLD

IV.10.1. The Shallow Official Attitude

Much of the criticism of architectural education stresses the uselessness of the newly qualified student in an office. His education has tried to develop his imagination, but it is said without harnessing it adequately to realistic requirements of the profession.

After five years of this it is very difficult or impossible to restructure the design skill in its full context. This is all the more serious as the ability to go on learning is not the end result of traditional education either. The student, as he "turns professional", becomes a haughty critic with a dash of cynicism about him, or he succumbs to the pressures of his office and begins to accept muddling through. He cannot easily bridge the gap between school and office. An analysis of this dilemma leads to a recognition of the vital omissions of the academic course, and this is tackled at the roots by the educreational attitude and detailed in the proposals of this chapter. But the R.I.B.A.'s view is different: with remarkable and well-documented chop-logic, it makes clear its intentions to try to improve the situation by pushing the student earlier, and for longer, into the very offices it has diagnosed as "urgently" in need of remedial action ". . . to improve the management efficiency."[i] How were these proposals arrived at?

(*a*) *Practical training: statutory obligations.*

"The education and training of the architect should be planned as an integrated whole, a seven-year period in which the stage or stages of practical training are co-ordinated with the School

(i) *The Architect and his Office*, R.I.B.A., London 1962, p. 185.

syllabus to ensure that both aspects are complementary and together cover the necessary ground.

"The profession should recognize that practical training of students in the office is an essential investment in the continuity of practice. There should be close co-operation between the office and the School, to ensure that the necessary standards are maintained throughout the training period, and that the experiences gained in each are integrated."[i]

These points were the guide to the Report on the Practical Training of Architects, also published in 1962 by the R.I.B.A. and accepted by the Council almost at once. The recommendations of the office survey were, to my mind, implemented unimaginatively and false criteria were applied.

Perhaps the most outstanding example of this is that a "rigorous examination" is envisaged at the end of the seven years recommended, new sets of hurdles to progress when development must become eminently feasible. It is typical of the type of thing described by Musgrove:

" . . . seniors protect their own position with a variety of stratagems, planned ostensibly in the best interests of the young . . . extended training schemes of neglible educational content which effectively delay the open competition of the young worker with his seniors."[ii]

It may be argued that an extra year in an office is not "negligible". But it can be said, on the other hand, that as the office survey found, most offices badly—"urgently in need of remedial action" as indeed one might find in any profession or trade—then it arises that, according to general experience, the student may in fact learn bad habits, become used to slovenly procedure and inefficiency rather than to a more positive approach than that currently found.

The Report on the Practical Training of Architects isolated training from education and did not see beyond the sort of conditions appertaining at the moment.

(i) *The Architect and his Office*, p. 65.
(ii) Musgrove F., *Youth and the Social Order*, p. 11.

Its pathetic recommendations could have been expected from a shallow investigation and conclusions drawn from this alone and slight "flirtations" with doctors and engineers in America and Germany. There was no basic or original thinking in the report on the educational aspect of a subject which is of such importance that at least an attempt should have been made to think afresh. There was not even a visit to a school which had, by that time, in a long article in the professional press, described a highly relevant course outlined later.[i]

The sad thing is not only that such a mediocre compromise of a proposal is now deeply buried in our system, to the fanfaronades of superlative congratulations (which the English reserve for moderate success), but that this has precluded thinking anew for some time, and all argument is now averted by pointing out that the new idea must have a chance to get into its stride, etc., etc. It will be forgotten that if you make a fuss about anything there is a stir and an improvement; that a whole extra year is a very large price to pay merely for some improvement; and that any improvement may have as much or more to do with changes in school training than with the extra office time. It will, finally, disappear from our memories that the argument, for one year in office after three years at school, was based on the observation that students had got bored with school in the past. This may be a condemnation of schools as seen, but it's not a valid argument for encouraging the jump from this frying pan into the fire of an inefficient office. Logically, it might also lead to recommendations for making courses stimulants rather than sedatives, tonics rather than slow poisons.

The architect and his office report showed inefficient offices and pointed out the need for radical changes. Is it really logical to expect that to steep students for two years in the traditional dye will bring them out the right colour for the future? I have posed this question frequently; there has never been an answer. An

(i) Ritter P., A New Course in the Theory and Practice of Building at Nottingham School of Architecture, *A.J.*, London, October 16, 1961.

obligatory extra year (if one was thought essential) of study and research, a critical view into architectural practice (nature and changes), might have made more sense in the circumstances of a rapidly transforming world. This would be entirely practicable on the basis of the staff atelier idea described later—and might have given a chance to do the vast research programme outlined as necessary by the Office Survey.

IV.10.2. An Educreational Course in Theory and Practice of Building

The idea described below is a way of introducing the real world and all aspects of practical training into the very essence of the architectural education.

In the field of architecture, it has for thousands of years been an obvious and basic requirement to understand about materials and the way they can be put together to good effect and best advantage.

No wonder that the lecture courses on BUILDING CONSTRUCTION which "covers" traditional and sometimes current ways of building, has been one of the most important ("rigorous!") courses of them all. It seemed impossible, and still seems so, to many a teacher with whom I have discussed it, that to do away with lectures, particularly in the early years, can result in anything but a disastrous lowering in standards. Know-how and ability of constructional design (where they can see this as a design field!) are bound to suffer, they think.

It was exceptionally fortunate that at Nottingham the Visiting Board of the R.I.B.A. managed to examine closely a course which had abolished the syllabus and four years of lecture courses as such, and pronounce the results "outstanding". It satisfied traditional and progressive standards.

How does this Theory and Practice of Building course work? To call it a course is a practical advantage. A day a week can be allowed for it on a time-table, and time-tables will be with us for some time. Though a course may be educreationally organized it is useful to be able to give the time-table picture as well when the administration needs it. And in terms of examinations, to specify a particular course makes things look tidy.

In practice, of course, the work done, the ways in which the student acquaints himself with the actual building process and all that it involves, cuts across his working week in many ways and links with other subjects. To set a day aside may have the real advantage in an institution's transition period that seminars involving many people may find them all free on the same day.

The Theory and Practice of Building course has as its context not a syllabus but the full S.F.B. list of the relevant subjects to building. With the table in front of him and his interests aroused by building that goes on around him, on his way to school or near his home, the student locates a building process he wants to study. The area he is about to explore is seen, possibly on an S.F.B.-type chart, as a tiny piece of knowledge in his sea of ignorance.

It is made clear to him that to watch an isolated building process will give him just that small pattern which puts it within his scope to observe, understand, record and report. This idea, of suggesting to students they look at one building process at a time, comes from my frustration, as student and lecturer on building visits. The party walked round, one made lots of points, but by and large it was all much too much, and the central aim for students was to take home a glass brick to use as an ashtray, or other such trophies.

The report, on the larger or smaller subjects—as the papers on other studies and in other fields—is presented to a seminar of interested people. A copy has previously been given to the critic who gives his comments on the report to start the discussion. The seminar has been charted on the person's work-progress chart and also perhaps in a special T.P.B. or Studies seminar chart, perhaps well in advance. For one of the functions of the report way of learning, it will be remembered, is to commit oneself to a finishing date and meet it, or be aware of not meeting it in the public eye, on the work-progress chart. If a special colour has to be used for revised dates it will soon be obvious to a student whether it is one of his weak points, not being able to predict his own work rate. He will learn accordingly, with his tutor's help. The functional virtue and common sense of reliability should become clear.

The process of this kind of study involves a great deal of contact with the real world normally closed to the student in traditional education.

1. The firm of architects to a building has to be asked for permission. Job architect and office are consulted.

2. Often, plans or relevant details of the building are asked for.

3. The people on the site, from clerk of works to labourer are met. Their own interpretations of drawings and the building process become clear.

4. A student learns to look at and see buildings under construction.

5. He becomes aware of his immediate environment and notes how buildings weather and stand up to wear.

6. A student learns much of the relationship between supplier, contractor, architects and others involved in building.

7. Delays and schedules as found on site become familiar to him. Critical path thinking is seen as a real need.

8. The whole business of specification writing and production of drawings (working drawings) takes on a note of reality and relevance.

9. To study many different drawings from many offices is enlightening. To study them in connection with a specific interest allows a good assessment of their qualities.

10. Technical literature is studied in context of the application of the information on a building. A first-rate bit of "reality training".

11. He gets to know the media of telephone and letter writing.

12. He finds lectures and films on specific subjects made available by the full range of facilities in the city can be used as part of his education.

13. He can see how architectural design is influenced by all the people involved in its realization.

14. The student becomes familiar with the time various processes take, including the relative times as proportions of the building time as a whole.

15. The professionals and trade people of the town will easily find relevance and interest in the school of architecture which helps the "professional evenings" described later.

16. The art of producing clear statements (other than essays) in writing, with illustrations, for easy reproduction, will be learned and developed in school .

17. Each person's experience rubs off to an increasing extent on others in the school, particularly because of the co-operative strategy.

18. The library of reports on local buildings gives an increasing reference for the study, at first hand, of any type of construction or material or finish, their history and performance.

19. The attention of the student body (and tact is one of the important things they learn in the field of human relations in this course) to the building trades, the contractors and the architects has its effect on the way these last persons carry out their work, believe or not. In spite of many disadvantages at Nottingham the course ran without major mishap, and nothing happened that a quick apology could not put right.

20. In judging the effectiveness of this way of teaching or learning it must be borne in mind that this process continues over five years.

The results as judged by the Visiting Board of the R.I.B.A. give only one side of the story. The more important point is the state of the mind of the student, which they did not inspect. We began to achieve an attitude to construction, as a field not divorced from, or thought of, after design, but as part of the pattern, making up the total design skill, involved in the design process at all times of this process.

The educreational attitude as described in its application to architecture in this book embraces so many aspects of management that after five years the graduate should be in a position far superior to those who had to try to pick up their management training at quick courses or merely from experience.

The attitude to management will be one of enlightened creative criticism. In other words, rather than work in an office which is run, as most are, in such a way that it is wide open to improvements, the students will look at the general problem in terms of many offices from the point of view of the emerging functional patterns. He can assess what changes are desirable, practicable, and how they can efficiently be introduced and at what level, and discuss these points with architects. This means the opposite of the young man fresh from college who "knows it all". This is the attitude of the young man from college who knows his areas of ignorance (and so those of others) better than those who have qualified before him.

Given reasonable sympathy for such a course by one or two staff in any school, I cannot see how lecture courses can still be defended in building construction. And just where some seem to think they are most necessary, at the beginning of a course, and dealing with "bricks and mortar", they are least valuable, most harmful, giving answers before questions have occurred.

This course, carried out in a fairly full-blooded manner, would have been an infinitely more valuable way of improving the professional capacities of young architects than the extra year, another "rigorous examination" and the log book, a dubious form-filling exercise—but agreed by the Council of the R.I.B.A. subsequent to the publication of the Report on Practical Training for Architects.

IV.10.3. The Professional Evening

Although the division into tutors and teaching consultants will bring into the school know-how of the experts in various professions, this influx can be put on an even broader basis with the professional evening. As run in Nottingham, this was one night a week when there was a permanent open invitation to all the professions and others concerned in the widest sense with building (anyone, in fact) could come. In the informality of the studio, and the framework of work in progress, to be seen there on the boards and tables, discussions took place. For some visitors attendance was due to the desire to influence or pass on lessons, others came to catch up and learn. Particular invitations can bring people together, informally, to whose conversation students can usefully listen and indeed join in. Fellow architects,[i] trades, sociologists, engineers, quantity surveyors, builders, etc., etc.

There is no reason why the nature of professional evenings should not vary a great deal. We had a great advantage in having all students working in one large studio. Informal groups discussing students' schemes and daily problems over a cup of coffee or a glass of cider,[ii] emerged naturally.

The atmosphere is as informal as that of a pub. But without the choking concentration of cigarette smoke and without the iniquitous social pressure that unless one drinks beer—and the more the better—one is not one of the lads. (I am not a teetotaller, but I have learned to hate the occurrence of so many things in pubs because they seem, quite wrongly, the only place to many where they can relax. Healthy young people can be zany without being drunk, sing and cheer without alcoholic help, and get the help to relax from being together in a group.)

The professional evening is part and parcel of the school's life— it is a matrix for innumerable different activities. It is a permanent sign of the openness of the school to professional help and advice. It is additional to any organized or paid lectures or other help by consultant teachers and others.

(i) " . . . I am convinced by the poignant observation of a famous architect and revered teacher of architecture: he needs to teach, he says, because with his students he can propose the ideal solutions of problems, rather than the routine compromises that he must submit to in the world as it is". —(GOODMAN P., *The Community of Scholars*, p. 16.)

(ii) Clandestinely only: request for permission to allow a keg of cider to be served to visitors as an alternative to cocoa had to be turned down by the Principal of the College, of course. Administration could not have allowed it. . . .

Out of it grow things like the Birmingham School's idea of attaching its fourth-year students to an office for the sake of having close professional contact in their efforts to solve the sort of design problem now normal for a fourth-year student. Advice of many kinds and knowledge of how an office might go about things were obtained and deemed worthwhile. I believe the success of this depends already to some extent on the ability to have a developed critical capacity as well as a healthy scepticism. To be ready to question office techniques, even if the offices chosen are famous for their quality.

IV.10.4. Offices in Schools

The obvious alternative or complement to sending students out into offices is to have offices in schools. "Live projects", design for actual building, again pioneered by the Birmingham School, can be run in many different ways. The Birmingham[i] way is one, the Nottingham one[ii] another, and the Sheffield one another still. In running live projects it is particularly important that the design and responsibility is left to the students to the maximum possible. The danger of mundane things being designed so that they are deemed easy enough for students to draw, specify and sometimes build is very real.

In an educreational set-up it follows that participation in the "life project" will be voluntary. It is difficult to see that unless a school is rather lucky in having one or two mature students, keen to control the job, that much will be gained if staff have to take command and students are merely employed. This is a mixing of teaching and professional activity, attitudes and motives fraught with danger.

Bringing the office into the school has a considerable history. But I am writing of the student's involvement in terms of education, not merely staff practising on the premises. The

(i) Birmingham Live Project, *A.J.*, London, April 3, 1958.
(ii) Detailed Description of Live Project, Nottingham School, *A.J.*, London, June 20, 1962.

latter may be legitimate but it's infuriating to students in need of help.

To have a staff atelier within the school, as D. W. Notley thought this out and planned it for Nottingham University, has rich educational and research content and has a proper place in a university. It would have meant an office within the school, which did not work under the normal pressures of existing, over-loaded offices with not enough time for analysis of their work methods. It would have been set up as an atelier which had time to think about what it did, it would have become a major research undertaking for office management, techniques, etc. Within such a critically orientated office, the students might have learned and the profession discovered and tested many innovations.

Co-ordinated Building Communication, for example (C.B.C.), as developed by Bindsley and published in the *Architects' Journal,* something which is sure to excite students because it is emerging, requires an open mind, critical appraisal and improvement, should become part of the study that goes on in the school. It is the responsibility of a seat of learning not to ignore innovations, because staff have no time to look at them, but to look at them as a matter of principle because it is a seat of learning, and to make time for this sort of thing. All people can't do everything, and just because of that, the value of many students doing many different things, not all the same, is so vital for vitality on a broad front.

"At Nottingham, I hope to start the experiment of having a teaching office on lines similar to the teaching hospital for medical students. Such an office in the university would give the students immediate on-the-spot contact with all stages of current practice, just as medical students would be able to go round the wards and watch operations. They would have seminars and lectures in relation to meetings with clients, site visits of office procedure. They would not take charge of jobs because at this stage they are not ready for it. It is more to their advantage to move around to get a varied experience. In this way I think it may be possible to combine the practical advantages of the articled pupilage system with the theoretical advantages of university training." The analogy with hospitals is entirely false, and what Prof. Ling did not say was that something similar and the space for it was worked out by Donald Notley (without any reference to Medical Education), the head of the School of Architecture at Nottingham before him, when the School was at the College of Art and Crafts.[i]

Notley's ateliers are those in which a tutorial professor might lead. Such ateliers, unlike the vast practices of professors divorcing them from their school work and educational responsibilities, could have immense benefits for students and fit admirably into an educreational framework. It could more than keep staff in touch with current practice (the old cry)—it would put them ahead. And that is what a place of learning ought to do, no less.

IV.11. AIDS: DESIGN SKILL IN THE DESIGN PROCESS

IV.11.1. Comment

With each step in the design process questions arise, the answers to which can fruitfully involve the use of aids. It is in response to such directly felt need that appreciation of aids lies. Though only some will be used in the first programme, their existence as a phenomenon, their inclusion in the student's pattern of design habits will be established, functionally, in a rational context.

The observation of seniors will give many clues and information, but it also entails the risk that use of aids becomes a meaningless routine, copied from others to "be with it". Hence, it is the specific usefulness of aids, the connection between them and design questions, that should be stressed.

The variety of aids is wide and the following classification may make it easier to recognize where they fit in.

(i) LING A., Thoughts on Architecture Education, Report on Lecture at B.A.S.A. Conference, Oxford, *A.J.*, March 1964.

There are aids to:
(a) Development of integrating capacity.
(b) Development of creative capacity.
(c) Aids to assessment and evaluation.
(d) Aids to memory.[i]

1. *Design integration aid* (*and techniques*)

The Gestalt techniques to be described are aids: with their help we can design better than without. They are aids of more general relevance than, say, a heliodon, and it is important that in spite of that they are seen as aids.

I had for some time felt that Gestalt psychology should lend itself to do very much more than to make the student aware of forms and their composition. It could bring a new discipline into the very process of evolving and evaluating ideas. It seemed fertile ground.

So I started my search. It seemed there must be something that had already been done in this field and had escaped my notice. But the learned works of Wolfkin,[ii] Gombrich,[iii] Arnheim,[iv] Norberg-Schulz[v] and others, though stimulating, did not give me what I was looking for. A letter from Professor Ruth Shaw, one of the authorities I consulted, suggested that I might look in vain: "My trouble is that people usually write on Psychology and Art or Art and Education and you want the two drawn together." Precisely, and what's more, I sought a dynamic interpretation for educreation.

The potential of using Gestalt psychology in educational and professional techniques for designers is to me quite obviously very great. And seemingly is quite unexplored. The promise of reward makes some systematic work in this field very attractive.

(i) This classification differs from that used in Chapter III.5.2, as it serves a different function.
(ii) WOLFKIN H., *Principles of Art*, London.
(iii) GOMBRICH E. H., *Art and Illusion*.
(iv) ARNHEIM R., *Art and Visual Perception*.
(v) NORBERG-SCHULZ, *Inventions in Architecture*, London 1964.

Whether the use of drawing or models is developed I think a criterion for effectiveness is to use an actual design problem in trying out Gestalt design aids. To abstract them, to create patterns as an end in themselves, like so many pseudo "Vision in Motion" or Bauhaus programmes[i] do in British schools, leaves the student no wiser. They may like what they have done, they may have liked doing it, and this is worth while, but it will not have become associated with the design process which is an important aspect of an aid, and that is a pity.

Lack of time has precluded the perfecting of techniques, but the tentative proposals offered are full of possibilities and invite, I hope, creative thinking of teachers in architecture.

IV.11.2. Design Integration Aids

I envisage the use of a transparent element like tracing paper in developing for the student or architect, a systematically integrating way of committing "building ideas" (designs) to paper. We are used to developing plans, sections, elevations. But if with each plan or elevation or section it was a regular habit to draw at *all* sketch design stages, on separate, overlayed transparent sheets the structural, service, finishes, even relative cost, aspects more or less abstracted, I think this would show profound advantages. The very fact that this idea is not entirely new suggests its usefulness. But it needs development. A systematic way of adopting this from the beginning of the training as a necessary (and not a special) design technique and communication, might have outstanding results in improving thinking in architecture. We know its failings so very often relate to the great gap between grand idea and realization in technical detail. The possibilities of early acquired integrated thinking curing this seem very good.

The technique need not take much time. If we draw to larger scales, with different symbols, many more, far more useful pieces

(i) Maholy-Nagy, *Vision in Motion*, Chicago 1941. Gropius, Gropius, Bayer, *Bauhaus*, 1919–28, New York 1938.

of communication between oneself and one's ideas, could be produced. And this frequent discourse is a substantial part of educreation in design and of design itself—for to each aspect of the building the aesthetic, economic, functional, and contructional viewpoints are applied as the parts of the complex skill.

From a developed Gestalt point of view this means that from the "ground" the existing total concept of a building at any point, each individual aspect of the building as drawn, is a Gestalt seen from a particular viewpoint. The Gestalt of the electrical line plan, the Gestalt of the ventilating system plan, the structural Gestalt and the Gestalt of the sculptural beauty of the building. The latter is in no way hindered by the multiple integrated depth approach. It will frustrate hasty students and architects used to what is now the norm. But when it comes to the translation of concept into building, the realization stage of design, the oft-repeated destruction of the sculptural-Gestalt through forgotten service or structural-Gestalts (becoming unexpectedly pronounced) —will be avoided. The use of overlays allows one to see the total picture—as we well know.

The Gestalt concept indicates that the abstracted aspect of the building makes sense in itself, has a meaningful form, i.e. Gestalt. The pipe system of a building is not something clipped to the walls and hidden, it is a meaningful system within other systems, it has a Gestalt of its own which the architect needs to be able to imagine, to know, feel, recognize, etc.

Looking at each superimposed Gestalt by itself has greater meaning if looked upon as a diagram which does or does not make sense in its own right, as well as part of the ground concept.

I think an exercise could be contrived where some students are confronted with a plan including all information, and some with diagrams showing certain aspects on each plan of similar simple buildings.

Subsequently, students are asked to write briefly on what they saw, i.e. a critical comment on the plan. This will show vividly how the same amount of information can be shown to good effect as a Gestalt or hidden in too complex a pattern for the observer to comprehend.

The following advantages accrue if the approach is thoroughly adopted:

(a) The complex composite design skill would be made explicitly composite and integrated habits of design thought would arise from this.

(b) It would introduce the student from the beginning in the way in which consultant firms and sub-contractors offer their contributions in practice and would keep the architect in functional command.

(c) The way each contribution goes towards the total concept would become vivid and imprinted. Industrialized processes not least of communication, follow naturally from this approach, and the ever-increasing function of services is not relegated to later years.

(d) The student's interest in the total nature of building, something that is surely there when he decides to study the subject, would be better satisfied.

Integrated thought—integrated communication—integrated building is a logical sequence. To teach it can be initiated by encouraging integrated communication—and so the need for the habit of integrated thinking is clear. And it is this very habit that carries him to a more satisfactory "grounding in fundamentals" than the mechanical sequence of "didactics then design" widely advocated and implemented. The real "grounding" lies in the development of integrated quality of thought and imagination in the service of the design skill.

We must develop techniques of drawing, to satisfy the new function. The "materials-Gestalt" drawing of a small shed is not a working drawing. It is a diagram that commits the student through symbols or colours (maybe allied to some such advanced communication system as C.B.C.) to what the roof, walls, etc., are supposed to be made of, etc. This brings the meaning of specification into focus long before the annotation of working details. This does not take long to draw. But it does entail its inclusion at the early design stages. Students will design in materials, in systems of construction, in actual services and not only in lines. Quite functionally the student will experience why he had to find his feet with simple buildings. Quite functionally will his studies of textbook and building processes and the real world follow the need expressed by this approach? Nor does this mean that he has to follow existing techniques invariably—but his original ideas will be of better quality.

This may seem similar, particularly in the eyes of the wishful thinker, to some services studies and structural studies now undertaken by many schools, so that the difference must be stressed. The studies above are already the painful cure of students who have not learnt to think in an integrated manner. And when they are asked to "consider" services, or structure, and make the study, it is, perhaps as a reaction, taken too far; most students copy textbooks, pipe sizes to the nearest thou', fix things into their designs, or forget design, when they draw services and structure. Integrated-design-skill is obscured by the detail and the exactness of the studies.

The drawing I have in mind, the diagrams that would aid thinking and imagination, might at first be labelled "hot; hot; cold," etc., not "three air changes and 58 degrees F". Finishes might be marked "hard; hard; soft; pleasure to touch; no maintenace allowed;" etc. etc. Our great designers' minds do work that way. It can be learnt as a matter of routine in educreational endeavours. Such presentation would also improve client–architect communication.

I remember that when we were set the first little garden shelter at Liverpool at the end of the first term, I was quite excited. I was also very interested in what was going on inside (as well as within) the walls. In fact I drew the plan (asked for without explanation, as usual) to eighth scale. I drew each brick to my wall; the bonding round corners fascinated me. And more than that, I drew each joint in double lines, carefully to scale (eighth scale, remember!) using the hardest, sharpest pencil I could find.

I even remember distinctly not being quite happy about the dead straight lines, as I knew bricks and joints were not. However, as can be imagined, such naïvety got me no credit, nor did what I thought was an important idea, using the existing garden wall as part of the structure—thus making it obviously much cheaper. No, this was quite immaterial in the marking. The stolid Georgian little shelters with drawings of gorgeously rendered brickwork got the high marks and praise and my envy. But they had no idea I thought of what went on "inside" their walls. My naïve, searching approach was knocked out of me until, in the fifth year, I saw the light again thanks to a real teacher, Colin Rowe, who was only a little older than myself and who had at that time done no practical architecture at all. This is important because there are too many people who do not understand that a good teacher need not necessarily practice.

The idea of integrating design drawing encourages all that inventiveness I have found emerging from students' work again and again in terms of better kinds of drawing communication. But these, instead of being critically developed by staff, are beaten back as "scruffy" and "no good" merely because staff have become too rigid to appreciate new forms, patterns and approaches, all too often.

A major break-through was achieved for us at Nottingham[i] when their own dye-line print-machine was hired and placed in the studio by the students for their own use. With one stroke communication in the school became orientated towards what is normal in the outside world. The crinkly white paper which has driven so many students into near bankruptcy both in terms of money and in terms of presentation techniques (Whatman, etc., my memory is blocked with unpleasant associations)—became the very special form—not the norm, as before.

From what has been written, tracing paper and printing techniques combined have a powerful future not yet properly analysed or creatively developed.

(i) Bowler D. A., Prints for Ninepence, *A.J.*, London, May 2, 1962.

IV.11.3. Aesthetic Gestalt Abstraction

In aesthetic aspect of design with models or with elevations, plans and sections, if that's the way your training has made you think, the same ground-Gestalt approach of abstracting one Gestalt at a time could clarify the intentions and help the imagination into fruitful channels.

Let us assume that the criteria have been arrived at; say that a building should be simple, have the stress on horizontal lines and have contrast not within itself, but with its surroundings. Then the design aid suggested to the first year student, from the first design on, may look like this:

GESTALT 1.   What are useful means for obtaining simplicity and unity for this building, obviating need for contrast within it?

GESTALT 2.   How could horizontality be established and worked right through from general lines to detail?

As the imagination produces proposals and they are drawn, the Gestalt approach can become a sort of checklist for the imagination.

As applied to Gestalt 1.   Can the simplicity and unity of the sketch be further enhanced? What are the influence on this of the other components of the design skill? Here we can use the systematic tracing overlay approach, of course.

Applied to Gestalt 2.   Can the horizontality be further enhanced by, for example, contribution from the other aspects of the design skill? (A horizontal pipe rather than a vertical one!) This is using what can only be fed into a computer as a "constraint", as a catalyst to man's imagination.

The tracing paper overlay design evolving technique, as indeed widely used for a very long time, but still not as a matter of course by many students, gains invaluable, clear direction. The aim is pronounced, the means of the development are suggested and the criteria for evaluating and judging ideas are there to use at any stage.

These techniques can become habits of a distinctly more useful kind than those learnt traditionally, making the imagination productive, and development of ideas economic in time and energy, without restricting creativity.

A query to a tutor such as, "Do you like my fenestration?" should be met with, "How have you evolved it?" and "Towards what goal with what criteria for judgement?" Not "Yes" or "No, I would do something like this"—taking pencil, sketching something for student. He may like it and use it without understanding why he likes it better—that's not very useful in the teaching process. Or he may dislike it and guiltily reject it (hoping there will be no hard feelings), but he does not know why he dislikes it; again, no educational value.

In this context my only encounter with Professor Reilly is relevant. It made a deep impression on me. The first design of a bungalow (adapting an existing stone lighthouse) at the end of the first year, made me want to use arches. I have never liked straight lines that much, and as there was a long elevation to the south I wanted to give my bungalow (sorry, single-storey house among competitors!) a "rhythm" of arches. I drew them and drew them and they did not look right. I asked the studio instructors I could get hold of, I asked senior students—but always the same: "Why don't they look right?" I would ask, and instead of an answer—"I tell you what I would do . . . I'd have lintols . . .".

Well, Professor Reilly, retired by then, came to visit the school, and walked round the studio. Always an opportunist, I asked him could HE tell me why the arches looked wrong, and not what to do instead. Immediatelly he responded: "Such masonry arches are meant to carry weight. In your design they seem to carry nothing." And this made excellent sense not only for me but all the studio instructors whom I told. "Of course", they said!

If I had been asked to look upon arches as a Gestalt, meaningful abstraction, and had checked with the past that had shaped our feelings towards arches, I might have discovered the answer without asking a tutor.

IV.11.4. Aids to Inspiration

Although a number of design methods include the idea of "brainstorming" to encourage originality, the theory and techniques of Synectics seem the best developed.[i] In an age that is infatuated with computers this is a magnificent antidote; ironically, it comes from Harvard like the teaching machine. Its educreational orientation is quite remarkable.

"Synectics research hinges on the following assumptions:

"(i) that the creative process in human beings can be concretely described and, further, that sound description should be usable in teaching methodology to increase the creative output of both individuals and groups. This assumption places Synectics theory in direct conflict with the theory that any attempt to analyse and train imagination and those aspects of the human psyche associated directly with the creative process threatens the process with destruction. In other words, true analysis of the creative process is considered impossible since if the individual attempts to examine himself in process the process ceases immediately, and his examination is bankrupt. This theory implies that illumination is destructive. At present this prejudice seems groundless. Synectics attempt to illuminate the creative process have resulted in several working hypotheses which are useful in practice and have increased markedly the creative output of both individuals and groups;

"(ii) that the cultural phenomena of invention in the arts and in science are analogous and are characterized by the same fundamental psychic processes;

"(iii) that individual process in the creative enterprise enjoys a direct analogy in group process."[i]

The theory of Synectics, which has been experimentally vindicated for many years, holds that:

"(i) creative efficiency in people can be markedly increased i they understand the psychological process by which they operate

(i) GORDON J. J., *Synectics, Development of Creative Capacity,* Londor 1961, p. 5.

"(ii) in creative process the emotional component is more important than the intellectual, the irrational more important than the rational;

"(iii) it is these emotional, irrational elements which can and must be understood in order to increase the probability of success in a problem-solving situation."[i]

The process of working with the emotional and intellectual elements in the irrational as well as rational form is followed under the following headings:

Phases of Synectics process:

1. Problem as given.
2. Making the strange familiar.
3. Problem as understood.
4. Operational mechanisms.
5. The familiar made strange.
    (i) Personal analogy.
    (ii) direct analogy.
    (iii) symbolic analogy.
    (iv) phantasy analogy.
6. Psychological states.
7. States integrated with problem.
8. Viewpoint.
9. Solution or research target.

These chapter headings indicate instructions on how "free association" can be made systematically productive in groups— they are charmingly and humorously illustrated with examples of sessions.

In a simple, jargon-free way, Gordon's clear, short book will help students greatly, particularly in a school where co-operation is the matrix of learning. It would be a great pity if the strangeness of the word Synectics put anyone off. The word does not reflect an abstruse text. On the contrary, any student (or even tutor) could follow it. Deliberate attempts to develop such a technique among designers is obviously right.

(i) GORDON J. J., *Synectics*, p. 6.

IV.11.5. Calculation and Measurement Aids

It is in this context, as an aid to design, that surveying equipment should become familiar and understood and used. It is in this sense that measured drawing exercises can be undertaken: the tape is meant to aid one's appreciation of how good proportion arises, and to appreciate distances in relation to buildings outside and inside.

Above all, it is in this way that the cost side of building becomes familiar, from the beginning. To be able to estimate cost as you go along is a help—not a bind—to design. The use of the calculating machine, little modest but efficient things, as a matter of course in the studio, the easy use of slide rules, taught particularly to the non-maths trained students as an extremely useful gadget without knowing how it works, all this is now neglected.

The aids such as heliodon[i] ripple tank, and wind-tunnel allow measurement as well as graphic description of what happens to buildings under various conditions. How we can still ignore these aids instead of using them as a matter of course is difficult to understand. Acoustics, even of small rooms, matters, and the windswept surroundings of our high buildings, make this more than urgent by now.

The heliodon, particularly, is such a cheap and straightforward aid that to place it in "science departments" of universities is all wrong. It should be by the studio, like the library, an immediately available aid. Professors of Environmental Design and professors of other aspects of architecture must be integrated as consultants into the course designed by the permanent Professor of Architectural Education.

IV.11.6. Memory Aids—Check Lists

Memory-aids are perhaps the best developed and the most rapidly developing of all the aids. Check-lists of very many kinds

(i) MILLARD C. J., *Every School Should have at Least One Heliodon*, *A.J.*, November 22, 1961.

an be found comprehensively developed in the technical sections
f the R.I.B.A. journals, particularly the *Architects' Journal*.

The use of such check-lists as a design aid does not follow
rom their existence. Each student will get used to the lists in his
wn way. He should experience the need for them and use them
n his own design process.

The argument for using these lists is, in the last resort, one of
esponsibility. They are an insurance not to forget aspects of
lesign which should have been borne in mind from the point of
iew of the client. Of course, omissions affect everyone in the
uilding team—It's like checking the parachute before you
ump—it's a self-discipline, but overwhelmingly worth while.

The first-year student might be overwhelmed with the compre-
ensive check-lists useful later. First, he must see the wood *and*
he trees. The following design process check-list is the sort that
ill let him see the basic idea. This is, it should be made plain,
he "material" that arises to be processed by the design skill along
he design process described before. This is the grist to the mill.
he student can practise what use the three-beat formula is on
uch an undifferentiated list (beyond the first basic rhythm).
deally, I think such lists should be worked up in seminar—
hrough an analytical approach, "What does architectural design
ntail, on the basis of the three-beat formula?" This would
tick in the student's mind and make better working sense than
o confront him with a list; answer before question to be avoided.
t is given here because in transition stages at schools this is much
etter than nothing. It does give the student an immediate
ealistic work programme.

Attraction—Analysis

Read or hear client's statement, or assume it.

Analysis of the brief or problem and requirements as
expressed, both in functional and material terms. Discussions and clarifications with client.

Re-statement of needs to satisfy enlightened attitude of
architect and client. Open questions where these are

reasonable. Programme: present the re-statement in such a manner so that it represents a clear frame of reference to client and architect.

Functional elements of brief enlarged and detailed.

Investigation into functional factors. E.g. kinds of possible accommodating spaces; of structural possibilities; of site usage; of services; of appropriate character; of economic variations; of special user requirements and creative possibilities; problems in previous solutions of the problem; special decisive fittings.

Classification, interrelation, interconnection between various factors: crystallizations of the criteria of design. Programme: clear statement of design criteria, in principle.

Fusion—Creative Activity

Schedule of accommodation in volumes, groups in basic service requirements, etc.

Interconnections.

Ideas combining the various criteria stated.

General concepts tried out for satisfaction of all requirements of structural solution, services, etc.

Solution of best solution and perfection of same—criticisms checking back to criteria.

Clear description of the design and the way it can be carried out—the way in which it still needs elaboration and detailed consideration, and the reasons for its nature.

Liberation—Realization

Communications to whom and what for?

Inquiry into usual manner of communication consideration of improvements if they seem desirable. Possible techniques.

Schema for the presentation of information.

Produce drawings, models, essays, reports, films, photographs, spoken records, tapes, slides, mock-ups, analyses of various, as required.

IV.12. RESEARCH

IV.12.1. Present Pathetic Position

Not much needs saying on research in schools of architecture. It has become clear that educreation would encourage and develop research mindedness through the orientation towards: asking questions; recognition of areas of ignorance as well as areas of knowledge; dealing with working difficulties when they arise; and by increase in the inventive capacity.

When people like Professor Page lament that it takes three years to train a research man and that immediate post-graduates let alone students, prove insufficient, we must, once again, beware, of the same old mistake: he is applying to the future and making a general principle out of that which is clearly seen as an outcome of the limitations and specific orientations of traditional education. Professor Page not so much trains as un-trains his workers, I think, from the inhibiting education they have received.

Research problems may occur and be examined during undergraduate years: particularly in architecture, where the course is ive years in many places and ought to remain so; particularly where diversification according to desire is possible early, and where special interests may grow for long periods, with a possible esearch content—side by side with the more general education nd training in design skill. Where post-graduate research is in rogress within the school, and such workers belong to tutorial roups, the participation in research work by the undergraduates ill be quite spontaneous and likely. If nothing else, the young udent becomes clearly aware of what is involved. Long training in-training, brain washing) should not be necessary for anyone ho wishes to carry out postgraduate research.

At the moment research at schools of architecture, and probably general, is severally pathetic. On the one hand, as Professor ernal says: "In the early stages of practical invention, when e smallest sum of money can achieve the greatest results, ere is the greatest difficulty in getting money; but in the later stages, after a clear breakthrough, there is always plenty of money."[i]

A slightly different twist to this story depresses me most: vast sums for research are allocated to famous professors on the basis of pathetically generalized aims for research, presumably because they are famous professors. Their research intentions certainly do not impress anyone who has ever been active in this way. Too often the intentions announced at the inception sound as either virulent megalomania or else crass ignorance of the limitations of research in terms of time, money, techniques and personnel.

Sadder still, the professors have nothing to do with working on the research. They advertise, hire people to do "their research" for them. This is the grossest misunderstanding or mishandling of the research process.[ii] The poor results from this kind of thing are the proof of this putrescent pudding.

Although the fashion is to urge more and more research funds, I am very worried about the allocation of more funds thither where waste and famous names share prominence.

Those who are seemingly in the forefront of research pronounce on the subject in a manner which certainly inspires no confidence in me. What is happening is directly related to the chaotic and one-sided approach to the subject.

The Minister of Housing and Local Government recently appointed a committee to advise him on what kind of research needs to be done. As this is one of the central issues of a "science of science", the opinions of a committee can hardly take the place of what requires exceptionally inspired research. We shall get lists so general they are meaningless, except for eliciting funds, with public approval, because of their evocative, promising sound and as a monumental example of intellectual, academic vested interest.

(i) BERNAL J. D., Towards a Science of Science, *Science Journal*, London, March 1965.
(ii) Reference to the analysis of the research process in Chapter III.4. will show exactly why.

IV.12.2. Proposals

The cure lies, I believe, in adopting Professor Page's advice to give the young chaps with good ideas the money and let them get on with it. (And I would not exclude professors with good ideas.) However, I would define this a little more carefully. First, I do not see how this tallies with Professor Page's pronouncement that it takes him three years to train his research staff. Secondly, I believe that the person who has shown the ability to ask naïve and original questions and who has shown ability for hunches, the person who has discovered the specific problem he wishes to solve, he is the man who should be given the money. What is more, though he may well work with the possibility to consult a professor who is experienced in research, he would be his own master. The present servitude of research scholars to their professors is monstrous and unproductive. The threat of punishment by forfeiting your Ph.D. is not an empty one either.

We could not waste more money. Eager minds searching for solutions to real problems are bound to be better than the hired labour of today, working doggedly, if mathematically, at establishing the Professor's claims that research is taking place in his establishment: the status symbol of university life.

I think the outlook for research is black while it is professor-orientated. These are normally people who have asked their brilliant question and have had their hunches, but are now deeply involved in "affairs of state". You can't get further from research-mindedness.

A science of science, as Professor Bernal champions, is badly needed to clarify the bleary view of those who set themselves up as the experts in research in the architectural profession; who try to intimidate the rest by their alleged scientific methods, rigorous mathematical application and intellectual superiority to emotion and creative acts. Let us read Bernal. He writes, as many of the eminent people who really do know about research and science, and I submit the quotation below as a grave warning so those who are enamoured by the "rigorous" rationality of science:

"What the reader rarely discovers is why or how the scientist did his work, because the logical steps described in his paper are quite different from the steps which he actually took. Sometimes these steps are the result of hunches, and hunches are very often useful as much when they are wrong as when they are right. In a science of science these real activities would be just as much an object of study as would the formal, logical research presented in the scientific literature."[i]

And for those who suffer from the extreme hubris of science, imagining that objectivity has reality, let them take in the comment below—one of many I could quote—which puts the scientific understanding of man and his scientific endeavours in the world, at its actual and inadequate level of development.

Taylor[ii] quotes research which shows that exposure to adult blood serum inhibits lupin seedling growth. And further quotes recent research (45 years after the other had virtually been forgotten) to indicate that with the blood serum of children, ages nine months to twenty-three years, "the degree of inhibition rose with increasing donor age and height".

Taylor speculates on aspects of unity and common principles in the universe that scientists have not yet fathomed and which are severally indicated. In this book we assume the unity as a fact and proceed from the discovered common functioning principles. But the above quotation of the lupins being more inhibited from growing by older blood than by younger might be directly applied to research!

Once the principal is established that young people should have funds to evaluate their hunches or have time to formulate their questions, I believe that it is possible for juries to allocate money more fairly than we do now. It could hardly be worse. But one proviso should surely be made. Namely that there is a premium on those who bridge disciplines.[iii] Not only have those

(i) BERNAL J. D., *Science Journal*, March 1965.
(ii) TAYLOR G. R., Focus, *Science Journal*, March 1965.
(iii) "A man who only knows his own science, does not even know that He has no fertility of thought, no power of quickly siezing the bearing of alien ideas. He will discover nothing, and be stupid in practical application".—(WHITEHEAD A. N., *The Aims of Education*, p. 62.)

who do so been shown to be the most inventive but, thanks to the professorial protégé system, they have been in an impossible position to get funds: one subject at a time, dead specialization rather than creative generalization. This is a remarkable phenomenon worth bringing to the notice of the foundations who give the money, to the juries who allocate it, and to the universities who largely waste it on impotent collections of statistics, however rigorously their mathematical accuracy is checked. (It is interesting to note, by the way, that the "recent coherent theory for sub-atomic particles, long needed to resolve chaos in theoretical physics was so long in coming because a plus was mistakenly put in place of a minus!" Everybody silly sometimes— however rigorous!)

IV.13. THE PLACE
IV.13.1. Work Needs

One can make much of any kind of accommodation. I believe that it is fallacious to wait for the provision of splendid accommodation before embarking on an educational development.

However, this does not preclude the formulation of views with regard to the best kind of accommodation for the sort of education envisaged in this book.

Basic needs to be satisfied by accommodation are:

1. To allow feeling of belonging to:
    (a) the school,[i]
    (b) the year,
    (c) the group,
    (d) the seminar or work group,
    (e) oneself—privacy.

2. To have at hand as many aids as possible:
    (a) tutorial head and staff and consultants,
    (b) libraries,
    (c) research rooms,
    (d) secretarial help, telephones,

(i) See Chapter IV.1.

- (e) print machines,
- (f) heliodon, wind tunnel,
- (g) physics lab.,
- (h) chemistry lab.,
- (i) model building workshop,
- (j) mock-up space, indoor and outdoor,
- (k) acoustic laboratory,
- (l) light laboratory,
- (m) heat laboratory,
- (n) radio room,
- (o) darkroom,
- (p) T.V. cubicle,
- (q) seminar rooms,
- (r) lecture room.

3. To give the right atmosphere: the studio is a place where one likes to be, where things happen, where one likes to do things, where work is attractive, not divorced from fun. A place which, through space, allows the imagination to expand and the soul to rise; which excites to creation within the space.

The studio is a background in which the students should form their environment, private and corporate. In physical terms the answer can be quite simple and economic. This does not exclude highly exciting and luxurious possibilities. But where the luxury is imposed, I think a challenge and important aspect of adventure can be lost.

Pointers to physical requirements:

We need high halls to take the unit of about 150 students; a "school". There may be several schools in one place closely connected and sharing ancillary accommodation.

Within this high hall the groups compose and the individual has his own place: home. Within the hall there may be a number of small decks or mushrooms, connected to the main space and the circulation, large enough for a group of about fifteen students to have their "office" or den.

The individual obtains his own privacy in simple ways similar to ideas used for the acoustic telephone booths. The furniture should give him easy choice whether he wants to concentrate alone or in a group.

The high hall would dominate not by its very size only, but by its function. This is where my concept differs radically from solutions physically similar in the States: there we have a fine central space but it is not the studio. It is for formalized circulation, exhibition and between-work meeting as, for example, at Minneapolis.

Two extremes exemplify the variety of possible applications of the idea. On the one hand, we have the converted Victorian Protestant chapel, with its high hall, highly ornate ceiling and decorous ventilators, balconies and organ loft. In Nottingham or at Leeds or Sheffield, there were such spaces which had the qualities described. An inspired choice: it can't just have been the only accommodation available.

Twelve years in Nottingham, my five in the School of Architecture at Liverpool with separated year studios, a year in the Department of Civic Design, Liverpool, and many shorter stays in dozens of other schools all over the world, persuaded me that the large, highly articulated space is the right solution.

Rudoph's School of Art and Architecture at Yale, which I saw only under construction, has the same theme. Two floors are devoted to architecture and planning. Here the drawing tables have provision for privacy, just as suggested in this book, and various levels make the large volume exciting.

"The drafting room is metropolitan: all the architectural students, plus most city planners, work in the one large, layered space . . . the space is about 80ft wide and 130ft long, and its ceiling height in the centre is close on 23ft.

". . . each of the five years has its own platform, but the drafting room [studio] is still a single room taking up the entire floor so as to facilitate interchange of ideas between students and faculty."[i]

(i) *Architectural Forum*, New York, February 1964, p. 73.

The Yale building, opened in November 1963, has been heralded as a great building. That may be its defect! I would doubt whether such a strong permanent personal expression of one architect is the ideal background for the training of architectural students. What in Britain would be described as the "studio" is thus described:

"The drafting room ceiling is 22 ft 5 ins. in the center diminishing gradually in the lateral spaces to an ultimate 6 ft 6 ins. in the upper mezzanine. Light influx from four sides, broken by varying textures on columns and parapets, creates space units interlocked by the movement of the users. Within each level, shallow steps change the eye focus, as on a Piranese engraving, making vertical and horizontal dynamics a self-sufficient perspective experience. Applied to teaching spaces, this learning-in-motion is as old as Aristotle's peripatetic method.

"It remains to be seen whether the work habits of the students will be moulded by this continuous process of group interchange in the high open spaces, and concentrated isolation during the design formulation process under the confining ceilings of the side spaces; where, in other words, individual concepts or solutions can be hoisted like building parts from level to level to fuse in the total fabric of architectural education. One thing is sure: this experiment of learning from each other with virtual liquidation of class differentiations, will do more to arouse in the creative individual respect for the collective task of environment making than all the impotent attacks on 'prima donna architecture'."[i]

It is interesting to note that the school has 136 students so that the size, not only the spatial arrangements and not only the critics' optimism coincide with my own proposals.

Whether one creates a monument like the Yale school, or whether one invents or adapts a prefabricated system, the idea of a large space and ancillary accommodation stays practical and valid. I personally favour the prefabricated solution for new

(i) *Architectural Forum*, p. 78.

schools because of its flexibility, its lack of architectural domina-
tion, and the possibilities of inviting students to participate in
making the school.

I realize that endless argument and disagreement are likely
on this score but this is independent of the rightness of the
basic concept.

The high hall would probably have top light in the main, with
a sense of enclosure, with perhaps no views out except to the
sky, with direct connection maybe to an "outlook tower" with a
commanding view. It can then be surrounded at two levels by
the ancillary accommodation, tutorial staff, consultants' places,
staff atelier, and the many aids, or as many of them as the school
can afford. In a live school the amount of equipment that can
be gained from industry, and through student work and interest
and perhaps in conjunction with the local professions, who might
make use of the facilities, should be very extensive, and the
sources are quite unexploited.

This has obvious relevance to the professional evenings when
use of the equipment might be encouraged on an informal basis.
Architects could learn watching students use new design aids and
techniques.

To have the ancillary accommodation with the teaching aids,
from books to heliodon next to the studio means their frequent
use, as a matter of course as part of the process of design. It also
means that the use can be observed and learnt by new students
or when any particular item becomes relevant, or if a special
event occurs it is easy to see and to attend to. What's more,
points in seminars sometimes require elucidation with the help
of equipment. For lectures to the whole school on formal
occasions, a lecture theatre of the university would no doubt be
available.

There should be easily, possibly directly, accessible, an
expansive open area, part under cover if possible for students to
play and work with building material and climate as well as
enjoy good weather for talks, seminars and other functions.

Roofs can provide many of these needs, but it is very desirable that some areas at ground level should be available for loading and unloading of heavy things and for many other reasons people will be able to think of. If room for expansion is allowed, there should be no difficulty on this score for a long time to come.

It seemed reasonable, and it certainly worked with my group at Nottingham, that a desk should be provided for the tutor within the group space, like that of the students. To what extent he can work there will depend on the person and his circumstances, and the tutors' room should, of course, be available also.

In Nottingham, where the whole staff shared one small room, quite normal still in British schools of architecture, and where we did not even have a drawer to call our own, greater privacy in many senses can be obtained in the very large room than in the small staff room. The close presence of other members of staff can be far more inhibiting than the presence of students.

I feel that a tutor, and this includes the Head, like the student, should have option to be private or not. This could be indicated in a glass connecting panel between the staff rooms and the central studio. The curtains drawn could indicate the member of staff is trying to concentrate. The open curtain invites consultation. Exceptional acoustic insulation of the tutors' rooms is important from the point of view of therapeutic outbursts by students who should, on the one hand, not be inhibited, and on the other, not disturb the student body in any way.

It would be quite a reasonable idea to combine a certain amount of residential accommodation with a studio. This would have several functions:

(a) Visitors could very conveniently remain until late, when the discussion is best.
(b) Students who wish to work late could get some sleep.
(c) Staff likewise.

It is clear that this accommodation might be very basic, tiny bunks and cubicles with washing facilities, youth hostel style, with one or two better visitors' rooms.

IV.13.2. A Wider View

It is surely in the best traditions to combine work place and living place to a certain degree. It may even be tried out to combine these things to a large degree—in one or two schools to see the reactions—and possibilities. But the more the student is centred around his studio the more important it becomes that outside interests are attractive also. When one thinks how the sleeping accommodation would facilitate the exchange of students and staff from different schools, the imagination can delight in lively prospects.

With regard to catering, the skill of producing decent nourishing food from raw materials is usually of interest to quite a few people of both sexes. Thus, the baking of bread taught at Nottingham was taken up by numbers of students. This wholemeal delicious basic food is the kind of thing to make the catering in a studio such as the one described really worthwhile.

Why should not students bake bread, make jams, bottle fruit, keep chickens, do gardening, and the Lord knows what—as well or instead of playing billiards, table tennis, watching television? All this is in the best modern tradition of giving the variety required to keep minds creative and original. What is more, it demonstrates to a society giving up quality in its food, air and love just what is involved. All this makes real the ideal that education is really learning to live. The professional aspect of it is just one. If the cynic comments that with all this jam making, sheep shearing and milking, when is there to be time for architecture? Let us remind him of all the time he spent—not on architecture during his training. He will have to concede it was enormous, and that it was not very productive or very enjoyable.

If education is to make sense in societies of increasing affluence it must give not only the possibilities to specialize in new ways but also to remain the whole man.

At the Darmstadt Technical University the studios for the third, fourth and fifth years have stainless steel sinks and draining boards, arrangements for cooking, enormous fridges for drinks and the odd couch. One has a fully-fledged dining kitchen, student built, run and fully used. This is valuable pioneering.

As the distinction between working and living quarters may dissolve, so perhaps, should our strict division of work rooms. The distinction between studio and laboratory becomes increasingly artificial.

It's high time we had the rooms where art and science could meet, marry and multiply by mixed offspring. If this is sailing uncharted seas, I name the ship *Labudio*.

FIG. 22.   The Place. The basic studio unit for 150 students is a high hall with most students at ground level but two or three groups on platforms at first floor level. (Labudio.)

All ancillary accommodation, staff rooms, libraries, print rooms, building science laboratories, workshops and so on are directly accessible from the hall or its gallery. On one side the studio faces onto open space for open air experiments, etc.

To this basic unit can be added halves or wholes of such units, as the school size is planned to increase. Units of 150 students will again be in tall studios and have their own ancillary accommodation. However, there now exists the possibility to increase the size of some of the ancillary rooms which need to be larger to serve more students, being shared by the two "schools" of 150 students each. It will be readily understood that endless architectural ways exist to compose two or more units, vertically perhaps, but best horizontally in any of many ways.

The simple basic principle is one space for the "school of 150" subdivided into the tutorial groups by whatever means is deemed best. And immediate access, without corridors, to the ancillary accommodation, staff and aids.

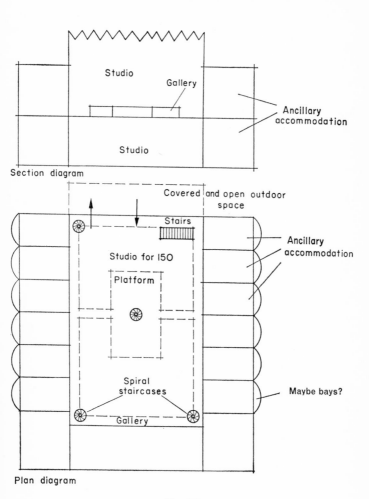

Section diagram

Plan diagram

FIG. 22.

V.
Bibliography

V.1. General

ABERCROMBIE M. L. J., *The Anatomy of Judgement*, London 1960.
ALEXANDER M. F., *The Universal Constant of Living*, London 1941.
ARNHEIM R., *Art and Visual Perception*, London 1956.

BARZUN JACQUES, *The House of Intellect*, London 1959.
BRAATOY T., *Fundamentals of Psycho-Analytic Technique*, London 1954.
BRISALIEVITCH M., *The Golden Number*, London 1958.
BROADBENT D. E., *Perception and Communication*, London 1958.
BROWN B. F., *The Non-grade High School*, New Jersey 1963.
BURGESS W., *Mental Health and Mental Disorder*, London 1956.
BURNS and STALKER, *The Management of Innovation*, London 1961.
BURTON W. K., Theory of Crystal Growth, Penguin *Science News* 21, August 1951.
BURTON KIMBALL AND WING, *Education for Effective Thinking*, New York 1960.

CHANDLER G., *How to Find Out*, Oxford 1963.
COOK T. A., *The Curves of Life, being an Account of Spiral Formations, their Application to Growth in Nature, to Science and to Art*, London 1914.
COOK T. A., *Spirals in Nature and Art*, London 1903.
COWAN P., and CASSIDY M., *The Transactions of the Bartlett Society, 1962–63*, Bartlett School of Architecture, London.
CRILE G., *The Phenomena of Life, a Radio-electric Interpretation*, London 1936.
CRAWSHAY-WILLIAMS R., *The Comforts of Unreason*, London 1948.

DEUTSCH J. A., *A Structural Basis of Behaviour*, Cambridge 1960.
DEWEY J., *The School and Society*, Chicago 1949.
DOUGLAS J. W. B., *The Home and the School*, London 1964.
DOXIADIS C. A., *Architecture in Transition*, London 1963.
DUNCKER K., *On Problem Solving*, Washington 1945.

EHRENFELS V., *Sexualethik*, Vienna 1907.
ELLIS W. D., *A Source Book of Gestalt Psychology*, London 1938.

FELDENKRAIS M., *Body and Mature Behaviour*, London 1954.
FERENCZI S., *The Further Development of an Active Therapy in Psycho-Analysis*, New York 1953.
FOULKES and ANTHONY, *Group Psychotherapy*, London 1957.
FOWLER W. S., *The Development of Scientific Method*, Oxford 1962.

FREUD S., *Civilization and Its Discontents*, London 1938.
FREUD S., *Civilized Sexual Morality and Modern Nervousness in Sexual Problems*, 1908.
FREUD S., *A Philosophy of Life, New Introductory Lectures on Psycho-analysis*, 1908.
FROMM E., *The Fear of Freedom*, New York 1954.
FROMM E., *Sane Society*, London 1956.
FURNEAUX W. D., *The Chosen Few*, Oxford 1961.

GETZELS J. W., and JACKSON P. W., *Creativity and Intelligence*, New York 1962.
GOMBRICH E. H., *Art and Illusion, A Study in the Psychology of Pictorial Representation*, London 1960.
GOODMAN P., *Growing Up Absurd*, New York 1956.
GOODMAN P., *The Community of Scholars*, New York 1962.
GORDON W. J. J., *Synectics, The Development of Creative Capacity*, New York 1961.

HADAMARD J., *The Psychology of Invention in the Mathematical Field*, Princetown 1949.
HALL, *Report of the Joint Committee on Training in the Building Industry*, London 1964.
HALLIDAY J. L., *Psycho-social Medicine*, London 1948.
HALMOS P., *Solitude and Privacy*, London 1952.
HALSEY A. H., FLOUD J. E. and ANDERSON C. A., eds., *Education, Economy and Society*, Glencoe Free Press.
Health of the School Child, The, H.M.S.O., London 1962 and 1963.
HORNEY K., *The Neurotic Personality of Our Time*, New York 1939.
HILL W., *Learning: a Survey of Psychological Interpretations*, San Francisco 1963.

INFIELD HENRICK F., *Utopia and Experiment, Essays in the Sociology of Co-operation*, New York 1955.

JACKSON B., *Streaming, An Education System in Miniature*, London 1964.

KARDINER A., *Psychological Frontiers of Society*, New York 1945.
KLEIN J., *The Study of Groups*, London 1956.
KOESTLER A., *The Act of Creation*, London 1964.
KÖHLER W., *Gestalt Psychology*, London 1930.
KOFFKA K., *Principles of Gestalt Psychology*, New York 1935.
KRIS E., *Psychoanalytic Explorations in Art*, London 1953.
KROPOTKIN P. A., *Mutual Aid, a Factor of Evolution*, London 1902.

LAWRENCE D. H., *The Man Who Died*, London 1931.
LELLO J., *The Official View of Education*, Oxford 1964.
LEWIN K., *Field Theory in Social Science*, New York 1951.

LEWIN K., *Resolving Social Conflicts*, New York 1948.
LOWEN A., *Physical Dynamics of Character Structure*, London 1958.
LUMSDAINE and GLASER, *Teaching Machines and Programmed Learning*, a source book, Department of Audio-Visual Instruction, National Education Association of the United States, Washington 1960.
LYWARD G. A., *Respite from Pressure*, 1963.

MAHOLY-NAGY, *Vision in Motion*, Chicago 1947.
MARRIS P., *The Biology of Art*, London 1962.
MARRIS P., *The Experience of Higher Education*, London 1964.
MCDOUGALL W., *The Energies of Men*, London 1932.
MCHALE J., *Buckminster Fuller*, New York 1962.
MCKENZIE R. F., *A Question of Living*, London 1963.
MOORE H. T., *The Intelligent Heart, The Story of D. H. Lawrence*, London 1955.
MORENO J. L., *Who Shall Survive?* New York 1953.
MORRIS D., *The Biology of Art*, London 1962.
MUSGROVE F., *Youth and the Social Order*, London 1964.

NEILL A. S., *Hearts not Heads in School*, London 1944.
NEILL A. S., *That Dreadful School*, London 1948.
NEILL A. S., *The Problem Child*, London 1929.
NEILL A. S., *The Free Child*, London 1953.
NEILL A. S., *Summerhill*, London 1964.
NEWSON J. and E., *Patterns of Infant Care in an Urban Community*, London 1963.
NORBERG-SCHULZ C., *Intentions in Architecture*, London 1963.

PARKINSON C. N., *Parkinson's Law*, London 1958.
PAVLOV J. P., *Conditioned Reflexes*, Oxford 1927.
PEARSE and CROCKER, *The Peckham Experiment*, London 1943.
PEARSON N., *Education for Planning*, New York 1963.
PEDLEY F. H., *The Educational System in England and Wales*, Oxford 1964.
PERLS F., HEFFERLINE and GOODMAN, *Gestalt Therapy*, Julian Press, U.S.A. 1951.
PETERMAN P., *Gestalt Theory*, London 1932.
PETTIGREW J. B., *Design in Nature*, London 1908.
PINION F. B., *Educational Values in an Age of Technology*, Oxford 1964.
PORTERFIELD A. L., *Creative Factors in Scientific Research*, Durham 1941.

READ H., *Education through Art*, London 1946.
REICH W., *Character Analysis*, London 1958.
REICH W., *Cosmic Superimposition*, Rangeley, U.S.A. 1951.
REICH W., *Die Naturliche Organisation der Arbeit*, Arbeitsdemokratie, Oslo 1939.
REICH W., *Ether, God and Devil*, Maine, U.S.A. 1949.
REICH W., *Function of the Orgasm*, New York 1945.

REICH W., *Mass Psychology of Fascism*, New York 1946.
REICH W., *The Emotional Plague of Mankind*, Rangeley, U.S.A. 1953.
REICH W., *The Sexual Revolution*, London 1951.
REILLY Sir C., *Scaffolding in the Sky*, London 1938.
R.I.B.A., Office Survey, London 1962.
RITTER P. and J., *The Free Family, a Creative Experiment in Self-regulation for Children*, London 1959.
ROBBINS, *Higher Education Report*, H.M.S.O., London 1963.
ROBERTSON H., *Architectural Composition*, London 1938.
ROSENTHAL H. WERNER, *Structural Decisions*, London 1962.
RUGG H., *Immigration*, London 1963.
RUSSELL B., *An Outline of Philosophy*, London 1927.

SANFORD N., ed., *The American College*, New York 1962.
SCHWARTZ C. and B., *Moments of Discovery*, New York 1958.
SHARP T., *Anatomy of the Village*, London 1946.
SITTE C., *The Art of Building Cities*, Vienna 1889, London 1949.
SKEMP Dr. R. R., *Understanding Mathematics*, London 1964.
SKINNER B. F., *The Behaviour of Organisms*, New York 1938.
SKINNER B. F., *The Science of Learning and the Art of Teaching*, 1945.
SKINNER B. F., *Walden Two*, New York 1948.
SKINNER B. F., *Science of Human Behavior*, New York 1953.
SKINNER B. F., *Cumulative Record*, New York 1959.
SNOW C. P., *The Two Cultures and the Scientific Revolution*, Cambridge 1959.
SPROTT W. J. H., *Human Groups*, London 1958.
STANFORD N., ed., *The American College*, Stanford University, U.S.A. 1962.
SUMMERSON J., *Heavenly Mansions*, London 1947.

TATE and MUSICK, *Adjustment Problems of College Students, Social Forces*, 1954.
TAYLOR C. W., *Creativity*, London 1964.
THELAN A. H., *Dynamics of Groups at Work*, Chicago 1954.

WERTHEIMER M., *Productive Thinking*, New York 1954.
WILSON C., *Town*, London 1964.
WHITEHEAD A. N., *The Aims of Education*, New York 1949.
WHITEHEAD A. N., *Nature and Life*, Cambridge 1934.
WHYTE L.-L., ed., *Aspects of Form*, London 1951.
WHYTE L. L., *The Next Development in Man*, London 1944.
WHYTE L. L., *The Unitary Principles in Physics and Biology*, London 1949.
WILLS W. D., *Homer Lane*, London 1964.
WITKIN DYK, FABERSON, GOODENOUGH, KARP, *Psychological Differentiation*, London 1962.
WÖLFFIN H., *Principles of Art*, London 1915.

ZWEIG F., *The Student in the Age of Anxiety*, London 1963.

V.2. *Articles, Reports, etc., with special reference to the development of architectural education*

ABERCROMBIE Dr. M. L. J., The Anatomy of Judgement, *A.J.*, B.A.S.A. Supp., March 14, 1962, and B.A.S.A. Sheffield Conference Report.

ABERCROMBIE Dr. M. L. J., and HUNT S. M., Selection for Entry to a School of Architecture, *R.I.B.A. Journal*, March 1964.

Acquiring a Creative Mind—Can it be Cultivated? *A.J.*, February 6, 1963.

A.I.P. and American Society of Planning Officials, Professional Planning Education in the U.S. and Canada, January 1962.

ALLEN W. A., Science in Schools of Architecture, *R.I.B.A. Journal*, August 1953.

ALLEN W. A., Modern Architect: the Decisive Decade, *The Builder*, January 1962.

ALLEN W. A., Training and Education of the Architect, *A.A. Journal*, April 1962.

ALLEN W. A., The Robbins Committee and Afterwards, *R.I.B.A. Journal*, May 1964.

ALLEN W. A., The Training and Education of Architects, February 1962.

ALLEN W. A., Training and Education of Architects, *A.J.*, Supp., March 7, 1962.

ALLEN W. A., Training and Education of Architects, letter, *A.J.*, March 28, 1962.

ALLSOPP BRUCE, Architectural Education in the Future, *A.J.*, September 2 and 9, 1964.

ALLSOPP BRUCE, Universities and a Planned Environment, *R.I.B.A. Journal*, October 1964.

Annual Statistics, Growth of Full Time Education, *R.I.B.A. Journal*, March 1964.

ANSELL W. H., Architectural Education, *R.I.B.A. Journal*, April 4, 1936.

Anthropometry, First-year Study at the A.A., The Creative Process, First-year Students' Work, B.A.S.A. Supp., *A.J.*, March 6, 1963.

Approach to Science and Structural Mechanics in the Architect's Training, papers read by staff of the Hammersmith School of Building and Arts and Crafts at the Architectural Teachers' Conference 1951, *R.I.B.A. Journal*, September 1951.

ARCHER B., Design Programmes, *A.J.*, September 16, 1964.

Architects Journal, eds. The Hardest Education of All, March 7, 1962.
    A Practical Masterpiece (on Layton Report), October 10, 1962.
    Getting Into Training, September 4, 1963.

Architects of Tomorrow, *A.J.*, June 17, 1964.

Architectural Education, Interim Report, *A.J.*, B.A.S.A. Supp., October 6, 1960, and September 1961.

Architectural Education in the United Kingdom, *R.I.B.A. Journal*, November 1963.

Architectural Education, Joint Committee on the Training and Qualifications for Associate Membership of the R.I.B.A., Report (Chairman, D. H. McMorran), *R.I.B.A. Journal*, February 1955.

Architectural Education, papers, *Architectural Design*, July 1955.
Architectural Education, Report of the Special Committee, *R.I.B.A. Journal*, September 1946.
Architectural Group:
  Group Study 1, Architectural Education, presented at Inaugural Meeting, September 28, 1962.
  Group Study 2, Architectural Education, presented at Conference, Queen's University, July 6, 1963.
Architectural Schools in Great Britain (special number), *Architecture and Building*, February 1958.
Architecture as a Career, Career Masters' Conference Report, *R.I.B.A. Journal*, March 1963.
Association of Building Technicians', Architects' Training and Efficiency in the Building Industry, Report, *A. and B.N.*, March 6, 1952.
ASTRAGAL, Robbins Reflections, *A.J.*, July 22, 1964.

BAINES G. G., Architects as Builders See Them, *A.J.*, July 31, 1958.
BAINES G. G., Learning to Design, *A.J.*, September 16, 1964.
BANISTER T. C., The Architect at Mid-Century, *A.I.A.*, 1950.
BARRACLOUGH Prof. G., *Times Educ. Supp.* Jubilee No., December 2, 1960.
B.A.S.A. Conference, Durham, Structure of Education for the Building Service, Aims for Architectural Education, *A.J.*, August 15, 1962.
B.A.S.A. Conference, Pattern of Education, *A.J.*, October 3, 1962.
B.A.S.A. Report 1961, An Interim Report on Architectural Education, London 1961.
B.A.S.A. Report 1962, Building for People, London 1962.
B.A.S.A. Report 1963, Aims and Methods, London 1963.
B.A.S.A. Report on Conference on Educreation, London 1965.
BERESFORD-PITE, Prof., A Review of the Tendencies of Architectural Education, *R.I.B.A. Journal*, May 1924.
BERNAL J. D., Towards a Science of Science, *Science Journal*, London, March, 1965.
BINDSLEV B., Drawing Practice, 1, Rationalisation and C.B.C., *A.J.*, October 14, 1964.
Board of Education, Committee of Secondary School Examinations Council, Report (Norwood), *R.I.B.A. Journal*, September 1943.
BONDI Prof. H., Turning a Training into an Education, *The Observer*, January 7, 1962.
BOWLER DAVID, A1 Prints for 9*d.*, *A.J.*, *Architectural Education Supp.*, May 2, 1962.
BRANDON-JONES J., The Education of Architects, II, *A. and B.N.*, April 24, 1952.
BRANDON-JONES J., The Education of Architects, III, *A. and B.N.*, May 8, 1952.
BRIGGS M. S., Architectural Education, *R.I.B.A. Journal*, June 1951.
BRITCH A. LANCASTER, Quantity Surveying of Electronic Computers, *A.J.*, March 27, 1963.

BROWN Prof. R. GORDON, Architectural Education, *A. and B.N.*, August 14, 1952.

BUDDEN L. B., The Future of Architectural Education, *R.I.B.A. Journal*, July 1945.

BUDDEN L. B., Letter on above topic, *R.I.B.A. Journal*, August 1947.

BURROUGH J. H., General Theories and Practice of Education, Dept. of Education, University College, London, B.A.S.A. Oxford Conference Report, 1960.

BUSSAT PIERRE, The Beaux Art System, *A.J.*, May 5, 1960.

CAMPBELL KENNETH, Trends in Architectural Practice, B.A.S.A. Oxford Conference Report, 1960.

CARDY D., FUSSELL W. F. J., and TSAKOK P., Practical Training Outside Architecture, *A.A. Journal*, March 1964.

CASSIDY M., History of Architectural Education in the 20th Century, *A.J.*, B.A.S.A. Supp., December 1, 1960.

CASSIDY M., Thoughts on Education, *A.J.*, B.A.S.A. Supp., June 1, 1961.

CASSON Sir H., Living, Learning and Leisure, The Planning of New Universities, lecture reprint, Royal Society of Arts, March 3, 1965.

CHAPMAN Dr. DENNIS, People, B.A.S.A. York Conference Report, London 1962.

CLAXTON K., and HARVEY M., Pool of Lecturers, *A.J.*, April 7, 1960.

COLE MARGARET, Integrated Training, letter, *A.J.*, October 10, 1962.

COLLINS PETER, Architectural Education 200 Years Ago, *R.I.B.A. Journal*, April 1955.

Commission for Education of the Architect, report, I.U.A., Prague, August 1962, *R.I.B.A. Journal*, November 1962.

Computer—A New Tool for the Architect, *R.I.B.A. Journal*, October 1964.

COOKE HENNESSEY, WARDLOW, NEUF BRISACH, *R.I.B.A. Journal*, February 1965.

COWAN H. J., The Place of Science in Architectural Education, reprint, *Architectural Science Review*, Sydney, November 1960.

COWAN H. J., The Architectural Science Laboratory of the University of Sydney, reprint, *Architectural Science Review*, July 1961.

COWAN H. J., Some Applications of the Use of Direct Model Analysis in the Design of Architectural Structures, Sydney, September 1961.

COWAN P., Research, *R.I.B.A. Journal*, April 1961.

COWAN P., Communication or Conflict, *The Lancet*, November 4, 1961.

COWAN P., The Search for Creativity, *A.J.*, December 23, 1964.

COWAN P., and WATSON N., Teaching and Learning, *A.J.*, August 8, 1961.

CURTIS E., Teachers Meet at Coventry, report, *A.J.*, September 1, 1962.

CURTIS E., KAIN A., and PERRY B. A., Student Viewpoint, interview at the Northern Polytechnic, *A.J.*, September 12, 1962.

CURTIS E., and ROSENTHAL H. WERNER, Teaching of Structural Design, *A.J.*, Supp., March 7, 1962.

DAINES J. W., The Need for a Philosophy of Education, *Nottm. Univ. Bulletin*, September 1960. (Special Studies in Education.)

DAVIES R. LLEWELLYN, Deeper Knowledge: Better Design, *A.J.*, May 23, 1957.

DAVIES R. LLEWELLYN, The Education of an Architect, *A.J.*, November 17, 1960.

DAVIES R. LLEWELLYN, Inaugural Address, Bartlett School of Architecture, *A.J.*, November 17, 1960.

DAVIES R. LLEWELLYN, Sources of Architectural Inspiration, lecture delivered at University College, London, October 10, 1961.

DAVIES R. LLEWELLYN, How Much Research? *R.I.B.A. Journal*, April 1963.

DAVIES R. LLEWELLYN and COWAN P., The Future of Research, joint paper, *R.I.B.A. Journal*, April 1964.

DAVIES R. LLEWELLYN and WEEKS J., Education for Building, report on the new Bartlett course, *A.J.*, September 13, 1961.

DAVY J., Can Exams Ever be Fair? *The Observer*, February 14, 1965.

Diversification: The End of a New Problem? *A.J.*, January 13, 1965.

DOME LOVING, *A.J.*, August 28, 1963.

ELLIS J. R., *The Times*, September 25, 1961.

FORWARD A., Seminar on Teaching Methods, *A.J.*, June 10, 1964.

FRANK L. K., *American Journal of Sociology*, Vol. 42, New York 1936.

Frustrated Staff at Universities, *The Guardian*, December 11, 1964.

FURNEAUX W. D., The Psychologist and the University, *University Quarterly*, 1962.

FULLER J. B., World Design Science Decade, 1965–1975, Phase 1 (1964), Document 2, The Design Initiative, Illinois 1964.

GARDNER-MEDWIN R., Profession and University, *R.I.B.A. Journal*, March 1964.

GIBSON Sir DONALD, Building Research and Technological Development, paper to the A.A., *The Builder*, March 15, 1963.

GILLESPIE J., Towards Freedom in Work, *Anarchy*, Vol. 47, January 1965.

GLASS RUTH, The Architects' Responsibilities, B.A.S.A. Oxford Conference Report, 1960.

GLICKMAN M., The Log Book—A Reaction, *A.J.*, November 20, 1963.

GOSS A., The Two Trends Contested, *A.J.*, September 20, 1961.

GOSS A., Realistic Projects at Birmingham, *A.J. Supp. on Architectural Education*, April 4, 1962.

GOWAN J., Curriculum: Discussion on What and How Architecture Can Be Taught in Schools, *Architectural Review*, December 1959.

GOWAN J., Architectural Educational and its Technical Aspects, paper at B.A.S.A. Conference 1960, *A.J.*, November 3, 1960.

GREENE W. CURTIS, Architectural Education in the Present in England, *R.I.B.A. Journal*, August 16, 1924.

GROPIUS W., The Architect in Society, *A.A. Journal*, January 1962.

GROPIUS, GROPIUS, and BAYER, *Bauhaus*, 1919–28, New York 1938.

The Guardian, March 13, 1965: And End to Finals Terrors.

Bibliography 369

HALL DENIS CLARKE, A Point of Contraflexure, A.A. Inaugural Address on Architectural Education, *A. and B.N.*, November 5, 1958.

Hammersmith School of Building and Arts and Crafts, Approach to Science and Structural Mechanics in the Architect's Training, papers by staff at Architectural Teachers' Conference, 1951, *R.I.B.A. Journal*, September 1951.

HANSON N. L., The Architect—Is He Really Necessary? Report on lecture, *R.I.B.A. Journal*, July 1964.

HARDY ALEXANDER, Environmental Physics in the Subjective Design Synthesis, *A.J.*, February 6, 1963.

HARPER D., A New Educational Framework, *R.I.B.A. Journal*, June 1960.

HARPER D., Some Notes on the Education of the Architect and his Technical Assistant, *R.I.B.A. Journal*, October 1964.

HARRIS A. J., Architectural Misconceptions of Engineering, *A.J.*, December 29, 1960; *R.I.B.A. Journal*, February 1961.

HAWKINS G., Ideal Architectural Course, letter, *A.J.*, March 11, 1964.

HENDRY A. W., University Research in Building Science, *A.J.*, June 13, 1962.

HINTON D., Live Projects by the Birmingham School of Architecture, *A.J.*, April 3, 1958.

HINTON D., Birmingham, the 5th Year, *R.I.B.A. Journal*, February 1963.

HODGES W. A., Education of the Specialist; a Humanist View (part 1), *A.J.*, September 12, 1962, and November 21, 1962.

HOLFORD Sir W., Address to students, *R.I.B.A. Journal*, March 1961.

HOLFORD Sir W., Keynote Address on Architectural Education, *R.I.B.A. Journal*, July 1962.

HOWARD T., letter on John Weeks on Indeterminacy, *A.J.*, October 28, 1964.

HOYLE, Prof. F., Science: A Vocation in the 60s, *The Observer*, January 8, 1961.

HUDSON L., Intelligence, Divergence and Potential Originality, *Nature, Lond.*, Vol. 196, 4854, pp. 601–2.

HUTTON G. H., Education in the Building Industry: A Suggestion, *A.J.*, November 21, 1962.

HUXLEY ALDOUS, *The Observer*, October 22, 1961.

INFIELD H., Co-operative College Papers; the Sociological Study of Co-operation, Loughborough 1956.

JACKSON B., Britain's University Throw-outs, *The Observer*, April 11, 1965.

JACQUES P., A Method of Assessing Studio Work of Architectural Students, *R.I.B.A. Journal*, October 1964.

JANDER and VOSS, Die Bedeutung von Streifenmustern fur das Formsehen der Roten Waldameise (*Formica rufa* L.), *Zeitschrift fur Tierpsychologie*, June 1963.

JAY P. A., The A.A. and the I.C.S.T., *A.J.*, June 10, 1964.

JEANES R. E., Critical Path Method Applied to the Overall Process of Building, *Building Research*, Design Series 11.

JENSEN R., Educational Reforms in an Australian School, *R.I.B.A. Journal*, August 1964.

JOHNSON-MARSHALL P., From Schools of Architecture to a New University Faculty, *A.J.*, June 6, 1957.
JONES FRANCIS M., Production, *A.J.*, Student Section, April 2, 1960.

KAY Prof. H., Machines for Teaching, extract from paper at B.A.S.A. Conference 1962, *A.J.*, March 14, 1962.
KAY and MEDD, A New Approach to Primary School Design, *A.J.*, February 17, 1965.
KELSALL R. K., Getting on at the Grammar, *Times Ed. Supp.*, March 15, 1963.
KLEIN R., *The Observer*, February 2, 1965.
Kneale Committee Report on Examinations, Oxford 1965.
KNIGHT Prof. C. R., Architectural Education in the British Empire, *R.I.B.A. Journal*, November 22, 1937.
KRETCHMER W., Control of Architectural Education, *R.I.B.A. Journal*, February 1963. Education and the Industrialization of Building, *A.J.*, June 3, 1964.
KRETCHMER W., and THOMAS F., Joint Education, evidence submitted to the Robbins Committee, *A.J. Supp. on Architectural Education*, December 27, 1961.

Lancaster Will Give Teaching a New Look, *Sunday Telegraph*, March 3, 1963.
LAYTON ELIZABETH, Practical Training of Architects, *A.J.*, October 10, 1962, *A.J.*, January 30, 1963.
LAYTON ELIZABETH, Questions on the Future, at the A.A., 1964.
LEA Dr. F. M., Advanced Training, Research and Development (paper read at Oxford conference), *R.I.B.A. Journal*, November 1958.
LEE A. MC., The Clinical Study of Society, *American Sociological Review*, Vol. 20, No. 6, December 1955.
LEONES R. E., Critical Path Method Applied to the Overall Process of Building, Current Papers, D.S.I.R., Watford 1964.
LEVIN P. H., Use 'G' Graphs to Decide the Optimum Layout of Buildings, *A.J.*, October 7, 1964.
LIBBY W., The Scientific Imagination, *Scientific Monthly*, Vol. XV, 1922.
LING ARTHUR, Thoughts on Architectural Education, *A.J.*, March 11, 1964.
LISBORG N., and MYERS B., Structures—A Qualitative Approach (discussion of first-year programme), *A.A. Journal*, January 1960.
LISBORG N., and MYERS B., Letter, B.A.S.A. Supp., *A.J.*, January 12, 1961.
Liverpool School of Architecture, Changed Course of Studies, *A.J.*, December 5, 1962.
LOCKE J., *Essay Concerning Human Understanding*.
LYNN R., Environmental Conditions Affecting Intelligence, *Educational Research*, Vol. 1, No. 3, June 1959.
LYNN R., Two Personality Characteristics Related to Academic Achievement, *Brit. Journal of Ed. Psych.*, 1959.

MACE RODNEY, Architectural Education Prior to 1900, B.A.S.A. Oxford Conference Report, 1960.

MACKAY-LEWIS J., Examinations, B.A.S.A. Oxford Conference Report, 1960.

MADGE J., The Contribution of Human and Social Sciences to Management, *R.I.B.A. Journal*, November 1964.

MALCZEWSKI A., The New Degree Course, B.A.S.A. Supp., *A.J.*, August 4, 1960.

MANNING PETER, Publication of Reports on Architectural Research, *A.J.*, December 18, 1963.

MARTIN BRUCE, Trends in the Building Industry, B.A.S.A. Oxford Conference Report 1960.

MARTIN Sir LESLIE, Conference on Architectural Education, Oxford 1958, *R.I.B.A. Journal*, June 1958.

MARTIN Sir LESLIE, An Overall View of the Architect's Training, paper at B.A.S.A. Conference, 1960, *A.J.*, November 3, 1960.

MAXWELL R., Architectural Directions, *A.A. Journal*, September 1963.

MICHAEL I., Teaching and Learning, *A.J.*, July 19, 1961.

MICHAEL I., Concept of Education, extract from paper at B.A.S.A. Conference, 1962, *A.J.*, February 14, 1962.

MILLARD C. J., Every School Should Have at Least One Heliodon, *A.J.*, November 22, 1961.

MILLER R., Architectural Education, letter, *A.J.*, June 10, 1964.

"Mr. Ritter is Right", a student, letter, *A.J.*, December 13, 1956.

MONK T., and MUSSON C., Wider Aspects of Education, B.A.S.A. Oxford Conference Report, 1960.

MOOR ROBERT, Education, Society and the Architect, *A.J.*, B.A.S.A. Supp., June 20, 1962.

MORGAN R. STANLEY, Upper School Conglomerate Demonstration Frame, *A.J.*, September 20, 1961.

MUSSON CHRIS, A Survey of Architectural Education, B.A.S.A. Bristol Conference, *A.J.*, March 30, 1960.

MUSSON CHRIS, Memorandum to R.I.B.A. on publicity to secondary schools, November 1961.

National Union of Students, memorandum to the Committee on University Teaching Methods, London.

Nature and Nurture of Architects, *A.J.*, June 10, 1964.

NEWBY F., Lecture on Architectural Education at Queen's University, Belfast, 1963.

NICHOLSON C., *The Observer*, June 7, 1964.

NOBLE JOHN, The How and Why of Behaviour, Social Psychology for the Architect, *A.J.*, March 6, 1963.

Northern Polytechnic School, *A.J.*, B.A.S.A. Supp., March 2, 1961.

Nottingham School of Architecture, Detailed Description of Live Project, *A.J.*, June 20, 1962.

NUTALL J. F., Optional Research in Building in Europe, *Building Research*, Construction Series 6.

NUTT B. B., and PEARSON D. C., Computer Conference, *A.J.*, September 30, 1964.

ODDIE G., Analysis, *A.J.*, Student Section, April 2, 1960.
Oxford Architectural Education Conference, Committee Report, *R.I.B.A. Journal*, November 1959.

PAGE Prof. J. K., Teaching Environmental Physics, extract from paper at B.A.S.A. Conference, 1962, *A.J.*, March 14, 1962.
PAGE Prof. J. K., Environmental Research Using Models, *A.J.*, March 11, 1964.
PAGE Prof. J. K., New Year Number on Research, *A.J.*, January 20, 1965.
PAINE R. W., Canterbury School of Architecture, *R.I.B.A. Journal*, March 1963.
Perception, B.A.S.A. Supp., *A.J.*, April 10, 1963.
PEVSNER N., The Training of Architects, Interim Report, *Architectural Review*, June 1950.
Planning Research Advisory Group, *A.J.*, March 10, 1965.
POTTS E. W. MAYNARD, The Calibre of the 6th Former, *A.J.*, June 15, 1961.
Practical Experience for A.A. Students, *A.A. Journal*, 1964.
Practical Training of Architects, Elizabeth Layton's Report, *A.J.*, October 10, 1962.
Practical Training of Architects, The report of meeting held at R.I.B.A., *R.I.B.A. Journal*, April 1963.
PRYDE ANN, Collaborative Projects at the Northern Polytechnic, *A.J.*, February 2, 1961.

REDFERN EWART B., Architectural Education, letter, *A.J.*, June 15, 1961.
REICH W., *The Murder of Christ*, Rangeley, U.S.A. 1953.
REICH W., *Listen Little Man*, New York 1949.
REICH W., *Weitere Probleme der Arbeitsdemokratie*, Oslo 1941 (manuscript only).
RENSCH B., Die Wirksamkeit ästhetischer Faktoren bei Wirbeltieren, Sonderdruck, *Zeitschrift fur Tierpsychologie*, Vol. 15, No. 4.
RENSCH B., Malversuche mit Affen *Zeitschrift fur Tierpsychologie*, Sonderdruck, Vol. 10, No. 3.
Research in Progress (12), *A.J.*, August 19, 1964.
R.I.B.A., Diversification, a Report to the Board of Architectural Education, December 1964, London.
R.I.B.A. Education Report, comments on, *R.I.B.A. Journal*, May 1947.
R.I.B.A. Conference, October 1961, Report, Postgraduate Training.
R.I.B.A. Glasgow Conference, Final Report, *A.J.*, May 20, 1964.
R.I.B.A., *The Guide to Group Practise and Consortia*, London 1965.
R.I.B.A. Practical Experience for Students, *A.J.*, April 3, 1963.
R.I.B.A. Seminar Report, The Teaching of Structure in Schools of Architecture, October 1960.
R.I.B.A. Special Committee on Architectural Education, Interim Report, *R.I.B.A. Journal*, March 1942.
R.I.B.A. Statistics on Architectural Education, London 1963, 1965.
R.I.B.A. Testimonies of Study, notes for the guidance of students preparing intermediate and final testimonies of study, *R.I.B.A. Journal*, March 1954.

R.I.B.A., *The Architect and his Office*, London 1962.

RICHARDSON, Prof. A. E., Papers Read at the Architectural Teachers' Conference, 1951, *R.I.B.A. Journal*, September 1951.

RITTER P., Architectural Education, a New Approach, *A.J.*, November 22, 1956.

RITTER P., A Teaching Technique, *Architecture and Building*, May 1960.

RITTER P., *A New Course in the Theory and Practice of Building*, October 18, 1961.

RITTER P., *Function of Architecture, Role of Architect*, February 7, 1962.

RITTER P., Five Realities on Architectural Education, *A.J.*, May 2, 1962.

RITTER P., Ritter and the Board, letter, *A.J.*, February 24, 1965.

RITTER P., Bio-Functional Planning, Part IV, Enclosure, Ritter Press, Nottingham.

RITTER P., Change of Panel Policy, *A.J.*, Architectural Education Supp., November 11, 1961.

RITTER P., Medical Education Criticized, *A.J.*, November 22, 1961.

RITTER P., Testing of Model Beams, *A. and B.N.*, April 9, 1953.

RITTER P., and WILLIAMS H. D. L., Teaching Methods, B.A.S.A. Oxford Conference Report, 1960.

ROSENTHAL H. WERNER, Education for Architects, *A. and B.N.*, January 24, 1952.

RUSHOLME Lord J., JOHNSON-MARSHALL S., and MATTHEW Sir R., report of discussion between, *R.I.B.A. Journal*, July 1964.

SAYERS C., and others, Pupilage System, *A.J.*, February 2, 1961.

SCHER PETER, Training for an "A.R.I.B.A.", *A.J.*, September 12, 1957.

SCHER PETER, Architectural Education, letter, *R.I.B.A. Journal*, August 1961.

Schools in the U.S.A., *M.O.E. Building Bulletin*, No. 18, July 1961.

SCOTT J. M., Several Fundamental Questions Ignored, The Oxford Conference Criticized, *A.J.*, July 31, 1958.

SHEPARD H. A., Superiors and Subordinates in Research, Paper 12 of the Symposium on the Direction of Research Establishments, H.M.S.O., Department of Scientific and Industrial Research, 1956.

SIMMS J., and CURTIS E. J. W., Foundation Course: Northern Polytechnic, *A.J.*, September 20, 1961.

SMITH J., The Development of Architectural Education, *Architecture and Building*, May 1958.

SMITH J., May a Cat Look at a King? *A.J.*, B.A.S.A. Supp., June 20, 1962.

SMITH J., Special Number on Architectural Education Review of all British Schools, *Architecture and Building*, 1960.

STEWART C., Gentlemen versus Students, *R.I.B.A. Journal*, December 1952.

Striking a Hard Bargain, *A.J.*, May 27, 1964.

Structure of Building Courses, *A.J.*, July 17, 1963.

STUART W. L., Education: What is Required, *A.J.*, September 8, 1960.

STURGIS T., Bartlett School, Research on Students, December 5, 1962.

SUGDEN D., The Office Man's View of the New Graduate Architect, *A.J.*, August 5, 1964.

SUMPNER M., The Summer Vacation, *A.J.*, July 14, 1960.

Sunday Times, October 13, 1963: Oxbridge Students, Youth-Humbug!

SUTCLIFFE S., Architectural Education, letter, *R.I.B.A. Journal*, September 1964.

SUTCLIFFE S., Studio Work or Whatever, *A.J.*, September 16, 1964.

SVYADOSCCH A. M., Learning During Sleep, *The Science Teacher*, London, November 1963. See also *The Journal of the Sleep-Learning Association*, London 1964 (14 Belsize Crescent, N.W.3).

TAYLOR G. P. W., *Teaching Architecture*, letter, December 1, 1960.

TAYLOR G. P. W., Work of 20 Schools of Architecture, B.A.S.A. exhibition, *A.J.*, July 12, 1961.

TAYLOR G. R., Focus, *Science Journal*, March 1965.

Teaching Technique Reviewed, report on the Ministry of Education course for teachers of architecture, Leicester, *A. and B.N.*, June 5, 1952.

Technicians in Architects' Offices, report of R.I.B.A. discussion meeting, *R.I.B.A. Journal*, September 1962.

TEMPEST J., Place of Young Architect in R.I.B.A., *A.J.*, October 7, 1964.

THORNLEY D. G., Architectural Education in West Germany, *R.I.B.A. Journal*, January 1961.

T.P.I., Recruitment and Membership Report of a Special Committee under the chairmanship of Mr. L. W. Lane, May 1963.

Transfer A.A. School to I.C.S.T., *R.I.B.A. Journal*, editorial, September 1964.

Universities Central Council on Admissions, Second Report, 1963–4, London 1965.

WATSON J. B., Psychology as the Behaviourist Views it, *Psychol. Rev.*, *U.S.A.*, Vol. 20, 1913.

WATSON N., A Method of Assessing Studio Work of Architectural Students, *R.I.B.A. Journal*, August 1964.

WEBB M. E., First International Congress on Architectural Education, *R.I.B.A. Journal*, August 16, 1924.

WEEKS J., Indeterminate Architecture, report on lecture, *A.J.*, May 27, 1964.

WHITEHEAD A. N., The Rhythmic Claims of Freedom and Discipline, *Hibbert Journal*, July 1923.

WHITEIS U. E., Poor Scholarship in the College, *Harvard Educational Review*, Winter 1962.

WILSON COLIN ST. JOHN, Synthesis, *A.J.*, Student Section, April 2, 1960.

WILSON L. HUGH, The Practical Training of Architects, *R.I.B.A. Journal*, December 1962.

WOOD F., Architectural Education in Edinburgh, *A.J.*, B.A.S.A. Supp., August 4, 1960.

WRIGHT J. H. G., Learning to Design, *A.J.*, August 19, 1964.

Yale School of Architecture, Architectural Forum, New York, February 1964.

YOUNG Y. F., Sociology and the Practising Professions, *American Sociological Review*, Vol. 20, No. 6, December 1955.